The LIFE *of* IMAGES

Also by Charles Simic

POETRY

COLLECTIONS IN TRANSLATION

Vasko Popa, *Homage to the Lame
Wolf: Selected Poems*
Co-translator, Slavko Mihalić,
Atlantis
Tomaž Šalamun, *Selected Poems*
Ivan V. Lalić, *Roll Call of Mirrors*
Aleksandar Ristović, *Some Other
Wine and Light*
Slavko Janevski, *Bandit Wind*

Novica Tadić, *Night Mail:
Selected Poems*
*Horse Has Six Legs: Contemporary
Serbian Poetry*
Aleksandar Ristović, *Devil's Lunch*
Radmila Lazić, *A Wake for the Living*
Günter Grass, *The Günter Grass
Reader*

PROSE COLLECTIONS

*The Uncertain Certainty: Interviews,
Essays, and Notes on Poetry*
Wonderful Words, Silent Truth
*Dime-Store Alchemy: The Art of
Joseph Cornell*
*The Unemployed Fortune-Teller:
Essays and Memoirs*

Orphan Factory: Essays and Memoirs
A Fly in the Soup: Memoirs
The Metaphysician in the Dark
The Renegade

The LIFE of IMAGES

Selected Prose

CHARLES SIMIC

An Imprint of HarperCollins*Publishers*

Unless otherwise credited, photographs courtesy of the author.

THE LIFE OF IMAGES. Copyright © 2015 by Charles Simic. All rights reserved. Printed in the United States of America. No part of this book may be used or reproduced in any manner whatsoever without written permission except in the case of brief quotations embodied in critical articles and reviews. For information address HarperCollins Publishers, 195 Broadway, New York, NY 10007.

HarperCollins books may be purchased for educational, business, or sales promotional use. For information please e-mail the Special Markets Department at SPsales@harpercollins.com.

A hardcover edition of this book was published in 2015 by Ecco, an imprint of HarperCollins Publishers.

FIRST ECCO PAPERBACK EDITION PUBLISHED 2017.

Designed by Suet Yee Chong

Library of Congress Cataloging-in-Publication Data has been applied for.

ISBN 978-0-06-236473-9

17 18 19 20 21   ID/LSC   10 9 8 7 6 5 4 3 2 1

To Philip

Contents

The LIFE *of* IMAGES

from

WONDERFUL WORDS, SILENT TRUTH

WHY I LIKE CERTAIN POEMS MORE THAN OTHERS

I have a photograph of my father wearing a black tuxedo and holding a suckling pig under his arm. He's on stage. Two dark-eyed beauties in low-cut party dresses are standing next to him and giggling. He's laughing too. The pig has its mouth open, but it doesn't look as if it's laughing.

It's New Year's Eve. The year is 1926. They are in some kind of nightclub. At midnight the lights were turned off, and the pig was let go. In the pandemonium that ensued, my father caught the squealing animal. It was now his. After the bows, he got a rope from the waiter and tied the pig to the leg of their table.

He and the girls visited several other establishments that night. The pig went with them on a rope. They made it drink champagne and wear a party hat. "Poor pig," my father said years later.

At daybreak they were alone, the pig and my father, drinking in a low dive by the railroad station. At the next table a drunken priest was marrying a young couple. He crossed the knife and the fork to bless the newlyweds. My father gave them the pig as a wedding present. Poor pig.

*

Written in 1986 as an introduction to the issue of *Ploughshares* magazine which I edited.

That's not the end of the story, however. In 1948, when my father was already on his way to America and we were starving back in Belgrade, we used to barter our possessions for food. You could get a chicken for a good pair of men's shoes. Our clocks, silverware, crystal vases, and fancy china were exchanged for bacon, lard, sausages, and such things. Once an old gypsy man wanted my father's top hat. It didn't even fit him. With that hat way down over his eyes, he handed over a live duck.

A few weeks later his brother came to see us. He looked prosperous. Gold teeth in front, two wristwatches, one on each hand. The other brother, it seems, had noticed a tuxedo we had. It was true. We let these people walk from room to room appraising the merchandise. They made themselves at home, opening drawers, peeking into closets. They knew we wouldn't object. We were very hungry.

Anyway, my mother brought out the 1926 tuxedo. We could see immediately the man was in love with it. He offered us first one, then two chickens for it. For some reason my mother got stubborn. The holidays were coming. She wanted a suckling pig. The gypsy got angry, or pretended to. A pig was too much. My mother, however, wouldn't give in. When she set her mind to it, she could really haggle. Years later in Dover, New Hampshire, I watched her drive a furniture salesman nuts. He offered to give her the couch for free just to get rid of her.

The gypsy was tougher. He marched out. Then, a few days later, he came back to take another look. He stood looking at the tux my mother had in the meantime brushed off. He looked and we looked. Finally, he let out a big sigh like a man making a difficult and irreversible decision. We got the pig the next day. It was alive and looked just like the one in the picture.

READING PHILOSOPHY AT NIGHT

*It is night again around me; I feel as though there had been
lightning—for a brief span of time I was entirely in my element
and in my light.* —NIETZSCHE

*The mind loves the unknown. It loves images whose meaning is
unknown, since the meaning of the mind itself is unknown.*
—MAGRITTE

I wore Buster Keaton's expression of exaggerated calm. I could have
been sitting on the edge of a cliff with my back to the abyss trying to
look normal.

Now I read philosophy in the morning. When I was younger and lived
in the city it was always at night. "That's how you ruined your eyes,"
my mother keeps saying. I sat and read late into the night. The quieter
it got, the more clearheaded I became—or so it seemed to me. In a
sparsely furnished room above an Italian grocery, I would be struggling with some intricate philosophical argument that promised a magnificent insight at its conclusion. I could sense it with my whole being.

Written for the special issue of *Antaeus* on the pleasures of reading and first published in 1987.

I couldn't put the book away, and it was getting really late. I had to be at work in the morning. Even had I tried to sleep, my head would have been full of Kant or Hegel. So, I wouldn't sleep. At some point I'd make that decision. I'd be sitting there with the open book, my face reflected dimly in the dark windowpane, the great city all around me grown quiet. I was watching myself watch myself. A very strange experience.

The first time it happened I was twenty. It was six o'clock in the morning. It was winter. It was dark and very cold. I was in Chicago riding the El to work seated between two heavily bundled-up old women. The train was overheated, but each time the door opened at one of the elevated platforms, a blast of cold air would send shivers through us. The lights, too, kept flickering. As the train changed tracks, the lights would go out for a moment and I would stop reading the history of philosophy I had borrowed from the library the previous day. "Why is there something rather than nothing?" the book asked, quoting Parmenides. It was as if my eyes were opened. I could not stop looking at my fellow passengers. How incredible, I thought, all of us being here, existing.

Philosophy is like a homecoming. I have a recurring dream about the street where I was born. It is always night. I'm walking past vaguely familiar buildings trying to find our house, but somehow it is not there. I retrace my steps on that short block of only a few buildings, all of which are there except the one I want. The effort leaves me exhausted and saddened.

In another version of this same dream, I catch a glimpse of our house. There it is, at last, but for some reason I'm unable to get any closer to it. No lights are on. I look for our window, but it is even darker there on the third floor. The entire building seems abandoned. "It can't be," I tell myself in horror.

Once in one of these dreams, many years ago, I saw someone

at our window, hunched over as if watching the street intently. That's how my grandmother would wait late into the night for us to come home, except that this was a stranger. Even without being able to make out his face, I was sure of that.

Most of the time, however, there's no one in sight during the dream. The facades of buildings still retain their pockmarks and other signs of the war. The streetlights are out and there's no moon in the sky, so it's not clear to me how I am able to see all this in complete darkness. The street I am walking on is long, empty, and seemingly without end.

Whoever reads philosophy reads himself as much as he reads the philosopher. I am in dialogue with certain decisive events in my life as much as I am with the ideas on the page. Meaning is the matter of my existence. My effort to understand is a perpetual circling around a few obsessive images.

Like everyone else, I have my hunches. All my experiences make a kind of untaught ontology, which precedes all my readings. What I am trying to conceptualize with the help of the philosopher is that which I have already intuited.

That's one way of looking at it.

The Meditation of yesterday filled my mind with so many doubts that it is no longer in my power to forget them. And yet, I do not see in what manner I can resolve them; and, just as if I had all of a sudden fallen into very deep water, I am so disconcerted that I can neither make certain of setting my feet on the bottom, nor can I swim and so support myself on the surface. I shall nevertheless make an effort and follow anew the same path as that on which I yesterday entered, i.e., I shall proceed by setting aside all that in which the least doubt could be supposed to exist, just as if I had discovered that it was absolutely false; and I shall ever follow in this road until I have met with something which is certain, or at least, if I can do nothing else, until I have learned for certain that there's nothing in the world that is certain. Archimedes, in order that he might draw the terrestrial globe out of its place, and transport it elsewhere, demanded only that one point should be fixed and immovable; in the same way I shall have the right to conceive high hopes if I am happy enough to discover one thing only which is certain and indubitable.

I love this passage of Descartes; his beginning again, his not wanting to be fooled. It describes the ambition of philosophy in all its nobility and desperation. I prefer this doubting Descartes to the later one, famous in his certainties. The poetry of indeterminacy still casts its spell. Of course, he's greedy for the absolute, but so is everybody else. Or are they?

There's an Eastern European folk song that tells of a girl who kept tossing an apple higher and higher until she tossed it as high as the clouds. To her surprise the apple didn't come down. One of the clouds got it. She waited with arms outstretched, but the apple stayed up there. All she could do was plead with the cloud to return her apple, but that's another story. I like the first part when the impossible still reigns.

I remember lying in a ditch and staring at some pebbles while German bombers were flying over our heads. That was long ago. I don't remember the face of my mother nor the faces of the people who were there with us, but I still see those perfectly ordinary pebbles.

"It is not 'how' things are in the world that is mystical, but that it exists," says Wittgenstein. I felt precisely that. Time had stopped. I was watching myself watching the pebbles and trembling with fear. Then time moved on and the experience was over.

The pebbles stayed in their otherness, stayed forever in my memory. Can language do justice to such moments of heightened consciousness? Speech is always less. When it comes to conveying what it means to be truly conscious, one approximates, one fails miserably.

Wittgenstein puts it this way: "What finds its reflection in language, language cannot represent. What expresses 'itself' in language, we cannot express by means of language." This has been my experience many times. Words are impoverishments, splendid poverties.

I knew someone who once tried to persuade me otherwise. He considered himself a logical positivist. These are people who remind you, for example, that you can speak of a pencil's dimension, location, appearance, and state of motion or rest but not of its intelligence and love of music. The moment I hear that, the poet in me rebels and I want to write a poem about an intelligent pencil in love with music. In other words, what these people regard as nonsense, I suspect to be full of imaginative possibilities.

There's a wonderful story told about Wittgenstein and his Cambridge colleague, the Italian economist Piero Sraffa. Apparently they often discussed philosophy. "One day," as Justus Hartnack has it, "when Wittgenstein was defending his view that a proposition has the same logical form as the fact it depicts, Sraffa made a gesture used by Neapolitans to express contempt and asked Wittgenstein what the logical form of that was? According to Wittgenstein's own recollection, it was this question which made him realize that his belief that a fact could have a logical form was untenable."

As for my "logical" friend, we argued all night. "What cannot be said, cannot be thought," he claimed. And then—after I blurted out something about silence being the language of consciousness—"You're silent because you have nothing to say!" In any case, it got to the point where we were calling each other "you dumb shit." We were drinking large quantities of red wine, misunderstanding each other totally, and only stopped bickering when his disheveled wife came to the bedroom door and told us to shut up.

Then I told him a story.

One day in Yugoslavia, just after the war, we made a class trip to the town War Museum. At the entrance we found a battered German tank, which delighted us. Inside the museum one could look at a few rifles, hand grenades, and uniforms, but not much else. Most of the space was taken up by photographs. These we were urged to examine. One saw people who had been hanged and people about to be hanged. The executioners stood around smoking. There were piles of corpses everywhere. Some were naked. Men and women with their genitals showing. That made some kid laugh.

Then we saw a man having his throat cut. The killer sat on the man's chest with a knife in his hand. He seemed pleased to be photographed. The victim's eyes I don't remember. A few men stood around gawking. There were clouds in the sky.

There were always clouds, blades of grass, tree stumps, bushes, and rocks no one was paying any attention to. In one photograph the earth was covered with snow. A miserable, teeth-chattering January morning and someone making someone else's life even more miserable. Or the rain would be falling. A small, hard rain that would wash the blood off the hands immediately, that would make one of the killers catch a bad cold. I imagined him sitting that same night with feet in a bucket of hot water and sipping tea.

That occurred to me later. Now that we had seen all there was to see, we were made to sit on the lawn outside the museum and eat our lunch. It was poor fare. Most of us had plum jam spread on slices of bread. A few had lard sprinkled with paprika. One kid had nothing but bread and scallions. I guess that's all they had at his home that day. Everybody thought it was funny. Someone snatched his thick slice of black bread and threw it up in the air. It got caught in a tree. The poor kid tried to get it down by throwing stones at it. He kept missing. Then he tried climbing the tree. He kept sliding back. Even our teacher who came to see what the commotion was all about thought it was hilarious.

As for the grass, there was plenty of it, each blade distinct and carefully sharpened, as it were. There were also clouds in the sky and many large flies of the kind one encounters in slaughterhouses, which kept pestering us and interrupting our laughter.

And here's what went through my head just last night as I lay awake thinking of my friend's argument:

The story you told him had nothing to do with what you were talking about.

The story had everything to do with what we were talking about.

I can think of a hundred objections after all these years.

Only idiots want something neat, something categorical—and I never talk unless I know!

Aha! You're mixing poetry and philosophy. Wittgenstein wouldn't give you the time of day!

"Everything looks very busy to me," says Jasper Johns, and that's my problem, too.

I remember a strange cat, exceedingly emaciated, that scratched on my door the day I was scratching my head over Hegel's Phenomenology of the Spirit.

Who said, "Whatever can be thought must be fictitious"?

You got me there! How about a bagel Hegel?

Still and all . . . And above all! Let's not forget "above all."

Here's what Nietzsche said to the ceiling: "The rank of the philosopher is determined by the rank of his laughter." But he couldn't really laugh. No matter how hard Friedrich tried, he couldn't really laugh.

I know because I'm a connoisseur of paradox. All the good-looking oxymorons are in love with me and come to visit me in my bed at night.

Have a tomato Plato!

*

Wallace Stevens has several beautiful poems about solitary readers. "The House Was Quiet and the World Was Calm" is one. It speaks of a "truth in a calm world." It happens! The world and the mind growing so calm that truth becomes visible.

It must be late at night "where shines the light that lets be the things that are"—the light of insomnia. The solitude of the reader of philosophy and the solitude of the philosopher drawing together. The impression that one is thinking and anticipating another man's subtlest turns of thought and beginning to truly understand.

Understanding depends on the relationship of what we are to what we have been: the being of the moment. Consciousness stirring up our conscience, our history. Consciousness as the light of clarity and history as the dark night of the soul.

The pleasures of philosophy are the pleasures of reduction—the epiphanies of hinting in a few words at complex matters. Both poetry and philosophy, for instance, are concerned with Being. What is a lyric poem, one might say, but the recreation of the experience of Being. In both cases, that need to get it down to its essentials, to say the unsayable and let the truth of Being shine through.

History, on the other hand, is antireductive. Nothing tidy about it. Chaos! Bedlam! Hopeless tangle! My own history and the history of this century like a child and his blind mother on the street. She mumbles, talks to herself, sings and wails as she leads the way across some busy intersection.

You'd think the sole meaning of history is to stand truth happily upon its head!

Poor poetry. Like imperturbable Buster Keaton alone with the woman he loves on an ocean liner set adrift on the stormy sea. Or an even better example: Again drifting over an endless ocean, he comes across a billboard, actually a target for battleship practice. Keaton climbs it, takes out his fishing rod and bait, and fishes peacefully. That's what great poetry is. A superb serenity in the face of chaos. Wise enough to play the fool.

And always the contradictions: I have Don Quixote and his windmills in my head and Sancho Panza and his mule kicking in my heart.

That's just some figure of speech. Who could live without them? Do they tell the truth? Do they conceal it? I really don't know. That's why I keep going back to philosophy. I want to learn how to think clearly about these matters.

It is morning. It is night. The book is open. The text is difficult, the text is momentarily opaque. My mind is wandering. My mind is struggling to grasp the always elusive, the always hinting—whatever it is.

It, it, I keep calling it. An infinity of "it" without a single antecedent—like a cosmic static in my ear.

Just then, about to give up, I find the following on a page of Heidegger: "No thinker has ever entered into another thinker's solitude. Yet it is only from its solitude that all thinking, in a hidden mode, speaks to the thinking that comes after or that went before."

For a moment it all comes together: poetry, philosophy, history. I see—in the sense of being able to picture and feel—the human weight of another's solitude. So many of them seated with a book. Day breaking. Thought becoming image. Image becoming thought.

CHINESE BOXES AND PUPPET THEATERS

Consciousness is the only home of which we know.

—DICKINSON

Two images come to mind when I think of Emily Dickinson's poems: Chinese boxes and puppet theaters. The image of boxes inside boxes has to do with cosmology, and theaters and puppets with psychology. They're, of course, intimately related.

The intimate immensity of consciousness is Dickinson's constant preoccupation. I imagine her sitting in her room for hours on end, with eyes closed, looking inward. To be conscious is already to be divided, to be multiple. There are so many me's within me. The whole world comes into our inner room. Visions and mysteries and secret thoughts. "How strange it all is," Dickinson must have told herself.

Every universe is enclosed in some other universe. She opens boxes, Pandora's boxes. There's terror in one; awe and ecstasy in the next one. She cannot leave the boxes alone. Her imagination and love of truth conspire against her. There are so many boxes. Every so often, she may believe that she has reached the last one, but on closer examination it proves to contain still another box. The appearances deceive.

Written for an Emily Dickinson issue of the magazine *Ironwood* in 1986.

That's the lesson. A trick is being played on her as it is being played on all of us who wish to reach the truth of things.

"As above, so below," Hermes Trismegistus claimed. Emerson thought the same. He believed that clarity and heightened understanding would follow the knowledge of that primary law of our being. Dickinson's experience of the self is very different. The self for her is the place of paradoxes, oxymorons, and endless ambiguities. She welcomed every one of them the way Emerson welcomed his clarities. "Impossibility, like wine, exhilarates," she told us.

Did she believe in God? Yes and no. God is the cunning of all these boxes fitting inside each other, perhaps? More likely, God is just another box. Neither the tiniest one nor the biggest imaginable. There are boxes even God knows nothing of.

In each box there's a theater. All the shadows the self casts and the World and the infinite Universe. A play is in progress, perhaps always the same play. Only the scenery and costumes differ from box to box. The puppets enact the Great Questions—or rather Dickinson allowed them to enact themselves. She sat spellbound and watched.

Some theaters have a Christian setting. There is God and his Son. There is Immortality and the snake in Paradise. Heaven is like a circus in one of her poems. When the tent is gone, "miles of Stare" is what remains behind. In the meantime, the Passion and Martyrdom of Emily Dickinson go on being played under the tent and under the open skies. There's no question, as far as I am concerned, that real suffering took place among these puppets.

In some other theaters the scenery could have been painted by De Chirico. In them we have a play of abstract nouns capitalized and personified against a metaphysical landscape of straight lines and vanishing points. Ciphers and Algebras stroll along "Miles and Miles of Nought" and converse. "The Truth is Bald and Cold," she says. Truth is a terrifying mannequin, as Sylvia Plath also suspected. This is the theater of metaphysical terror.

Death is in all the plays and so is this woman. Death is a kind of master of ceremonies, opening boxes while concealing others in his pockets. The self is divided. Dickinson is both on stage and in the audience watching herself. "The Battle fought between Soul and No Man" is what we are all watching.

That she made all this happen within the length of a lyric poem is astonishing. In Dickinson we have a short poem that builds and dismantles cosmologies. She understood that a poem and our consciousness are both a theater. Or rather, many theaters.

"Who, besides myself, knows what Ariadne is," wrote Nietzsche. Emily Dickinson knew much better than he did.

NOTES ON POETRY AND PHILOSOPHY

*It is the hardship of the times that before an artist can fashion an
icon he must compose the theology that his icon will reinforce.*

—HAROLD ROSENBERG

Some sort of Academy of Fine Arts from which they stole the bust of
the philosopher Socrates so he may accompany them on what was to be
a night of serious drinking.

It was heavy. The two of them had to lug it together. They went
from tavern to tavern like that. They'd make Socrates sit in his own
chair. When the waiter came, they'd ask for three glasses. Socrates sat
over his drink looking wise.

Later, in a low dive where gypsies were playing, a couple of
drunken women joined them. They loved their "friend." They kept
kissing Socrates and trying to make him drink wine. His mouth turned
red. He could have been bleeding.

They left Socrates, as the day was breaking, at a streetcar stop.
The number 2 would arrive full of sleepy factory workers, the doors
would open, and there'd be the Greek philosopher with his blind gaze
and his bloodied mouth, waiting on the sidewalk to be taken up.

Written as a commentary on an essay linking my own poetry with Heidegger's
philosophy for *New Literary History* in 1989.

KNIGHTS OF SORROWFUL COUNTENANCE
SITTING LATE OVER DOG-EARED BOOKS

That was my father's story. Philosophy intrigued him all his life. He loved it. He made fun of it. He was the one who gave me Heidegger's *Being and Time*. We read its most difficult passages together and discussed the book endlessly.

"Amateur philosophers, the worst kind!" he used to say about us.

I continued to read Heidegger as his various works became available in English. The attraction was strong for a Surrealist—which is what I considered myself in those days. "Avant-garde is revolt and metaphysics," says Rosenberg. You cannot have great poetry without at least an attempt at one. That's how I understood the legacy of Rimbaud and Stevens. Heidegger made my own intuitions about the philosophical ambitions of modern poetry clearer to me.

The other appeal of Heidegger was his attack on subjectivism, his idea that it is not the poet who speaks through the poem but the work itself. This has always been my experience. The poet is at the mercy of his metaphors. Everything is at the mercy of the poet's metaphors—even Language, who is their Lord and master.

"O PARADISO!" MY POP SANG IN THE SHOWER

The twentieth-century poet is "a metaphysician in the dark," according to Wallace Stevens.

That sounds to me like a version of that old joke about chasing a black cat in a dark room. The room today is more crowded than ever. In addition to Poetry, Theology is also there, and so are various representatives of Western and Eastern Philosophies. There's a lot of bumping of heads in the dark. The famous kitty, however, isn't there. . . . Still, the poets continue to cry from time to time: "We got her, folks!"

Unless, of course, it's the Devil himself they've got by the tail instead!

THE FISH IS SPHINX TO THE CAT

There is a major misunderstanding in literary criticism as to how ideas get into poems. The poets, supposedly, proceed in one of these two ways: they either state their ideas directly or they find equivalents for them. What is usually called philosophical poetry seems to be either a poetry of heightened eloquence or some variety of symbolism. In each case, the assumption is that the poet knows beforehand what he or she wishes to say and the writing of the poem is the search for the most effective means of gussying up these ideas.

If this were correct, poetry would simply repeat what has been thought and said before. There would be no poetic thinking in the way Heidegger conceives of it. There would be no hope that poetry could have any relation to truth.

IN A HEAD THIS OLD THERE'S A BLIND HEN THAT OCCASIONALLY FINDS A KERNEL OF CORN AND HER NAME IS LOVE

My poems (in the beginning) are like a table on which one places interesting things one has found on one's walks: a pebble, a rusty nail, a strangely shaped root, the corner of a torn photograph, etc., . . . where after months of looking at them and thinking about them daily, certain surprising relationships, which hint at meanings, begin to appear.

These *objets trouvés* of poetry are, of course, bits of language. The poem is the place where one hears what the language is really saying, where the full meaning of words begins to emerge.

That's not quite right! It's not so much what the words mean that is crucial, but rather, what they show and reveal. The literal leads to the figurative, and inside every poetic figure of value there's a theater where a play is in progress. The play is about gods and demons and the world in its baffling presence and variety.

In its essence an interesting poem is an epistemological and meta-physical problem for the poet.

THE WAY A CHILD STUDIES THE MINUTE HAND OF HIS WATCH

Back in 1965 I sent some of my object poems ("Fork" among them) to a literary magazine. They came back with a letter that said something like this: "Dear Mr. Simic . . . you're obviously a sensible young man, so why do you waste your time by writing about knives, spoons, and forks?"

I guess the editor's premise was that there were things worthy of poetry and that the fork in my hand was not one of them. In other words, "serious" subjects and "serious" ideas make "serious" poems, etc. He was just trying to give me fatherly advice.

I was surprised by the resistance some people had to these poems. "Back to things themselves," said Husserl, and the Imagist had the same idea. An object is the irreducible itself, a convenient place to begin, it seemed to me.

What appealed to me, too, was the discipline, the attention required, and the dialectics that went with it. You look and you don't see. It's so familiar that it is invisible, etc. I mean, anybody can tell when you're faking it. Everybody is an expert when it comes to forks.

Plus, all genuine poetry in my view is antipoetry.

*

LIKE A BARBER COLLEGE HAIRCUT

Poets think they're pitchers when they're really catchers.

—JACK SPICER

Everything would be very simple if we could will our metaphors. We cannot.

This is true of poems, too. We may start believing that we are recreating an experience, that we are making an attempt at mimesis, but then the language takes over. Suddenly the words have a mind of their own.

It's like saying, "I wanted to go to church but the poem took me to the dog races."

When it first happened I was horrified. It took me years to admit that the poem is smarter than I am. Now I go where it wants to go.

A SHORT-ORDER COOK PEELING METAPHYSICAL ONIONS

Heidegger says that we will never understand properly what poetry is until we understand what thinking is. Then he says, most interestingly, that the nature of thinking is something other than thinking, something other than willing.

It's this "other" that poetry sets traps for.

ETERNITY, THE PRESENT MOMENT, PLAYING WITH EACH OTHER

My hunch has always been that our deepest experiences are wordless. There may be images, but there are no words to describe the gap between seeing and saying, for example. The labor of poetry is finding ways through language to point to what cannot be put into words.

Robert Duncan had this to say about the pronoun "it," which for him was the most interesting word in the language, as it is for me:

> The gnostics and magicians claim to know or would know *Its* real nature, which they believe to be miswritten or cryptically written in the text of the actual world. But Williams is right in his "no ideas but in things"; for *It* has only the actual universe to realize *Itself.* We ourselves in our actuality, as the poem in its actuality, its thingness, are facts, factors, in which *It* makes *Itself* real.

Duncan is speaking out of the Romantic and occult tradition, but here he's close to Heidegger, who speaks of the "It" that gives Being, the "It" that gives Time.

The poem that thinks is a place where we open to "It." The poem's difficulty is that it presents an experience language cannot get at. Being cannot be represented or uttered—as poor realists foolishly believe—but only hinted at. Writing is always a rough translation from wordlessness into words.

VERY QUIET. PSSST.

We cannot say what reality is, only what it seems like to us.
—GASTON BACHELARD

Every new metaphor is a new thought, a fragment of a new myth of reality.

Metaphor is a part of the not-knowing aspect of art, and yet I'm firmly convinced that it is the supreme way of searching for truth. How can this be? I don't know. I have never been able to figure it out to my satisfaction.

Poetry attracts me because it makes trouble for thinkers.

TO UNDERSTAND, IS THAT AGAINST NATURE, AGAINST GOD?

I like a poem that understates, that leaves out, breaks off, remains open-ended. A poem as a piece of the unutterable whole. To "complete," to pretend that it is possible to do so (and here, too, I'm following Heidegger), is to set arbitrary boundaries to what is boundless.

Emily Dickinson's poems do that for me. Her ambiguities are philosophical. She lives with uncertainties, even delights in them. To the great questions she remains "unshielded," as Heidegger would say. The nature of presence itself is her subject. The awe of . . . the supreme mystery of consciousness watching itself.

Ideally then, a poem that speculates is full of mirrors . . . it measures the gap between words and what they presume to name . . . the gap between being and being-said.

LIKE THOSE BEAUTIFUL WOMEN ASLEEP A HUNDRED YEARS?

Something must be for something to be said.

—PAUL RICOEUR

The world was going up in flames and I was making screeching noises on my violin. The baby Nero. Once walking to the market I saw people in a ditch with their throats cut. Then I got lice wearing a German helmet.

This used to be a famous story in my family. I remember those cold, hungry winters just after the war, with everybody huddled around the coal stove, talking and worrying late into the night. Sooner or later, inevitably, someone would bring up my German helmet full of lice as comic relief. Old people would have tears of laughter in their eyes. A kid dumb enough to walk around with a German helmet full of lice. They were crawling all over it! A blind man could see them!

I sat there saying nothing, pretending to be equally amused, nodding my head in agreement while thinking to myself, what a bunch of idiots! They, of course, had no idea how I got the helmet, and I wasn't about to tell them.

It was the day after the liberation of Belgrade. I was up in the fairgrounds by St. Mark's church with a few older boys, more or less snooping around. Then, all of a sudden, we saw them! Two German soldiers, obviously dead, stretched out on the ground. We drew closer to take a better look. They had no weapons. Their boots were gone, but there was a helmet, which had fallen off to the side. I don't remember what the others did, but I went for the helmet. I tiptoed so as not to wake the dead men. I also kept my eyes averted. I never saw their faces, even if sometimes I think I did. Everything else about that moment is still intensely clear to me.

GIUSEPPE VERDI, THE FAMOUS
CHINESE-AMERICAN VENTRILOQUIST...

Poetry is not just "a verbal universe that looks inwardly on itself," as someone said. Neither is poetry merely a recreation of experience. "It was and it was not," is how the old storytellers used to begin their tales. It lies to tell the truth.

Mallarmé thought there were two kinds of language: *parole brute*, which names things, and *parole essentielle*, which distances us from things. One serves representation and the other the allusive, fictive world of poetry. He's wrong. It's not that clear-cut. If anything, it's both. Poetry is impure. I don't think Heidegger understands this either.

The poem is an attempt at self-recovery, self-recognition, self-remembering, the marvel of being again. That this happens at times, happens in poems in many different and contradictory ways, is as great a mystery as the mystery of being itself and cause for serious thought.

from

THE
UNEMPLOYED
FORTUNE-TELLER

THE FLUTE PLAYER IN THE PIT

I say the word or two that has to be said . . . and remind every
man and every woman of something.

—WALT WHITMAN

Thirty years ago in New York City I used to stay up late almost every night listening to Jean Shepherd's rambling soliloquies on the radio. He had a show with a lot of interesting talk and a little music. One night he told a lengthy story, which I still remember, about the sacred ritual of some Amazon tribe. It went roughly like this:

Once every seven years, the members of this remote tribe would dig a deep hole in the jungle and lower their finest flute player into it. He would be given no food, only a little water and no way of climbing out. After this was done, the other members of the tribe would bid him good-bye, never to return. Seven days later, the flute player, sitting crosslegged at the bottom of his hole, would begin to play. Of course, the tribesmen could not hear him, only the gods could, and that was the point.

According to Shepherd, who was not above putting on his audience of insomniacs, an anthropologist had hidden himself during the ritual and recorded the man playing the flute. Tonight Shepherd was going to play that very tape.

Written as an introduction to *The Best American Poetry 1992*.

I was spooked. Here was a man, soon to die, already dizzy with hunger and despair, summoning whatever strength and belief in gods he had. A New World Orpheus, it occurred to me.

Shepherd went on talking until finally, in the wee-hour silence of the night and my shabby room on East 13th Street, the faint sound of the otherworldly flute was heard: its solitary, infinitely sad squeak with the raspy breath of the living human being still audible in it from time to time, making the best of his predicament. I didn't care then nor do I care now whether Shepherd made up the whole story. We are all at the bottom of our own private pits, even here in New York.

All the arts are about the impossible predicament. That's their fatal attraction. "Words fail me," poets often say. Every poem is an act of desperation or, if you prefer, a throw of the dice. God is the ideal audience, especially if you can't sleep or if you're in a hole in the Amazon. If he's absent, so much the worse.

The poet sits before a blank piece of paper with a need to say many things in the small space of the poem. The world is huge, the poet is alone, and the poem is just a bit of language, a few scratchings of a pen surrounded by the silence of the night.

It could be that the poet wishes to tell you about his or her life. A few images of some fleeting moment when one was happy or exceptionally lucid. The secret wish of poetry is to stop time. The poet wants to retrieve a face, a mood, a cloud in the sky, a tree in the wind, and take a kind of mental photograph of that moment in which you as a reader recognize yourself. Poems are other people's snapshots in which we recognize ourselves.

Next, the poet is driven by the desire to tell the truth. "How is truth to be said?" asks Gwendolyn Brooks. Truth matters. Getting it right matters. The realists advise: open your eyes and look. People of imagination warn: close your eyes to see better. There's truth with eyes open and there's truth with eyes closed and they often do not recognize each other on the street.

Next, one wishes to say something about the age in which one lives. Every age has its injustices and immense sufferings, and ours is scarcely an exception. There's the history of human vileness to contend with and there are fresh instances every day to think about. One can think about it all one wants, but making sense of it is another matter. We live in a time in which there are hundreds of ways of explaining the world. Everything from every variety of religion to every species of scientism is believed. The task of poetry, perhaps, is to salvage a trace of the authentic from the wreckage of religious, philosophical, and political systems.

Next, one wants to write a poem so well crafted that it would do honor to the tradition of Emily Dickinson, Ezra Pound, and Wallace Stevens, to name only a few masters.

At the same time, one hopes to rewrite that tradition, subvert it, turn it upside down and make some living space for oneself.

At the same time, one wants to entertain the reader with outrageous metaphors, flights of imagination, and heartbreaking pronouncements.

At the same time, one has, for the most part, no idea of what one is doing. Words make love on the page like flies in the summer heat and the poet is merely the bemused spectator. The poem is as much the result of chance as of intention. Probably more so.

At the same time, one hopes to be read and loved in China in a thousand years the same way the ancient Chinese poets are loved and read in our own day, and so forth.

This is a small order from a large menu requiring one of those many-armed Indian divinities to serve as a waiter.

One great defect of poetry, or one of its sublime attractions—depending on your view—is that it wants to include everything. In the cold light of reason, poetry is impossible to write.

Of course, there would be no anthology of best poems if the impossible did not happen occasionally. Authentic poems get written, and that's the best-kept secret in any age. In the history of the world the poet is ever present, invisible and often inaudible. Just when everything else seems to be going to hell in America, poetry is doing fine. The predictions of its demise, about which we so often read, are plain wrong, just as most of the intellectual prophecies in our century have been wrong. Poetry proves again and again that any single overall theory of anything doesn't work. Poetry is always the cat concert under the window of the room in which the official version of reality is being written. The academic critics write, for instance, that poetry is the instrument of the ideology of the ruling class and that everything is political. The tormentors of Anna Akhmatova are their patron saints. But what if poets are not crazy? What if they convey the feel of a historical period better than anybody else? Obviously, poetry engages something essential and overlooked in human beings, and it is this ineffable quality that has always ensured its longevity. "To glimpse the essential . . . stay flat on your back all day, and moan," says E. M. Cioran. There's more than that to poetry, of course, but that's a beginning.

Lyric poets perpetuate the oldest values on earth. They assert the individual's experience against that of the tribe. Emerson claimed that to be a genius meant "to believe your own thoughts, to believe that what is true for you in your private heart is true for all men." Lyric poetry since the Greeks has always assumed something like that, but American poetry since Whitman and Emerson has made it its main conviction. Everything in the world, profane or sacred, needs to be reexamined repeatedly in the light of one's own experience.

Here, now, I, amazed to find myself living my life . . . The American poet is a modern citizen of a democracy who lacks any clear historical, religious, or philosophical foundation. Sneering Marxists used to characterize such statements as "typical bourgeois individualism." "They adore the smell of their own shit," a fellow I used to know said about poets. He was a Maoist, and the idea of each human being finding his or her own truth was incomprehensible to him. Still, this is what Robert Frost, Charles Olson, and even Elizabeth Bishop had in mind. They were realists who had not yet decided what reality is. Their poetry defends the sanctity of that pursuit in which reality and identity are forever being rediscovered.

It's not imagination or ideas that our poets primarily trust, but examples, narratives, or specific experiences. There's more than a little of the Puritan diarist still left in poets. Like their ancestors, they worry about the state of their inner lives in between entries about the weather. The problem of identity is ever present, as is the nagging suspicion that one's existence lacks meaning. The working premise, nevertheless, is that each self, even in its most private concerns, is representative, that the "aesthetic problem," as John Ashbery has said, is a "microcosm of all human problems," that the poem is a place where the "I" of the poet, by a kind of visionary alchemy, becomes a mirror for all of us.

"America is not finished, perhaps never will be," Whitman said. Our poetry is the dramatic knowledge of that state. Its heresy is that it takes a part of the truth for the whole truth and makes it a "temporary stay against confusion," in Robert Frost's famous formulation. In physics it is the infinitely small that contradicts the general law, and the same is true of poetry at its best. What we love in it is its democracy of values, its recklessness, its individualism, and its freedom. There's nothing more American and more hopeful than its poetry.

> *one dark, still Sunday*
>
> —H. D. THOREAU

The black dog on the chain wags his tail as I walk by. The house and the barn of his master are sagging, as if about to collapse with the weight of the sky. On my neighbor's porch and in his yard there are old cars, stoves, refrigerators, washing machines, and dryers that he keeps carting back from the town dump for some unclear and still undecided future use. All of it is broken, rusty, partly dismantled and scattered about, except for the new-looking and incongruous plaster statue of the Virgin with eyes lowered as if embarrassed to be there. Past his house, there's a spectacular winter sunset over the lake, the kind one used to see in paintings sold in back of discount department stores. As for the flute player, I remember reading that in the distant Southwest there are ancient matchstick figures on the walls of desert caves and that some of them are playing the flute. In New Hampshire, where I am now, there's only this dark house, the ghostly statue, the silence of the woods, and the cold winter night falling down in a big hurry.

FOOD AND HAPPINESS

Sadness and good food are incompatible. The old sages knew that wine lets the tongue loose, but one can grow melancholy with even the best bottle, especially as one grows older. The appearance of food, however, brings instant happiness. A *paella*, a *choucroute garnie*, a pot of *tripes à la mode de Caen*, and so many other dishes of peasant origin guarantee merriment. The best talk is around that table. Poetry and wisdom are its company. The true Muses are cooks. Cats and dogs don't stay far from the busy kitchen. Heaven is a pot of chili simmering on the stove. If I were to write about the happiest days of my life, many of them would have to do with food and wine and a table full of friends.

> *Homer never wrote on an empty stomach.*
>
> —RABELAIS

One could compose an autobiography mentioning every memorable meal in one's life and it would probably make better reading than what one ordinarily gets. Honestly, what would you rather have, the description of a first kiss or of stuffed cabbage done to perfection?

I have to admit, I remember better what I've eaten than what I've thought. My memory is especially vivid about those far-off days from

Written for the special issue of *Antaeus* on food, wine, and the art of eating and published in 1992.

1944 to 1949 in Yugoslavia, when we were mostly starving. The black market flourished. Women exchanged their wedding rings and silk underwear for hams. Occasionally someone invited us to an illicit feast on a day everyone else was hungry.

I'll begin with the day I realized that there was more to food than just stuffing yourself. I was nine years old. I ate Dobrosav Cvetković's *burek*, and I can still see it and taste it when I close my eyes.

A *burek* is a kind of pie made with phyllo dough and stuffed with either ground meat, cheese, or spinach. It is eaten everywhere in the Near East and the Balkans. Like pizza today, it's usually good no matter where you get it, but it can also be a work of art. My father said that when Dobrosav retired from his bakery in Skopje, the mayor and his cronies, after realizing that he was gone, sent a police warrant after him. The cops brought him back in handcuffs! "Dobrosav," they said visiting him in jail, "how can you do a thing like that to us? At least make us one last *burek*, and then you can go wherever your heart desires."

I ate that famous *burek* forty-four years ago on a cold winter morning with snow falling. Dobrosav made it illegally in his kitchen and sold it to select customers, who used to knock on his door and enter looking like foreign agents making a pickup. The day I was his guest—for the sake of my poor exiled father who was so good to Dobrosav—the *burek* came with meat. I ate every greasy crumb that fell out of my mouth on the table while old Dobrosav studied me the way a cat studies a bird in a cage. He wanted my opinion. I understood this was no fluke. Dobrosav knew something other *burek* makers did not. I believe I told him so. This was my first passionate outburst to a cook.

Then there was my aunt, Ivanka Bajalović. Every time I wiped my plate clean she shook her head sadly. "One day," she'd say to me, "I'll make so much food you won't be able to finish it." With my appetite in those days that seemed impossible, but she did it! She found a huge pot ordinarily used to make soap and filled it with enough beans to "feed an army," as the neighbors said.

All Serbians, of whatever gender or age, have their own opinion as to how this dish ought to be made. Some folks like it thick, others soupy. Between the two extremes there are many nuances. Almost everybody adds bacon, pork ribs, sausage, paprika, and hot peppers. It's a class thing. The upper classes make it lean, the lower fatty. My aunt, who was educated in London and speaks English with a British accent to this day, made it like a ditchdigger's wife. The beans were spicy hot.

My uncle was one of those wonders of nature everybody envies, a skinny guy who could eat all day long and never gain any weight. I'm sad to admit that I've no idea how much we actually ate that day. Anywhere between three and five platefuls is a good guess. These were European soup plates, nice and roomy, that could take loads of beans. It was a summer afternoon. We were eating on a big terrace watched by nosy neighbors, who kept score. At some point, I remember, I just slid off my chair onto the floor.

I'm dying, it occurred to me. My uncle was still wielding his spoon with his face deep in his plate. There was a kind of hush. In the beginning, everybody talked and kidded around, but now my aunt was exhausted and had gone in to lie down. There were still plenty of beans, but I was through. I couldn't move. Finally, even my uncle staggered off to bed, and I was left alone, sitting under the table, the heat intolerable, the sun setting, my mind blurry, thinking, This is how a pig must feel.

On May 9, 1950, I asked all my relatives to give me money instead of presents for my birthday. When they did, I spent the entire day going with a friend from one pastry shop to another. We ate huge quantities of cream puffs, custard rolls, *dobos torta,* rum balls, pishingers, strudel with poppy seed, and other Viennese and Hungarian pastries. At dusk we had no money left. We were dragging ourselves in the general vicinity of the Belgrade railroad station when a man, out of breath and carrying a large suitcase, overtook us. He wondered if we could carry it to the station for him and we said we could. The suitcase was very heavy and it made a noise as if it was full of silverware or burglar's tools, but we managed somehow to get it to his train. There, he surprised us by paying us handsomely for our good deed. Without a moment's thought we returned to our favorite pastry shop, which was closing at that hour and where the help eyed us with alarm as we ordered more ice cream and cake.

In 1951 I lived an entire summer in a village on the Adriatic coast. Actually, the house my mother, brother, and I roomed at was a considerable distance from the village on a stretch of sandy beach. Our landlady, a war widow, was a fabulous cook. In her home I ate squid for the first time and began my lifelong love affair with olives. All her fish was grilled with a little olive oil, garlic, and parsley. I still prefer it that way.

My favorite dish was a plate of tiny surf fish called *girice*, which were fried in corn flour. We'd eat them with our fingers, head and all. Since it's no good to swim after lunch, all the guests would take a long siesta. I remember our deliciously cool room, the clean sheets, the soothing sound of the sea, the aftertaste and smell of the fish, and the long naps full of erotic dreams.

There were two females who obsessed me in that place. One was a theater actress from Zagreb in the room next to ours who used to sunbathe with her bikini top removed when our beach was deserted. I would hide in the bushes. The other was our landlady's sixteen-year-old daughter. I sort of tagged along after her. She must have been bored out of her wits to allow a thirteen-year-old boy to keep her company. We used to swim out to a rock in the bay where there were wild grapes. We'd lie sunbathing and popping the little blue grapes in our mouths.

And in the evening, once or twice, there was even a kiss, and then an exquisite risotto with mussels.

> *He that with his soup will drink,*
> *When he's dead won't sleep a wink.*

—OLD FRENCH SONG

In Paris I went to what can only be described as a school for losers. These were youngsters who were not destined for the further glories of French education but were en route to being petty bureaucrats and tradespeople. We ate lunch in school, and the food was mostly tolerable. We even drank red wine. The vegetable soup served on Tuesdays, however, was out of this world. One of the fat ladies I saw milling in the kitchen must have been a southerner, because the soup had a touch of Provence. For some reason, the other kids didn't care for it. Since the school rule was that you had to *manger* everything on your plate, and since I loved the soup so much, my neighbors at the table would let me have theirs. I'd end up eating three or four servings of that thick concoction with tomatoes, green and yellow beans, potatoes, carrots, white beans, noodles, and herbs. After that kind of eating, I usually fell asleep in class after lunch only to be rudely awakened by one of my teachers and ordered to a blackboard already covered with numbers. I'd stand there bewildered and feeling sleepy while time changed into eternity and nobody budged or said anything. My only solace was the lingering taste in my mouth of that divine soup.

Some years back I found myself in Genoa at an elegant reception in Palazzo Doria talking with the Communist mayor. "I love American food," he blurted out to me after I mentioned enjoying the local cuisine. I asked him what he had in mind. "I love potato chips," he told me. I had to agree, potato chips were pretty good.

When we came to the United States in 1954, it now seems as if that's all my brother and I ate. We sat in front of the TV eating potato chips out of huge bags. Our parents approved. We were learning English and being American. It's a wonder we have any teeth left today. We visited the neighborhood supermarket twice a day to sightsee the junk food. There were so many things to taste, and we were interested in all of them. There was deviled ham, marshmallows, Spam, Hawaiian Punch, Fig Newtons, V-8 Juice, Mounds Bars, Planters Peanuts, and so much else, all good. Everything was good in America except for Wonder Bread, which we found disgusting.

It took me a few years to come to my senses. One day I met Salvatore. He told me I ate like a dumb shit and took me home to his mother. Sal and his three brothers were all well employed, unmarried, living at home, and giving their paychecks to Mom. The father was dead, so there were just these four boys to feed. She did not stop cooking. Every meal was like a peasant wedding feast. Of course, her sons didn't appreciate it as far as she was concerned. "Are you crazy, Mom?" they'd shout in a chorus each time she brought in another steaming dish. The old lady didn't flinch. The day I came she was happy to have someone else at the table who was more appreciative, and I did not spare the compliments.

She cooked southern Italian dishes. Lots of olive oil and garlic. I recollect with a sense of heightened consciousness her linguine with anchovies. We drank red Sicilian wine with it. She'd put several open bottles on the table before the start of the meal. I never saw anything like it. She'd lie to us and say there was nothing more to eat, so we'd have at least two helpings, and then she'd bring out some sausage and peppers, and after that some kind of roast.

After the meal we'd remain at the table, drinking and listening to old records of Beniamino Gigli and Ferruccio Tagliavini. The old lady would still be around, urging on us a little more cheese, a little more cake. And then, just when we thought she had given up and gone to bed, she'd surprise us by bringing out a dish of fresh figs.

*

My late father, who never in his life refused another helping at the table, had a peculiarity common among gastronomes. The more he ate the more he talked about food. My mother was always amazed. We'd be done with a huge turkey roasted over sauerkraut and my father would begin reminiscing about a little breakfastlike sausage he'd had in some village on the Romanian border in 1929, or a fish soup a blind woman made for him in Marseilles in 1945. Well, she wasn't completely blind, and besides she was pretty to look at—in any case, after three or four stories like that we'd be hungry again. My father had a theory that if you were still hungry, say for a hot dog, after a meal at Lutèce, that meant that you were extraordinarily healthy. If a casual visitor to your house was not eating and drinking three minutes after his arrival, you had no manners. Of people who had no interest in food, he had absolutely no comprehension. He'd ask them questions like an anthropologist, and go away seriously puzzled and worried. He told me toward the end of his life that the greatest mistake he ever made was accepting his doctor's advice to eat and drink less after he passed seventy-five. He felt terrible until he went back to his old ways.

One day we are walking up Second Avenue and talking. We get into an elaborate philosophical argument, as we often do. I feel as if I've understood everything! I'm inspired! I'm quoting Kant, Descartes, Wittgenstein, when I notice he's no longer with me. I look around and locate him a block back staring into a shop window. I'm kind of pissed, especially since I have to walk back to where he's standing, since he doesn't move or answer my shouts. Finally, I tap him on the shoulder and he looks at me, dazed. "Can you believe that?" he says and points to a window full of Hungarian smoked sausages, salamis, and pork rinds.

My friend, Mike DePorte, whose grandfather was a famous St. Petersburg lawyer and who in his arguments combines a Dostoevskian probity with his grandfather's jurisprudence, claims that such an obsession with food is the best proof we have of the existence of the soul. Ergo, long after the body is satisfied, the soul is not. "Does that mean," I asked him, "that the soul is never satisfied?" He has not given me his answer yet. My own notion is that it is a supreme sign of happiness. When our souls are happy, they talk about food.

THE LITTLE VENUS OF THE ESKIMOS

You just go on your nerve.

—FRANK O'HARA

In India, I remember reading as a child, there once lived people who were called Sciapodes. They had a single large foot on which they moved with great speed and which they also employed as an umbrella against the burning sun. The rest of their marvelous lives was up to the reader to imagine. The book was full of such creatures. I kept turning its pages, reading the brief descriptions and carefully examining the drawings. There was Cerberus, the dog with three heads, the Centaur, the Chinese Dragon, the Manticore, which has the face of a man, the body of a lion, and a tail like the sting of a scorpion, and many other wonders. They resembled, I realized years later, the creations of Cadavre Exquis, the surrealist game of chance. I was also reminded of Max Ernst's surrealist novels in collage where bird wings sprout from people's backs and rooster-headed men carry off naked women.

The history of these fabulous beings is dateless. They are found in the oldest mythologies and in all cultures. Their origins vary. Some are very probably symbolic representations of theological ideas by long-forgotten sects and alchemist schools for whom the marriage of

---

Written in 1993 for an exhibition at the Drawing Center in New York City called *The Return of Cadavre Exquis*.

opposite elements was the guiding idea. Others, I'd like to believe, are the products of sheer fantasy, the liar's art, and our fascination with the grotesque image of the body. In both cases, they are the earliest instances of the collage aesthetic. Mythological zoos testify to our curiosity about the outcome of the sexual embrace of different species. They are the earliest examples of the collaboration of dream and intellect for the sake of putting appearances into doubt.

Were these visual oxymorons of ancient bestiaries first imagined and then drawn, or was it the other way around? Did one start drawing a head and the hand took off on its own, as it does in automatic writing? It's possible, although I don't have a lot of faith in automatic writing, with its aping of mediums and their trances. All my attempts at opening the floodgates of my psyche were unimpressive. "You need a certain state of vacancy for the marvelous to condescend to visit you," said Benjamin Péret. Very well and thanks for the advice, but I have my doubts. The reputation of the unconscious as the endless source of poetry is over-rated. The first rule for a poet must be, cheat on your unconscious and your dreams.

It was Octavio Paz, I believe, who told me the story about going to visit André Breton in Paris after the War. He was admitted and told to wait because the poet was engaged. Indeed, from the living room where he was seated, he could see Breton writing furiously in his study. After a while he came out, and they greeted each other and set out to have lunch in a nearby restaurant.

"What were you working on, maître?" Paz inquired as they were strolling to their destination.

"I was doing some automatic writing," Breton replied.

"But," Paz exclaimed in astonishment, "I saw you erase repeatedly!"

"It wasn't automatic enough," Breton assured the young poet.

I must admit to being shocked, too, when I heard the story. I thought I was the only one who did that. There have always been two opposite and contradictory approaches to chance operations. In the first, one devises systems to take words at random out of a dictionary or writes poems with scissors, old newspapers, and paste. The words found in either manner are not tampered with. The poem is truly the product of blind chance. All mechanical chance operations, from Dada's picking words out of a hat to the compositions of John Cage and the poems of Jackson Mac Low, work something like that. There is no cheating. These people are as honest and as scrupulous as the practitioners of photo-realism. I mean, they are both suspicious of the imagination. They handle chance with a Buddhist's disinterestedness of mind and do not allow it to be contaminated by the impurities of desire.

My entire practice, on the other hand, consists of submitting to chance only to cheat on it. I agree with Vicente Huidobro who said long ago: "Chance is fine when you're dealt five aces or at least four queens. Otherwise, forget it." I, for example, may pull a book from my bookshelf and, opening it anywhere, take out a word or a phrase. Then, to find another bit of language to go along with my first find, I may grab another book or peek into one of my notebooks and get something like this:

> he rips some papers
> forest
> whispers
> telephone book
> a child's heart
> the mouse has a nest
> concert piano
> lost innocence
> my mother's mourning dress

Once the words are on the page, however, I let them play off each other. In the house of correction called sense, where language and art serve their sentences, the words are making whoopee.

Innocence

Someone rips a telephone book in half.
The mouse has a nest in a concert piano.

In a forest of whispers,
A child's heart,
The mother's mourning dress.

This is more interesting. I'm beginning to feel that there are real possibilities here. To see what comes next, I'll call on chance for help again. My premise in this activity is that the poet finds poetry in what comes by accident. It's a complete revision of what we usually mean by creativity.

Twenty years ago, James Tate and I collaborated on some poems in the following manner: We'd take a word or a phrase and then we'd turn ourselves into a "pinball machine of associations," as Paul Auster would say. For example, the word "match" and the word "jail" would become "matchstick jail." At some point we'd stop and see what we had. We'd even do a bit of literary analysis. We'd revise, free-associate again, and watch an unknown poem begin to take shape. At some moments we felt as if we were one person; at others, one of us was the inspired poet and the other the cold-blooded critic.

Russell Edson, who with James Tate and John Ashbery is one of our greatest believers in lucky finds, says, "This kind of creation needs to be done as rapidly as possible. Any hesitation causes it to lose its believability, its special reality." I have the same experience. One doesn't come up with phrases like Tate's "the wheelchair butterfly" or Bill Knott's "razorblade choir" by way of a leisurely Cartesian meditation. They are as much a surprise to the poet as they will be to the future reader.

I open myself to chance in order to invite the unknown. I'm not sure whether it's fate or chance that dogs me, but something does. I'm like a reader of tea leaves in that store on the corner. In Madame Esmeralda's metaphysics, there is a recognition scene, too. Clairvoyants believe that there are lucky days, moments when one's divinatory abilities are especially acute. Today, one says to oneself, I'm the waking dream, the source of the magical river! I see the hand that guides fate. The miraculous thing is that the tea leaves and the poem always end up by resembling me. Here is a near-portrait, the story of my life, and I've no idea how they got there.

If you worship in the Church of Art with a Message, stay away. Chance operations make trouble, promote ambiguity, spit on dogmatism of any kind. Everything from our ideas of identity to our ideas of cause and effect are cheerfully undermined. Surrealist games are the greatest blasphemy yet conceived by the arts against the arts. In them, the disordering of the senses is given ontological status. Chance brings a funhouse mirror to reality. They used to burn people at the stake for far less.

There has never been a poet who didn't believe in a stroke of luck. What is an occasional poem but a quick convergence of unforeseen bits of language? That's what Catullus and Frank O'Hara are all about. Only literary critics do not know that poems mostly write themselves. Metaphors and similes owe everything to chance. A poet cannot will a memorable comparison. These things just pop into somebody's head. In the past one thanked the gods or the Muse for it, but all along chance has been passing out freebies. Pierce claimed that only by granting the occurrence of chance events can one account for the diversity of the universe. The same is true of art and literature.

How does one recognize that blind accident has given one poetry? This is what puzzles me. What is it that guides the eye or the ear to accept what appears at first ugly or nonsensical? One says to oneself many times while writing, what I have here I do not understand at all, but I'm going to keep it no matter what.

> Painter of doll faces
> Here's a window where my soul
> Used to peek out at night
> At the quickly improvised gallows

If there's no such thing as an aesthetic sense, how does one pick and choose among the various products of chance and decide some are worthless and some are not? Obviously, the history of modern art and literature has accustomed the eye and ear to the unexpected. We are happy, or so we believe, to reorient our vision, to accept any outrage. Is it still our old fascination with freak shows that drives us, or are formal aesthetic considerations just as important?

No doubt both. Successful chance operations stress the ambiguous origin and complex nature of any work of art or literature. The art object is always a collaboration of will and chance, but like our sense of humor, it eludes analysis. There has never been an adequate definition of why something is funny or why something is beautiful, and yet we often laugh and make poems and paintings that reassemble reality in new and unpredictably pleasing ways.

What shocks us more in the end, what we see or what we hear? Is the ear more avant-garde or the eye? Surrealist art has found more admirers than surrealist poetry, so it must be the eye. It's the new image that both painters and poets have dreamed of in this century, an image that would be ahead of our ideas and our desires, an image magnificent in its shock and its irreverence. Perhaps some new Temptation of Saint Anthony, in which the holy martyr praying in the desert would be surrounded by the rioting menagerie of exquisite corpses instead of traditional demons?

Surrealists intuited that the creation of the world is not yet finished. The Chaos spoken of in ancient creation myths has not said its last word. Chance continues to be one of the manifestations of cosmic mystery. The other one is mathematics. We are crucified in awe between freedom and necessity. The future is the forever unfolding game of Cadavre Exquis.

In the meantime, like the song says, "I've got my mojo working."

FRIED SAUSAGE

It is a fact, you singers of the lilies of the field, that the smell of fried sausage means nothing to you.

—UNKNOWN AUTHOR

The word *nature* has always had for me, a city boy, unpleasant didactic connotations. It was the place where our mothers and our schools took us occasionally so we could get some fresh air. We'd be led to a spot with lots of trees and a pretty view, where we would be ordered to breathe deeply and cleanse our lungs of the foul city air. "Isn't nature beautiful?" my mother or my schoolteacher would exclaim. And we pretended to agree, thinking meanwhile, Times Square on a Saturday night is the place to be. A city with its crowds, traffic, movies, saloons, jazz clubs, beggars, muggers, and yes, the smell of fried sausage, has always been more attractive to me. Nature is where yokels lived, *idiotikos,* as ancient Greeks used to call the unfortunates who lived outside the polis. I don't mind the middle of the ocean, or a garden choked with hot peppers, eggplants, and tomatoes, but idealized nature has always struck me as a fool's paradise.

> The cow lets fall an even
> Golden stream of shit,

Written in 1992 for the special issue of the *Ohio Review* on art and nature.

Terence, you lie under
And never mind a bit of it.

I forget where I read this gem, but these verses always come to my mind when I read pastoral poetry. Very nice, one says to oneself, but what about the farmer beyond that gorgeous meadow who works seven days a week from morning to night and is still starving? What about his sickly wife and their boy, who tortures cats? As my father used to say, if country living was any good, all these cities would not be so packed.

Now, of course, I live in the boonies. I have been in New Hampshire almost twenty years and in my walks through the woods I regularly bump into Emerson and Thoreau. We nod to each other in a friendly way and go our separate ways. It's true I've often made fun of them behind their backs. I've imagined Waldo as the cow certain poets milk. I've guffawed at some of Henry's rhapsodizing. I could never free myself from the thought that Nature is that which is slowly killing me. In addition, any philosophy of Nature that doesn't include nude picnics and rolling in the hay leaves me cold. Still and all, living here as I do, where their feet and eyes have roamed, who else do I have to argue with but these two illustrious and fine old neighbors?

This is how I see it. There are three ways of thinking about the world. You can think about the Cosmos (as the Greeks did), you can think about History (as the Hebrews did), and since the late eighteenth century you can think about Nature. The choice is yours. Where do you prefer to find (or not find) the meaning of your life? And do you include God on the menu? I myself fancy the cosmic angle. The brain-chilling infinities and silences of modern astronomy and Pascalian thought impress me deeply, except that I'm also a child of History. I've seen tanks, piles of corpses, and people strung from lampposts with my own eyes. As for Nature so-called, it's a product of Romantic utopias: noble savage, Rousseau, earthly paradise in the manner of Gauguin, the projects of Charles Fourier, our Transcendentalists, and so forth.

No longer the golden city but a lush meadow where happy humans and sheep gambol.

Most American writers on Nature partake of that utopian strain and its Manichaeanism. It's always the machine versus the garden, freedom versus confinement, God in Nature and the devil in the city. The city with its contradictions, its history, its freedom and exhilaration is godless and un-American. Only a few of our poets have praised it. Frank O'Hara comes to mind, but while he sipped beer at Cedar Tavern, it seems that all his contemporaries went fishing.

Can we have modern literature without a city? Can we write about History without quarreling with Nature? Plenty of poets think we can, but I doubt it.

Until we resolve these questions, a nap in a hammock on a summer afternoon is highly recommended. "The universe is breaking up, losing all hope of a single design," I read somewhere recently. History has not ended, despite recent predictions to the contrary, but is proceeding, as it always has, on its bloody way. Our options are limited. We can either sing hymns or grind our teeth, as Zbigniew Herbert pointed out. I do both.

"A sausage of angel and beast," Nicanor Parra called human beings. Is that why the sows are sighing in the afternoon heat in their pens across the road? They know the score. Pigs, I'm convinced, despite what Plato said about dogs, are the most philosophical of all animals. Such a fine brain, such an alert beginning, but then all that gluttony leading to the abyss of laziness. If a sow can still in rare moments ponder, what tragic, Shakespearean peaks it must reach. I, too, as a late-twentieth-century sufferer of all the unforeseen consequences of all the utopian projects of the last two hundred years, have a horror of generalizations, especially when they come wrapped in good intentions. Nature as experience—making a tomato salad, say, with young mozzarella, fresh basil leaves, and olive oil—is better than any idea about Nature.

"It is a bone on which reason breaks its teeth," Machado said of the otherness of everything we see. Not only reason, I want to shout, but our hearts too. When it comes to Being and Nature and even History, all of us are toothless. In the meantime, here's a Polish song to sing in a hammock while falling asleep and dreaming of that tomato salad:

> Down the road the children go,
> a sister and a brother,
> and they cannot help but wonder
> at the beauty of the world.

ELEGY IN A SPIDER'S WEB

In a letter to Hannah Arendt, Karl Jaspers describes how the philosopher Spinoza used to amuse himself by placing flies in a spider's web, then adding two spiders so he could watch them fight over the flies. "Very strange and difficult to interpret," concludes Jasper. As it turns out, this was the only time the otherwise somber philosopher was known to laugh.

A friend from Yugoslavia called me about a year ago and said, "Charlie, why don't you come home and hate with your own people?"

I knew he was pulling my leg, but I was shocked nevertheless. I told him that I was never very good at hating, that I've managed to loathe a few individuals here and there, but had never managed to progress to hating whole peoples.

"In that case," he replied, "you're missing out on the greatest happiness one can have in life."

I'm surprised that there is no History of Stupidity. I envision a work of many volumes, encyclopedic, cumulative, with an index listing

A shorter version of this essay appeared in the *New Republic* in 1993.

millions of names. I only have to think about history for a moment or two before I realize the absolute necessity of such a book. I do not underestimate the influence of religion, nationalism, economics, personal ambition, and even chance on events, but the historian who does not admit that men are also fools has not really understood his subject.

Watching Yugoslavia dismember itself, for instance, is like watching a man mutilate himself in public. He has already managed to make himself legless, armless, and blind, and now in his frenzy he's struggling to tear his heart out with his teeth. Between bites he shouts to us that he is a martyr for a holy cause, but we know that he is mad, that he is monstrously stupid.

People tell me I predicted the tragedy years ago. This required no extraordinary wisdom. If our own specialists in ethnic pride in the United States ever start shouting that they can't live with each other, we can expect the same bloodshed to follow. For that reason, what amazed me in the case of Yugoslavia was the readiness with which our intellectuals accepted as legitimate the claim of every nationalist there. The desirability of breaking up into ethnic and religious states a country that had existed since 1918 and that had complicated internal and outside agreements was welcomed with unreserved enthusiasm by everybody from the *New York Times* to the German government. It probably takes much longer to get a fried chicken franchise than it took to convince the world that Yugoslavia should be replaced by as many little states as the natives desired.

> *Isn't "we" the problem, that little word "we" (which I distrust so profoundly, which I would forbid the individual man to use).*
> —WITOLD GOMBROWICZ

Dr. Frankenstein's descendants do not dig up fresh graves anymore on dark and stormy nights to make monsters. They stay home and

study national history, making up lists of past wrongs. We hear people say in Yugoslavia, "I didn't used to hate them, but after I read
what they've been doing to us, I'd like see them all dead."

Nationalism is a self-constructed cage in which family members
can huddle in safety when they're not growling and barking at someone outside the cage. One people baring their teeth at all comers is the
dream of every nationalist and religious fanatic the world over. The
real horror movie monsters would run at the sight of these people, who
only yesterday were someone's quiet and kind neighbors and who will
probably resume being that after the killing is done.

What are you? Americans ask me. I explain that I was born in Belgrade, that I left when I was fifteen, that we always thought of ourselves as Yugoslavs, that for the last thirty years I have been translating
Serbian, Croatian, Slovenian, and Macedonian poets into English, that
whatever differences I found among these people delighted me, that I
don't give a shit about any of these nationalist leaders and their programs . . .

"Oh, so you're a Serb!" they exclaim triumphantly.

I remember an old interview with Duke Ellington, the interviewer saying to him with complete confidence, you write your music
for your own people, and Ellington pretending not to understand, asking what people would that be? The lovers of Beaujolais?

I have more in common with some Patagonian or Chinese lover
of Ellington or Emily Dickinson than I have with many of my own
people. The proverbial warning "Too many cooks spoil the broth"
was the way I was concocted. I have always considered myself lucky
to be that way.

The strange thing is that I find more and more people who do not
believe me, who assure me that life has no meaning outside some kind
of tribe.

*

Five of us were sitting in the Brasserie Cluny in Paris writing a protest letter to Milošević and arguing about the wording when one of us remembered that Tito conducted his illegal business for the Comintern in the same brasserie before the war.

Does this crap ever end? someone wondered aloud.

Over the last forty years I've known Russians, Yugoslavs, Hungarians, Poles, Argentines, Chinese, Iranians, and a dozen other nationalities, all refugees from murderous regimes. The only people of honor on the whole planet.

This summer in Paris and Amsterdam I met more "traitors," men and women who refused to identify themselves with various nationalist groups in Yugoslavia. They wanted to remain free, outside tribal pieties, and that was their heresy. They are the other orphans of that civil war.

One Sunday on the metro I heard an accordionist play a Serbian song, struck up a conversation with him, and found out he was a war refugee from Croatia. "One of these days," he whispered to me in parting, "the French will get rid of us too and then where will we go?"

His name, to our mutual astonishment, turned out to be Simic too.

> *Sacrifice the children—an old story, pre-Homeric—so that the nation will endure, to create a legend.*
>
> —ALEKSANDER WAT

The destruction of Vukovar and Sarajevo will not be forgiven the Serbs. Whatever moral credit they had as the result of their history they have squandered in these two acts. The suicidal and abysmal idiocy of nationalism is revealed here better than anywhere else. No human being or group of people has the right to pass a death sentence on a city.

"Defend your own, but respect what others have," my grandfather used to say, and he was a highly decorated officer in the First

World War and certainly a Serbian patriot. I imagine he would have agreed with me. There will be no happy future for people who have made the innocent suffer.

Here is something we can all count on. Sooner or later our tribe always comes to ask us to agree to murder.

"In the hour of need you walked away from your own people," a fellow I know said to me when I turned down the invitation.

True. I refused to turn my conscience over to the leader of the pack. I continued stubbornly to believe in more than one truth. Only the individual is real, I kept saying over and over again. I praised the outcast, the pariah, while my people were offering me an opportunity to become a part of a mystic whole. I insisted on remaining aloof, self-absorbed, lovingly nursing my suspicions.

"For whom does your poetry speak when you have no tribe anywhere you can call your own?" my interlocutor wanted to know.

"The true poet is never a member of any tribe," I shouted back. It is his refusal of his birthright that makes him a poet and an individual worth respecting, I explained.

This wasn't true, of course. Many of the greatest poets in the history of the world have been fierce nationalists. The sole function of the epic poet is to find excuses for the butcheries of the innocent. In our big and comfy family bed today's murderers will sleep like little babies, is what they are always saying.

On the other side are the poets who trust only the solitary human voice. The lyric poet is almost by definition a traitor to his own people. He is the stranger who speaks the harsh truth that only individual lives are unique and therefore sacred. He may be loved by his people, but his example is also the one to be warned against. The tribe must pull together to face the invading enemy while the lyric poet sits talking to the skull in the graveyard.

For that reason he deserves to be exiled, put to death, and remembered.

> *Mistaken ideas always end in bloodshed, but in every case it is someone else's blood. This is why our thinkers feel free to say just about everything.*   —CAMUS

"There are always a lot of people just waiting for a bandwagon to jump on either for or against something," Hannah Arendt said in a letter. She knew what she was talking about. The terrifying thing about modern intellectuals everywhere is that they are always changing idols. At least religious fanatics stick mostly to what they believe in. All the rabid nationalists in Eastern Europe were Marxists yesterday and Stalinists last week. The freedom of the individual has never been their concern. They were after bigger fish. The sufferings of the world are an ideal chance for all intellectuals to have an experience of tragedy and to fulfill their utopian longings. If in the meantime one comes to share the views of some mass murderer, the end justifies the means. Modern tyrants have had some of the most illustrious literary salons.

Nationalism as much as Communism provides an opportunity to rewrite history. The problem with true history and great literature is that they wallow in ambiguities, unresolved issues, nuances, and baffling contradictions. Let's not kid ourselves. The Manichaean view of the world is much more satisfying. Any revision of history is acceptable providing it gives us some version of the struggle between angels and devils. If, in reality, this means dividing murderers in Yugoslavia into good and bad, so be it. If it means weeping from one eye at the death of a Moslem woman and winking from the other at the death of her Orthodox husband, that's the secret attraction of that model.

Our media, too, treat complexity the way Victorians treated sexuality—as something from which the viewer and the reader need to be protected. In the case of Yugoslavia, where nothing is simple, the consequences are more evil. Our columnists and intellectuals often have views identical to their nationalist counterparts in various parts of that country. In an age of PC, they miss hate and lynching mobs. The democratic forces in Yugoslavia can expect nothing from either side. At home they'll be treated as traitors and abroad their version of events will be greeted by silence for making the plot too complicated.

So what's to be done? people rightly ask. I've no idea. As an elegist I mourn and expect the worst. Vileness and stupidity always have a rosy future. The world is still a few evils short, but they'll come. Dark despair is the only healthy outlook if you identify yourself with the flies as I do. If, however, you secretly think of yourself as one of the spiders, or, God forbid, as the laughing philosopher himself, you have much less to worry about. Since you'll be on the winning side, you can always rewrite history and claim you were a fly. Elegies in a spider's web is all we bona fide flies get. That and the beauty of the sunrise like some unexpected touch of the executioner's final courtesy the day they take us out to be slaughtered. In the meantime, my hope is very modest. Let's have a true ceasefire for once, so the old lady can walk out into the rubble and find her cat.

SHOP, LE BACARÈS
Pyrénées-Orientales, France, 1950

> *At the moment the writer realizes he has no ideas he has become*
> *an artist.*
> —GILBERT SORRENTINO

A shop in a town of twisting streets. The hour of siesta and immense heat. The street as empty as the Sahara.

"I didn't meet a soul," says the madman who walks in the midday sun.

A greengrocer's shop with its sign almost faded. A shop inviting reverie with its empty crates and baskets, its three closed doors and black cat.

They were selling beans for cassoulet here while Napoleon was retreating from Russia, dunking bread in the wine while the Arabs were still in Spain.

How cool must be the leaves of young lettuce in the dark shop with its low ceiling and thick walls! Are there baskets of eggplants and peas still in their pods left unsold? I'm sure there's an old-fashioned scale in there with its golden pans balanced and empty in the half-darkness.

The one who feeds the cat is lying down in the upstairs bedroom.

Written for a book of essays on the life and work of the photographer Paul Strand.

She is a huge fat woman with enormous naked arms and one eye open. She has heard steps.

The eye is wiser than the tongue even in the land of Descartes and Mallarmé. "The eye has knowledge the mind cannot share," says my friend Hayden Carruth. That knowledge must have made the photographer stop.

What photography and modern poetry share is the belief in the chance encounter. The image is presented without commentary—as in this old poem by William Carlos Williams, which Paul Strand, too, must have known.

> Between Walls
>
> the back wings
> of the
>
> hospital where
> nothing
>
> will grow lie
> cinders
>
> in which shine
> the broken
>
> pieces of a green
> bottle

The painter De Chirico says: "Then I had the strange impression that I was looking at these things for the first time and the composition of my picture came to my mind's eye. Now each time I look at this painting I again see the moment. Nevertheless, the moment is an enigma to me, for it is inexplicable. And I like also to call the work which sprang from it an enigma."

He is talking about familiar things restored to their strangeness, becoming, indeed, a school of metaphysics. The image is what we think about in its all-night classes.

It is not so much that all ages are contemporaneous, as Ezra Pound claimed, but that all the present moments certainly are. The trust in the present moment and the visible truth is what American poetry shares with photography. The present is the only place where we experience the eternal. The eternal shrinks to the size of the present because only the present is humanly graspable.

Peeling walls, a worn-out sign, nothing prosperous about the shop except for the balcony with its wrought iron railing and the finely carved heavy door. Did the house once belong to a rich merchant?

One must resist this temptation to "read" the photograph further and further, for its power lies precisely in its remaining always on the verge of being "read." With Baudelaire we say that a closed door is much more interesting than an open one.

Just then, as if on cue, a black cat came out to look at something to the side of the photographer.

The cat is the X in this equation. I expect never to get her out of my mind.

NO CURE FOR THE BLUES

*It seems that we learn something about art when we experience
what the word solitude is meant to designate.*

—MAURICE BLANCHOT

A cold and windy day in New York City thirty years ago. Outside an
A&P market plastered with signs of that day's specials, a beautiful old
black man with a beat-up guitar, dark glasses, tin cup, and an equally
ancient seeing-eye dog lying at his feet. He sings in high tenor voice:

> "Santi Claus, Santi Claus,
> Won't you please hear my lonesome plea.
> I don't want nothing for Christmas,
> But my baby back to me."

Later that day, crossing Central Park, I see a young woman lying
on a bench, her face hidden in her hands, her white party dress just
covering the backs of her knees, one of her red shoes fallen off to the
side. She is sleeping, or more likely pretending to. In any case, I feel
obliged to walk past her almost on tiptoes.

No one else is around, and it's still cold and windy. I walk briskly,

Written for a special issue of *Antaeus* on music and published in 1993.

looking back now and then, the last time when there's no chance I can see her from so far away.

"Doing something wrong," sings Walter Davis.

> You show your linen to any man . . .
> You come home walking like a goose
> As if somebody turned you loose.

The chief preoccupation of much country and urban blues is the relationship between men and women. Love, unfaithfulness, jealousy, hard times, good times, happy sex, bad sex, and everything else that keeps people awake tossing and turning at night, is the subject.

> You'll need me some morning when I won't need you.

Or,

> You've been a good ole wagon, Daddy,
> But you done broke down.

Or, there's the blues song Jelly Roll Morton claims is the first one he ever heard back in New Orleans in the early years of this century:

> Stood on the corner
> With her feet soaking wet,
> Begging each and every man
> That she met.
>
> If you can't give a dollar,
> Give me a lousy dime.

> I want to feed
> That hungry man of mine.

That's the blues at its most tragic. But the same Morton can also sing on another occasion:

> If you must go, sweet baby,
> Leave a dime for beer.

A kind of comic realism is at work in many of the songs, especially when the subject is love or sex. No wonder churchgoers called it devil's music. Everybody knows the devil likes to fool around. The comic seriousness of these songs understands the coexistence of misfortune and laughter. It is in that joyful irreverence and freedom that one must seek their truth.

> Your nuts hang down like a damn bell clapper,
> And your dick stands up like a steeple,
> And your asshole stands open like a church door,
> And crab walks in like people.

This is from the blues singer Lucille Bogan, who sang about sex with such abandon and humor that it seemed her purpose was to intentionally terrify the prudes.

There was a commercial angle to it, of course. How else do you entertain a bunch of drunks in a dive? The critics who say sexual themes were forced on black performers are talking nonsense. I guess they were forced on poor Boccaccio and Rabelais, too. Money is not the whole explanation. There is poetry in some of that smut.

"I have something between my legs to make a dead man come," I overheard a woman once say to the young preacher at a wake which had turned boisterous with drink and good food. It was improper, but very funny, like this music, which knows only the truth of laughter and no inhibition.

They played blues records in Berlin in the 1920s. They heard "Jazzin' Babies Blues" on the banks of the Nile, "Mean Old Bedbug Blues" by the Yangtze River. I first heard the blues in Belgrade in 1947–48 when one could go to jail for listening to American music. We heard Louis Armstrong sing "St. James Infirmary." We lay on the floor next to the record player with the sound turned down low and the mother of my friend fretting in the next room.

> Some people call me a hobo, some call me a bum,
> Nobody knows my name, nobody knows what I've done.

Bessie Smith, Eva Taylor, Bertha Chippie Hill, Alberta Hunter, Sippie Wallace, Ada Brown, Ida Cox, Victoria Spivey—addicts of the blues know them all. I played Ethel Waters's "One Man Nan" till it hissed and skipped terribly. I could not play that record or most of my other records for anyone else. They would not understand my forbearance. At their best my records would sound like rain, a summer downpour in the city when everyone runs for cover, at their worst like a sausage patty being fried in a pan. It didn't matter. Sadness and happiness would well up in me with the first few notes. Why is it, I said to myself one night, that listening to the music I feel a homesickness for a vanished world that I was never a part of?

The blues prove the complete silliness of any theory of cultural separatism which denies the possibility of aesthetic experience outside one's race, ethnicity, religion, or even gender. Like all genuine art, the blues belong to a specific time, place, and people which it then, paradoxically, transcends. The secret of its transcendence lies in its minor key and its poetry of solitude. Lyric poetry has no closer relation anywhere than the blues. The reason people make lyric poems and blues songs is because our life is short, sweet, and fleeting. The blues bears witness to the strangeness of each individual's fate. It begins wordlessly in a moan, a stamp of the foot, a sigh, a hum, and then seeks words for that something or other that has no name in any language and for which all poetry and music seek an approximation.

The friendship of solitude, late night, and the blues. In 1959, I lived in a fleabag hotel in Greenwhich Village in a room no bigger than a closet and just as dark. There was a window, but it faced a brick wall. My nights were interrupted by creaking beds, smokers' coughs, and moans of love-making. I didn't sleep much. I lay in bed reading, chain-smoking, and drinking wine. I had a radio and a cheap portable record player.

> Nobody loves me but my mother,
> And she could be jiving too.

Some old sage claims that the soul is made between one or two in the morning. I agree, especially if you're listening to the blues. I owned a few records, but it was the radio that brought me surprises and delights from time to time. Playing with the dial, I'd come across an unknown voice, a cornet, and a piano that would make me turn up the volume in my excitement. I lay with eyes closed, astonished that such a fine song existed and regretting already that it would end. Very often the D.J. would not even name the performer, and what I'd heard would haunt me for years, until in my manic record-buying I would come upon that very cut.

One night I was listening to a program devoted to Leroy Carr and Scrapper Blackwell, that great piano-and-guitar duo that made so many records back in the 1930s, when there was a soft knock on the door. It was a quarter to three. I thought somebody had complained to the night clerk about me, but why was he knocking so softly? I didn't budge. Carr could have been singing something like:

Ain't it lonesome
Sleeping by yourself
When the woman that you love
Is loving someone else?

Finally, I opened the door a crack. Outside, an old man stood as if shivering in his T-shirt, pants, and with nothing on his feet. "What's that beautiful music?" he asked me with a heavy Italian accent. I told him. Carr went on singing, so I let him in. He sat in my only chair and I sat on the bed.

In the wee midnight hour
Long before the break of day,
When the blues creep upon you
And carry your mind away.

My visitor listened with a serious, even pious expression. He didn't say much, except to call the music nice, very nice, much too nice. We parted when the program was over, and I never saw him again.

Some people tell me,
God takes care of old folks and fools,
But since I've been born,
He must've changed the rules.

The guitar player who sang this recorded, under the name Funny Papa Smith, some twenty sides between 1930 and 1931. They say he wore a stovepipe hat and work-overalls, but not in the picture I have of him, where he wears a suit, bow tie, and the kind of hat a traveling salesman might wear. A good-looking young fellow with a sensitive, even melancholy, expression. I can well believe he was a gambler, but I'm surprised to learn that he murdered a man. I read someplace that he ended up in the electric chair, but I've no idea if this is true. All I know is that he sang an astonishing two-part hoodoo blues called "Seven Sisters."

> They tell me Seven Sisters in New Orleans, that can really fix a
> man up right,
> And I'm headed for New Orleans, Louisiana, I'm traveling both
> day and night.
> I hear them say the oldest sister look like she's just twenty-one
> And said she can look right in your eyes and tell you exactly what
> you want done.
> They tell me they been hung, been bled and been crucified
> But I just want enough help to stand on the water and rule the
> tide.
> It's bound to be Seven Sisters 'cause I've heard it by everybody
> else.
> 'Course I'd love to take their word, but I'd rather go and see for
> myself.
> When I leave the Seven Sisters I'm piling stones all around
> And go to my baby and tell her there's another Seven-Sister man
> in town.
> Good mornin' Seven Sisters, just thought I'd come down and see
> Will you build me up where I'm torn down and make me strong
> where I'm weak?
> I went to New Orleans, Louisiana, just on account of something I
> heard.
> The Seven Sisters told me everything I wanted to know and they
> wouldn't let me speak a word.
> Now it's Sara, Minnie, Bertha, Holly, Dolly, Betty and Jane—
> You can't know them sisters apart because they all looks just the
> same
> The Seven Sisters sent me away happy, 'round the corner I met
> another little girl;

She looked at me and smiled and said: Go devil and destroy the
    world.
[Spoken: I'm gonna destroy it, too . . . I'm all right now.]
Seven times you hear the Seven Sisters, will visit me in my sleep,
And they said I won't have no more trouble, and said I'll live
    twelve days in a week.
Boy go down in Louisiana, and get the lead right outta your
    being.
If Seven Sisters can't do anything in Louisiana, bet you'll have to
    go to New Orleans.

Small masterpieces by nearly unknown performers are the rule
when it comes to the history of recorded blues. Again, it must have
been the usual makeshift recording studio in some hotel room on a
street of pool halls, whorehouses, and dance halls. The year was 1931.
Around the corner, probably, there was a soup kitchen with a line of
unemployed black men and, inside, a straight-backed chair and a bottle
of whiskey for the musician.

There was nothing customary about what Smith sang. Here was
a blues song about the secret world of voodoo, eroticism, crime, and
god-knows-what-else, in a lingo both poetic and obscure. In this blues,
as in many others, one glimpses an unknown America with an imagination and imagery all its own. The blues poet has been where we
are all afraid to go, as if there was a physical place, a forbidden place
that corresponds to a place in ourselves where we experience the tragic
sense of life and its amazing wonders. In that dive, in that all-night
blues and soul club, we feel the full weight of our fate, we taste the
nothingness at the heart of our being, we are simultaneously wretched
and happy, we spit on it all, we want to weep and raise hell, because the
blues, in the end, is about a sadness older than the world, and there's no
cure for that.

ORPHAN FACTORY

CHARLES THE OBSCURE

Late one night, as the half-moon rode high above the church of St. Mark, I grabbed my balls while passing a priest. This happened in Belgrade when I was twelve years old. I was skipping along without a care in the world when he came around the corner. He assumed I was about to greet him—he was even inclining his head benevolently—then I did what my friends advised me to do when meeting a priest. He stood there steaming in his cassock for a moment. Then it was my turn to be surprised. Plump as he was, he went after me with extraordinary quickness, waving his arms about and shouting: "You little creep! You little son of a bitch!" His cussing terrified me even more than the chase he gave me. I ran without looking back.

At home the photographs of my great-great-grandfathers and uncles awaited me on the living room walls. On my mother's side, I had several priests and one bishop in my ancestry. I've never seen a wanted poster with a more murderous collection of mugs. They had huge black-and-white beards that grew even sideways. Their eyes were bulging. The photographer must have warned them not to move, and they obeyed. Flies crawled inside of their ears during the long exposure. Their noses itched terribly. That evening, after the priest, their eyes followed me with unusual grimness. They all knew what I had done.

From *New Letters* 60, no. 4 (1994), written for the special issue on poetry and religion.

The meanest-looking of the lot was my grandfather's father. It was public knowledge that his children hated him. My grandfather did not permit any mention of priests or religion in our house when he was around. When my grandmother died, he informed the family that there would be no priest officiating in the cemetery chapel or at the grave site. A scandal, people whispered. Everybody crossed themselves just thinking about it. A couple of aunts decided to disobey his wishes. The priest would appear at the grave site while the coffin was being lowered; and my grandfather, so the theory went, would be too overwhelmed with grief and sorrow to object to a short prayer being said.

That's not what happened. Just as the gravediggers were fussing with the ropes, and the family and friends were standing with bowed heads, the priest materialized in his vestments, a prayer book in hand, already blessing us and mumbling a prayer. To everyone's astonishment, Grandpa lunged at him. Before we had time to realize what was happening, the old curmudgeon had the priest by the scruff of the neck and was marching him away from the grave. As if that wasn't enough, one of my weeping aunts ran after them, grabbed the tails of Grandfather's coat and started pulling him back. She had the strength of ten, and so did he. A tug-of-war ensued and lots of yelling. The old man was trying to kick her without turning and letting the priest go. Unfortunately, my mother rushed me and my brother away before we could see and hear more.

If you had asked anybody in my family if God exists, they would have given you a puzzled look. Of course he does, they would have replied. This meant, in practice, attending the church only to baptize, wed, and bury someone. Bona fide atheists probably mention religion and God more frequently than my mother ever did. My father, however, was a different story. He didn't mind entering churches. Russian churches, black churches, old Italian churches, austere New England churches, Byzantine churches, all were admirable. The same is true of me. He liked the pomp and music, but he liked an empty church even more. A few times I saw him get down on his knees to pray, but he had no use for organized religion, or for any other idea that has sought to take its place. As far as he was concerned, communism and fascism were versions of the nastiest aspects of Christianity. "All that orthodoxy, fanaticism, virtue by decree," he'd complain. They were all enemies of the individual, forever peddling intolerance and conformity. He had serious philosophical interest in Islam, Buddhism, Hinduism, and Christianity, but no desire to join any congregation of the faithful. Belief in God was something private, like sex. If you did not believe in anything, as I often told him was the case with me, that was all right, too.

"Come on," she yanked my arm. "Let's go. They're just a couple of hicks," she assured me, but I had to take a better look at the street preachers.

The young woman with thick glasses pressed a Bible to her heart; the horse-faced fellow by her side strummed a tuneless guitar at the edge of a large Saturday night crowd. They preached and sang hymns as if dogs were biting their asses.

My friend had had enough. Without my noticing, she split. I was left in custody of their Jesus, who, by the sound of it, had too many lost sheep already to worry about. His great love always spurned— "Sweet Jesus," they hollered, trying to drown out an ambulance crying its heart out somewhere in the dark city beyond the brightly lit movie houses and penny arcades all around us.

Hell! I was deeply moved.

America is God crazy, as everyone knows. It's impossible to be an American writer without taking that into account.

Driving just after daybreak early one spring morning through West Virginia, I'm listening to the radio. Someone is playing scratchy old black gospel records. The station is fading and coming clear in turn; the car is speeding down the empty road, and I'm wondering who is choosing the records so impeccably, so mysteriously, given the odd hour. Beyond the enjoyment, the emotion is gripping me, I have a sudden realization: They mean every word they say. Every word. They sing so beautifully, and so wildly, because they believe the Lord is in their midst right then and there.

It has always seemed obvious to me that we are alone in the universe. I love metaphysics and its speculations, but the suspicion at the core of my being is that we are whistling in the dark. Still, I have tears in my eyes every time I hear good church music. Never has the human heart been so pure, I think. Perhaps divinity can only be experienced by those who sing together? The God who comes or does not come to the solitaries is a different one.

"Without this mystery, the most incomprehensible of all, we are incomprehensible to ourselves," said Pascal, in a different context.

Sing and shout, Reverend! is my advice. Do that little dance step while the choir behind you sways and slaps its tambourines, and the old lady on the piano and the scrawny kid on the electric guitar nod to each other with approval. There's no doubt about it: "Except for music, everything is a lie," as Cioran says.

One day I finally admitted to myself that I'm hopelessly superstitious. You do not believe in God, I said to myself, so how come you believe in bad luck? I have no reply to that. Do we make our Fate, or is our Fate an independent agency? Calvin at least knew who arranged our destiny; I do not.

This head full of contradictions walking on two legs, is this the modern version of holy foolishness? Let's hope so.

In the meantime, the worries of a crumb overlooked on death's dinner plate . . .

*

I was always attracted to mystical and esoteric doctrines that propose the unknowingness of the Supreme Being, the ineffability of the experience of his presence and the ambiguity of our human condition. Ambiguity, that great carnivore. If I believe in anything, it is in the dark night of the soul. Awe is my religion, and mystery is its church. I include here equally the mysteries of consciousness and the torments of conscience.

If not for conscience would we ever consider the possibility of the independent existence of evil? Nothing explains the world and the people in it. This is the knowledge that makes us fall down on our knees and listen to the silence of the night. Not even a dog or an owl is brave enough to interrupt it tonight. Being and nothingness, those two abstractions, how real, how close they feel. In such moments I want to reach for my chessboard. Let them play each other, and I'll sit and watch until the first streak of light slips under the door and crawls to my feet without waking the dust.

Many years ago, Vasko Popa took me to visit the women's monastery Mesić, near his hometown, Vršac, on the Yugoslav-Romanian border. We had a long lunch at a young poet's house and did not leave till five in the afternoon. I don't remember much about the drive, since we were talking a lot, interrupting each other with stories and jokes; but all of a sudden there was a high wall at the end of a dirt road and a closed iron gate. We left the car outside the gate and pushed it open just enough to squeeze through. What we found inside was a veritable jungle, as if the grass had not been cut all summer, and the trees had grown wild over the years without being trimmed and thinned out. We followed what was once a road, and now a narrow path in the twilight calm broken occasionally by the sound of a bird or cricket. We did not speak. After a mile or so, we saw through the trees several large houses and a small Byzantine church. We walked to the largest of them, knocked, opened the door, peeked inside, even announced ourselves; but only silence came out to welcome us. It was so quiet, our steps became cautious. We walked on tiptoe on the way to the next house. Through the open door, we could see six nuns sitting in a circle with heads bowed. Vasko knew the name of the prioress and called out to her. She jumped, and the nuns followed after her in joy and delight to see him. The prioress, who was old, used to be in her youth a lady-in-waiting at the royal court, Vasko had told me, and was exceptionally well educated. Vasko sent her French books. She was just reading Camus and immediately wanted to talk about him with us.

We were then given a tour by the prioress and a tall, skinny young nun. We visited the church, which was under repair, to see some surprisingly fine frescoes, and then slowly, because of the prioress's age, we climbed to the small graveyard above the church. The sun had just set. "I'll be soon resting here," the prioress told us, laughing. We smiled in reply. One could almost envy the prospect.

Then we were led back to the large house we had first come to. This we heard was one of the local bishop's many summer residences. He had not stayed in it for the last thirty years, but everything was kept in readiness for his arrival. We sat in a large living room with the prioress and the skinny nun drinking homemade brandy, while being sternly examined by former bishops in sooty old paintings. Only one table lamp had been lit. Vasko talked and so did the old woman, but the rustling of so many leaves muffled their voices, and then all of a sudden, there was complete silence. Here was peace of a world outside time, the kind one encounters at times in fairy-tale illustrations, in which a solitary child is seen entering a dark forest of gigantic trees.

After a while I listened only to the silence deepen, the night continue to hold its breath.

"Every poem, knowingly, or unknowingly, is addressed to God," the poet Frank Samperi told me long ago. I remember being surprised, objecting, mentioning some awful contemporary poems. We were filing subscription cards in the stock room of a photography magazine and having long philosophical conversations on the subject of poetry. Frank had been reading a lot of Dante, so I figured, that's it. He is stuck in fourteenth-century Italy.

No more. Today I think as he did then. It makes absolutely no difference whether gods and devils exist or not. The secret ambition of every true poem is to ask about them even as it acknowledges their absence.

IN PRAISE OF INVECTIVE

. . . the tongue we use
When we don't want nuance
To get in the way.

—CORNELIUS EADY

At the end of a murderous century, let's curse the enemies of the individual.

Every modern ideologue and thought policeman continues to say that the private is political, that there is no such thing as an autonomous self, and if there is, for the sake of common good it is not desirable to have one. He or she who refuses to accept the idea that the self is socially constructed and that it can be manipulated to fit the latest theory of human improvement is everywhere the enemy. In the academy of lies where new enthusiasms and hatreds are being concocted, where "only children and madmen speak the truth," as Goebbels said, the unrepentant individual is the one standing in the corner with his face to the wall. Orthodoxy, groupthink, virtue by decree are the ideals of every religion and every utopian model of society. The only intellectual problem that the philosophers of such systems have is how to make conformism attractive. Ideologies from nationalism to racism are

From *Raritan* 14, no. 3 (Winter 1995): 60–64.

not really about ideas; they're revivalists' tents offering a chance to the righteous to enjoy their sense of superiority. "We will find eternal happiness and harmony by sacrificing the individual," every congregation of the faithful continues to rhapsodize.

Historical experience has taught me to be wary of any manifestation of collectivism. Even literary historians and critics, when they generalize, make me suspicious. Of course, young poets and painters do associate and influence each other and partake of the same zeitgeist, but despite these obvious truths, what literature worth anything is written by a group? Has any genuine artist ever thought of himself or herself exclusively as a part of a movement? Is anyone seriously a postmodernist, whatever that is?

I don't find systems congenial. My aesthetic says that the poet is true because he or she cannot be labeled. It is the irreducible uniqueness of each life that is worth honoring and defending. If at times one has to fall back on the vocabulary of abuse to keep those in the gumming business away, so be it.

The first and never-to-be-forgotten pleasure that language gave me was the discovery of "bad words." I must've been three or four years old when I overheard my mother and another woman use the word *cunt*. When I repeated it to myself, when I said it aloud for all to hear and admire, I was slapped by my mother and told never to use that word again. Aha, I thought, there are words so delicious they must not be said aloud! I had a great-aunt who used to use such language every time she opened her mouth. My mother would beg her, when she came to visit, not to speak like that in front of the children, but she paid her no mind. To have a temper and a foul mouth like that was a serious liability in a Communist country. "We'll all end up in jail because of her," my mother said.

There are moments in life when true invective is called for, when there comes an absolute necessity, out of a deep sense of justice, to denounce, mock, vituperate, lash out, rail at, in the strongest possible language. "I do not wish to be weaned from this error," Robert Burton wrote long ago in his *Anatomy of Melancholy*. I agree. If anything I want to enlarge and perfect my stock of maledictions.

This is what I learned from twentieth-century history: Only dumb ideas get recycled. The dream of a social reformer is to be the brains of an enlightened, soul-reforming penitentiary. Everyone vain, dull, peevish, and sexually frustrated dreams of legislating his impotence. Mao's uniforms: a billion people dressing the same and shouting from his little red book continues to be the secret hope of new visionaries.

Once one comes to understand that much of what one sees and hears serves to make fraud sound respectable, one is in trouble. For instance, long before Parisian intellectuals did so, my great-aunt had figured out that the Soviet Union and the so-called people's democracies were a scam and a lie from the bottom up. She was one of these women who see through appearances instantly. To begin with, she did not have a good opinion of humanity. Not because she was a sourpuss, a viper's nest of imaginary resentments. Far from it. She liked eating, drinking, a good laugh, and a quick roll in the hay behind her elderly husband's back. It's just that she had an unusually uncluttered and clear head. She would tell you that our revolutionary regime, which regarded loose tongues and levity as political crimes and those unfortunates caught in the act as unhealthy elements, was a huge pile of shit, and that included Marshal Tito himself. Her outbursts were caused by what she regarded as other people's gullibility. As far as she was concerned, she was surrounded by cowards and dunces. The daily papers and the radio drove her into verbal fury. "Admit it," she'd yell at my mother and grandmother. "Doesn't it turn your stomach to hear them talk like that?"

If they agreed, and confided in a whisper, that yes, indeed, these Commies are nothing but a bunch of murderous illiterate yokels, Stalinist stooges, and whatnot, she still wasn't happy. There was something about humans as a species that worried her to no end. It's not like they were different yesterday and the day before yesterday. This frenzy of vileness and stupidity started on day one. She'd throw her hands up in the air in despair again and again. She couldn't get over it. It was like she had an incurable allergy to everything false and slimy. It didn't lessen her zest for life, because she had a way of exorcising these evil spirits, but it was a full-time job. Cursing them, I imagine, gave her royal pleasure and, unknown to her, to me, too, listening behind the closed door with a shameless grin.

In a book entitled *Paradoxes of Gender,* Judith Lorber gives us a feminist version of this recurring madness:

> In a world of scrupulous gender equality, equal numbers of girls and boys would be educated and trained for the liberal arts and for the sciences, for clerical and manual labor and for all professions. Among those with equal credentials, women and men would be hired in an alternating fashion for the same types of jobs—or only men would be hired to do women's types of jobs until half of every workplace was made of men and half, women.

Very nice, one thinks, but what about the cops, the jailers, and the informers needed to enforce all of this? Will they be organized in units composed with strict gender equality? We hope so. Note, as is typical of all pious hypocrites and prophets of universal happiness, there's no mention of the individual.

How are we to defend ourselves against these monsters dividing the members of society into useful and useless? For them, the ideal citizen is a voluntary slave! America, or any other place on earth, must be a school of virtue where even the political meaning of a sunset in a poem will be carefully examined for unauthorized views!

I knew a thirteen-year-old who wrote a letter telling off President

Johnson about the conduct of the Vietnam War. It was some letter. Our president was an idiot and a murderer who deserved to be napalmed himself, and worse. One evening as the boy and his mother and sister, who told me the story, were sitting around the kitchen table slurping their soup, the doors and the windows leading to the fire escape opened at the same time and men with drawn guns surrounded the table. We are the FBI, they announced, and they wanted to know who was Anthony Palermo? The two women pointed at the boy with thick glasses and crossed eyes. Well, it took a while to convince them that he was the one who wrote the letter. They were expecting a full-grown Commie assassin with long hair and an arsenal of weapons and bombs by his side.

"What do you want from me, blood?" I heard an old woman shout once in a welfare office. She kept cussing them for another five minutes, not because she had any expectation that the wrongs done to her would be righted, but simply in order to make herself feel good and clean for one brief moment.

ORPHAN FACTORY

Experts in the manufacture of orphans.

—ANNA AKHMATOVA

The last time I talked to my mother, the day before she died at the age of eighty-nine in the winter of 1994, she asked me:

"Are those idiots still killing each other?"

I told her yes, and she sighed and rolled her eyes with exasperation. She had stopped watching television and reading the papers, but she had a pretty good idea what sort of dirty little war they were having in Yugoslavia. Every time I came to visit her in the nursing home, she'd ask me the same question, and I would give her the same answer. Despite being well educated and widely traveled, my mother had no understanding of the world. Wars, even those fought, supposedly, for the worthiest of causes, made no sense to her.

What about the Nazis, my brother and I would ask her. Surely those bastards were worth fighting?

She'd shrug her shoulders and wave us away. No heroes for her. Idiots killing idiots was how she saw it. When my brother was in Vietnam, she wrote a letter to President Johnson telling him that he had no business sending young people to die over there. She even called him a

---

From *Frankfurter Allgemeine Zeitung*, August 24, 1995.

lousy liar and a murderer of children. I was sure she'd get a visit from the FBI. Instead, she received a two-line form letter from the White House informing her that the president appreciated her interesting views.

"They are cutting someone's throat in Pera's cornfield." My young aunt ran into the house shouting at the top of her lungs.

"May I go and see?" I asked my mother, which made my aunt shriek even louder at the horror of it all. She didn't stop until they slapped her face and put her to bed.

I don't recollect that event well, but I have a clear memory of the view of the cornfield from our bedroom window. The corn in August 1944 was already high. At times I saw crows hover over it and dive quickly, but mostly the sky was empty and blue. Still, for days after, they would not let me come near that window, even though its heavy curtains were drawn as if it were wintertime.

Today when I watch the war in Yugoslavia on TV, I have the feeling I'm watching the reruns of my childhood. It's like the networks were all engaged in some far-out science fiction plot to pluck the images out of my head. The bombed buildings, the corpses lying in the streets of Sarajevo, the crowds of refugees are all frighteningly familiar.

My own home movie begins with the German bombing of Belgrade on April 6, 1941, when a bomb hit the building across the street. I flew out of my bed all the way across the room. I was three years old and more astonished than I actually was frightened by the flames that rose everywhere.

"How come these bombs hardly ever hit anything of military importance?" I asked the poet Richard Hugo, who had bombed me in Belgrade on a regular basis in 1944 for the American air force. He was terribly upset that he had bumped into someone, and someone he liked, who had actually been the recipient of his bombs, but I assured him that I bore no grudges. You, Yankees, were our dear allies, I explained to him. We were happy to be pounded by you. I just wanted to know the reason why all the important buildings and the old Gestapo headquarters were still standing and the poorest neighborhoods were in ruins?

What Hugo told me made sense. Their primary mission was the oil fields in Romania, which were heavily defended. They often lost a plane. On the way back to Italy, they were supposed to unload the remaining bombs over Belgrade. Of course, they took no chances. They flew high and dropped their loads in the general direction of the city. Understandably, they were in a big hurry to get back, kiss the ground, and thank the Lord for being alive, before rushing off to the beach with some nice Italian girl. As for murdering innocent folk, that's more or less what everybody expects everybody to do in a war.

Then, as now, in Yugoslavia, there was a nasty civil war in progress. It was not enough for us natives that the country was occupied by Germans, Italians, Bulgarians, and even Hungarians who were all no slouches when it came to murdering the innocent. We, the victims, spent four years trying to outdo our occupiers in cruelty. In the little town near Belgrade where my grandfather had a house and we went to take a breather from the bombings of the city, the main local pastime was murder. Mihailović's Chetniks were killing commies and the commies were killing Chetniks. In addition, we had the followers of the fascist general Ljotić; we had the collaborators of General Nedić; we had the White Russian troops who fought on the German side; and we had assorted other psychopaths who worked alone or in groups. We even had a couple of Italian soldiers who were disarmed and abandoned after the fall of Mussolini. They went knocking on people's doors and asking the kind signora for something to eat in exchange for doing any odd jobs. They were the only soldiers among the lot I liked and trusted.

Around the dinner table every night the talk turned to the day's horrors: The shoemaker and his family had their throats cut last night. The high school teacher of French was arrested. The Sava River was full of fresh corpses floating down from Croatia. There were four dead men lying in the ditch on the road to some village.

This wasn't just unfounded rumor. Running around the country-side, my friends and I saw plenty of corpses in the last months of war. I never went near them. The few who were bolder and did, tried to frighten the rest of us with gory details. All this seemed unsurpassably awful, until I heard the stories of what went on in Bosnia, Herzegovina, Krajina, and Montenegro. Horror, like anything else people do, has its degrees. I realized early on that my wartime experiences were comparatively idyllic. We always had the city to run back to, and the city despite the bombs has ways of protecting one that a small village in the wilds of Bosnia or Herzegovina just cannot do.

"I only regret not having had an opportunity to kill my father," a Montenegrin intellectual told me years later in New York. He had the face and a manner one would ordinarily describe as sensitive, so his words came as a great shock to me. The members of his family, as was often the case, took different sides in the civil war, and his father was on the wrong side. In him, and in so many others I encountered after the war, I sensed a hatred so huge, so vicious and mindless that any attempt to counter it with pleas for forgiveness and reasonableness was met with total incomprehension, and their hatred turning eventually against me. For my mother, the murderers of all nations belonged to a single nation, the nation of murderers, a view that I always found eminently sensible and regrettably in the minority. Still, I guess, if you know that your sister and mother were killed and raped by a Serb or a Croat, it's hard to confine your hatred to just that one Serb or Croat. Loathing and cries for vengeance do not distinguish between individual and collective responsibility.

The marching music of the next century will undoubtedly be religion and nationalism. The choir practice has already started. Children of light and children of darkness are already being sorted out everywhere. Brutality, violence, and inhumanity, as Simone Weil knew, have always had an immense and secret prestige. We now only require a new superior morality to justify them.

All that became obvious to me watching the dismemberment of Yugoslavia, the way opportunists of every stripe over there instantly fell behind some vile nationalist program. Yugoslav identity was enthusiastically canceled overnight by local nationalists and Western democracies in tandem. Religion and ethnicity were to be the main qualifications for citizenship, and that was just dandy. Those who still persisted in thinking of themselves as Yugoslavs were now regarded as chumps and hopeless utopians, not even interesting enough to be pitied. In the West many jumped at the opportunity to join in the fun and become ethnic experts. We read countless articles about the rational, democratic, and civilized Croats and Slovenes, the secular Moslems, who, thank God, are not like their fanatic brethren elsewhere, and the primitive, barbaric, and Byzantine Serbs and Montenegrins. This was supposed to explain the breakup and justify the creation of ethnic states. The concept of the free and unique individual ceased to exist. Someone intermarried and ethnically mixed was an impediment to cultural theory. The ideal was a revision of history that a lynch mob could understand.

Anyone who, like me, regularly reads the press of the warring sides in former Yugoslavia has a very different view. The supreme folly of every nationalism is that it believes itself unique, while in truth it's nothing more than a bad xerox copy of every other nationalism. Unknown to them, their self-delusions and paranoias are identical. The chief characteristic of a true nationalist is that special kind of blindness. In both Serbia and Croatia, and even in Slovenia, intellectuals are ready to parrot the foulest neofascist imbecilities, believing that they're uttering the loftiest homegrown sentiments. Hypocrites who have never uttered a word of regret for the evil committed by their side shed copious tears for real and imaginary injustices done to their people over the centuries. What is astonishing to me is how many in the West find that practice of selective morality and machismo attractive.

There's no better entertainment than a good bombing, Richard Burt and Richard Perle, sounding like the disciples of General Mladić, told us a while back on the op-ed page of the *New York Times*. "Air strikes, especially televised ones, would be dramatic, even exhilarating," the two distinguished civil servants claimed. What worries me is the ease with which people even in our democratic society recommend violence to accomplish certain ends, in this case as a bit of uplift and a curative for America's lack of military confidence after Vietnam.

In the meantime, columns of refugees. An old woman dressed in black is pulling by a rope a small suitcase that lies flat on the ground. Is she a Moslem from Srebrenica or Žepa, or she is one of two hundred thousand cleansed Serbs from Krajina? It makes no difference. I only catch a glimpse of her on TV, but she moves me as much as that woman suicide we all saw hanging from a tree did. Only a thoroughly evil brain could regard her limping along like that, black as a crow, along the side of a dusty road, and dragging that suitcase as necessary, but the same news program quotes a so-called government expert who sees this "exchange of population as facilitating the peace process." In other words: Innocents everywhere, watch your ass! We got big travel plans for you.

Of course, she reminds me of my mother and me carrying our heavy suitcases in 1948, through pitch-dark Slovenian woods, while sneaking across the border illegally into Austria. The suitcases contained, besides our clothes and a couple of salamis, the yellowed family photographs, the dog-eared diplomas, a few letters, a few other documents covered with rubber stamps, and finally my baby spoon. I wonder what that poor woman is carrying in her suitcase? I'm afraid it would break all our hearts if we found out.

I think this unknown woman's plight is much worse than my mother's and mine ever was. At least we knew that Hitler and Stalin packed our suitcases and Marshal Tito provided the rope. This woman, on the other hand, comes at the end of a long wicked century when everybody is already tired of hearing her rambling story.

THE TROUBLE WITH POETRY

The only thing poetry has always been good for is to make children hate school and jump with joy the day they no longer have to look at another poem. The whole world is in complete agreement on that subject. No one in their right mind ever reads poetry. Even among the literary theorists nowadays, it is fashionable to feel superior to all literature and especially poetry. That some people still continue to write it is an oddity that belongs in some "Believe It or Not" column of the daily newspaper.

When they praised the tribal gods and heroes and glorified their wisdom in war, poets were tolerated, but with the emergence of lyric poetry and the poet's obsession with the self, everything changed. Who wants to hear about lives of nobodies while great empires rise and fall? All that stuff about being in love, smooching, and having to part as the day breaks and the rooster crows is at best laughable. Schoolteachers, clergymen, and other policemen of virtue have always seen eye to eye with the philosophers. No model of ideal society since Plato has ever welcomed lyric poets, and for plenty of good reasons. Lyric poets are always corrupting the young, making them choke in self-pity and indulge in reverie. Dirty sex and disrespect for authority is what they have been whispering into their ears for ages.

From *Michigan Quarterly Review* 36, no. 3 (Winter 1997): 39–42, special issue "The Poet's Voice."

"If he writes verses, kick him out," a new father was counseled two thousand years ago in Rome. That hasn't changed a bit. Parents still prefer their children to be taxidermists and tax collectors rather than poets. Who can blame them? Would you want your only daughter to be a poet or a hostess in a sleazy night club? That's a tough one.

Even true poets have detested poetry. "There are more things beyond this fiddle," said our own Marianne Moore. She had a point. Some of the most idiotic things human beings have ever uttered are to be found in poetry. Poetry, as a rule, has embarrassed both individuals and nations.

Poetry is dead, the enemies of poetry have shouted happily for centuries and still do. Our classic poets, our trendy professors have told us, are nothing but a bunch of propagandists for the ruling classes and male oppression. The ideas once promulgated by the jailers and murderers of poets in the Soviet Union are now a big hit in American universities. Aestheticism, humor, eroticism, and all the other manifestations of the free imagination are suspect and must be censored. Poetry, that foolish diversion for the politically incorrect, has mostly ceased to exist for our educated classes. Nevertheless, as if to spite them, poetry keeps being written.

The world is always looking to reward conformity. Every age has its official line on what is real, what is good, and what is bad. A dish made up of dishonesty, ignorance, and cowardice served every evening with a serious mien and an air of highest integrity by the TV news is the ideal. Literature, too, is expected to go along with that. Your tribe is always trying to reform you and teach you manners. The poet is that kid who, standing in the corner with his back turned to his schoolmates, thinks he is in paradise.

If that were not enough, poets, as everybody knows, are champion liars. "You got to lie to stay halfway interested in yourself," says the novelist Barry Hannah. This is especially true of the writers of verse. Every fool one of them believes he perjures himself only to tell the truth. If we can't see the world for what it is in reality, it's due to the layers of dead metaphors poets have left around. Reality is just an old, peeling poetry poster.

Philosophers say that poets delude themselves when they dwell lovingly on particulars. The identification of what remains untouched by change has been the philosopher's task. Poetry and the novel, on the contrary, have been delighted with the ephemeral—the smell of bread, for instance. As far as poets are concerned, only fools are seduced by generalizations.

Heaven and earth, nature and history, gods and devils are all scandalously reconciled in poetry. Analogy says that each is all, all is each. Consequently, the best religious poems are full of the erotic. Subjectivity, so the poets claim, transcends itself by the practice of seeing identity in far-apart things. In a good poem, the poet who wrote the poem vanishes so that the poet-reader may come into existence. The "I" of a total stranger, an ancient Chinese, for instance, speaks to us from the most secret place within ourselves, and we are delighted.

The true poet specializes in a kind of bedroom and kitchen metaphysics. I'm the mystic of the frying pan and my love's pink toes. Like every other art, poetry depends on nuance. There are many ways to touch a guitar string, to kiss and nibble someone's toe. Blues musicians know that a few notes rightly placed touch the soul, and so do lyric poets. The idea is, it is possible to make astonishingly tasty dishes from the simplest ingredients. Was it Charles Olson who said that myth is a bed in which human beings make love to the gods? As long as human beings fall in love and compose love letters, poems, too, will get written.

Most poems are fairly short. It takes longer to sneeze properly than to read a haiku. Still, some of these "little" poems have managed to say more in a few words about the human condition than centuries of other kinds of writing. Short, occasional poems have survived for thousands of years when epics and just about everything else have grown unreadable. The supreme mystery of poetry is the way such poems cast a spell on the reader. The poem is perfectly understandable after one reading, and yet one immediately wants to reread it again. Poetry is about repetition that never gets monotonous. "More!" my sleepy children would nag after I had finished reading them some nursery rhyme. For them, as for all the lovers of poetry, there was only more, and never enough.

It is the paradoxical quality of poetry, precisely, that gives poetry its flavor. Paradox is its secret spice. Without its numerous contradictions and its impertinence, poetry would be as bland as a Sunday sermon or the president's State of the Union address. It's due to its many delicious paradoxes that poetry has continuously defeated and outlived its sternest critics. Any attempt to reform poetry, to make it didactic and moral, or even to restrict it within some literary "school," is to misunderstand its nature. Good poetry has never swerved from its purpose as an inexhaustible source of paradoxes about art and the human condition.

Only a style that is a carnival of styles to bring out poetry's irreverence seems appropriate to me today. A poetry, in short, that has the feel of cable television with more than three hundred channels, facts stranger than fiction, fake miracles and superstitions in supermarket tabloids. A poem that is like a sighting of Elvis Presley on Mars, the woman with three breasts, the picture of a dog who ate Shakespeare's best play, the news that hell is overcrowded, that blackest sinners are now being settled in heaven.

Here, for instance, comes a homeless fellow whose bald head once belonged to Julius Caesar. Didn't I see you holding up a Live Sex Show sign on Times Square yesterday? I ask him. He nods happily. Will Hannibal again cross the Alps with his elephants? is my next question. Watch out for the lady poet, is his reply. If she comes wheeling her shopping cart full of old books and old clothes, be ready to hear a poem.

That reminds me. My great-grandfather, the blacksmith Philip Simic, died at the age of ninety-six in 1938, the year of my birth, after returning home late one night from a dive in the company of gypsies. He thought they would help him fall asleep, but he passed away like that in his own bed with the musicians playing his favorite songs. That explains why my father sang gypsy songs so well and why I write poems, because like my grandfather I can't sleep at night.

CUT THE COMEDY

> *The cow that goes to heaven must take its body for not having enough brain to remember itself in spirit.*
>
> *It's an unhappy time of struggle. The cow mooing. It is no less difficult than a breech birth.*
>
> *But if a cow should die it must be raised toward heaven, lest it perish in forgetfulness, the sleep of pastures.*
>
> *The farmer is trying to get the cow into the hayloft, "nearer, my God, to Thee," pulling the cow with ropes; the cow trying to get a footing over the tractor and bales of hay piled for the ascension . . .*
>
> *—The cow mooing, the farmer praying, and his wife crying, scandal, scandal, scandal!*
>
> —RUSSELL EDSON, "THE ASCENSION OF THE COW"

If it's funny, then, obviously, it can't be serious, people will tell you.

I disagree. Comedy says as much about the world as does tragedy. In fact, if you seek true seriousness, you must make room for both comic and tragic vision. Still, almost everybody prefers to be pitied than to be laughed at. For every million poems lamenting the cruel

From *Harvard Review* 11 (Spring 1996).

fate of a much-misunderstood and endlessly suffering soul, we get one funny Russell Edson or Kenneth Koch poem.

The dirtiest little secret around is that there are as many people without a sense of humor as there are people with no aesthetic sense. How do you convey to someone that something is funny or that something is beautiful? Well, you can't. It's not often that one hears people confess that they don't understand jokes. Humorless folk regard the rest of us as being merely silly. Our verbal acrobatics and our faces distorted by laughter are annoying and childish. Only if they are vastly outnumbered do they plead to have the joke explained. Everyone has, at one time or another, witnessed or participated in such a hopeless attempt. It can't be done. You are better off telling a blind man about the glory of a sunset, and a deaf man about a Charlie Parker solo.

Aesthetic sense can be cultivated or developed, but what of the comic? Is one born with a sense of humor, or can it be acquired?

I suppose both, but it's not easy. If you love yourself too much, your chances are poor. The vainglorious want the world to tiptoe around them and draw near only to gaze at them in wordless admiration. The whole notion of hierarchy and its various supporting institutions depends on the absence of humor. The ridiculousness of authority must not be mentioned. The church, the state, and the academy are in complete accord about that. The emperor who has no clothes always strolls past silent courtiers. All that is spiritual, lofty, and abstract regards the comic as profane and blasphemous.

It is impossible to imagine a Christian or a fascist theory of humor. Like poetry, humor is subversive. The only remedy, the ideologue of all stripes will tell you, is complete prohibition. Moral uplift is a grim business, and the dictatorship of virtue, as we know, has the air of funeral home and graveyard about it. Irony and cutting wit are reserved solely for the superior classes and their closest flunkies. The servants of the mighty and their dogs are allowed to show their teeth and to bite when necessary.

We ordinarily anticipate good literature to be solemn, boring, and therefore edifying. I attended, for example, one of the first performances of Beckett's *Krapp's Last Tape* in New York. The audience in the small theater was made up of intellectual types of both sexes. Early on in the play, the old guy on the stage is trying to open the drawer of the desk he's sitting at. It's stuck. He's got to pull hard and rest between attempts. Finally, it comes loose. He opens the drawer halfway, looks at us, gropes inside and finds what he's looking for. We can't see it, of course, but he can, and he's very happy with his find. Slowly, he brings into view an ordinary banana. After a pause for dramatic effect, he begins to peel it.

At that point, a man sitting behind me began to cackle loudly. To my astonishment people started hissing "Pssst," some even turning around to shake their fists angrily in his face. "Stupid, stupid man," said the beautiful woman sitting next to me. She meant: no side-splitting hilarity allowed in the presence of high art. Like an obedient concertgoer snoozing through a Mahler symphony and awakening at the end to applaud vigorously, we are expected to submit to art and literature as joylessly as to a foul-tasting but beneficial medicine.

Serious literature, supposedly, has an important message to impart, and the problem with the comic is that it does not. In any case, if it has a "message," it's not the one we are comfortable with. The philosophy of laughter reminds us that we live in the midst of contradictions, pulled this way by the head, pulled that way by the heart, and still another way by our sex organs.

Don't forget the eternal shouts of the flesh: Oh! Ah! and Ha-ha!

If humor ever became extinct, human beings would be left without souls.

Philosophically, we must start with the idea of laughter. I cannot imagine anything more horrible than a society where laughter and poetry are prohibited, where the morbid self-absorption of the rich and the powerful and the hypocrisies of our clergymen and politicians go unchecked. Protecting from ridicule those who proclaim eternal truths is where most intellectual energy is expended in our world.

The Greeks, on the other hand, were able to poke fun at their gods.

I ask you, is there anything more healthy than that?

I would consider any society near-perfect where the arts of highest irreverence were practiced and Russell Edson was poet laureate.

THE POETRY OF VILLAGE IDIOTS

None of the willed imagination of the professionals. No themes, developments, construction, or method. On the contrary, only the imagination that comes from the inability to conform.
—HENRI MICHAUX

I dream of immense cosmologies, sagas and epics reduced to the dimension of an epigram. —ITALO CALVINO

Writing a prose poem is a bit like trying to catch a fly in a dark room. The fly probably isn't even there, the fly is inside your head; still, you keep tripping over and bumping into things while in hot pursuit. The prose poem is a burst of language following a collision with a large piece of furniture.

So, why do it? What is the attraction of such a seemingly idiotic undertaking?

In my own case, the so-called prose poems I wrote were the results of my attempt to get away from myself. To be free of my own imagination and my own brain, to embark on an adventure of unforeseeable consequences, continues to be my great dream.

From *Verse* 13, no. 1 (1996): 7–8, written for the special issue on prose poetry.

Others pray to God; I pray to chance to show me the way out of this prison I call myself.

A quick, unpremeditated scribble and the cell door opens at times. I have never had any idea how I accomplished what I accomplished. In such writing intuition rules. One depends on one's own literary savvy to make the right moves and to recognize the presence of a poem. For me, the prose poem is a pure literary creation, the monster child of two incompatible strategies, the lyric and the narrative. On one hand, there's the lyric's wish to make the time stop around an image, and on the other hand, one wants to tell a little story.

The aim, as in a poem written in lines, is to arouse in the reader an unconquerable desire to reread what he or she has just read. In other words, it may look like prose, but it acts like a poem. The second, the third, and the fiftieth reading will be even better. You'll never get tired of me, it promises. If you don't believe what I say, read some of Rimbaud's *Illuminations* or Russell Edson's finest poems. They are inexhaustible.

It's pointless to attempt to give guidelines for what is really the product of the free imagination, but I can say the following:

The secret of the prose poem lies in its economy and surprise. It must dazzle, and it must also have a lightness of touch. I regard the comic spirit as its true Muse. Playful and irreverent treatment of every subject is usually the custom. In order to free poetry of its mannerism and tics, the prose poem must not take itself too seriously. Impossible to write, illegitimate in the view of so many poets and critics, it must remain a pariah and an object of ridicule to survive.

FEARFUL PARADISE

We all came to America expecting to play a part in a Hollywood movie. Most of the American films were made in southern California, so if you were in Europe, watching those palm trees swaying in the wind with someone like Rita Hayworth gliding underneath them in a white convertible, you got all kinds of wonderfully wrong ideas about the place. Do people really live like that? I wondered. What will they say about my bad teeth and my funny accent? America was a fearful paradise.

It was reassuring to find that in Chicago, there were poor people, trash-strewn streets and laundry hanging from fire escapes, old men swaying on the corner drinking out of brown paper bags, kids pummeling each other in a school yard, even a few beggars. This I understood. I immediately felt at home.

Chicago in the fifties was still a town of factories. Its ugliness and squalor brought to mind Dostoyevsky's descriptions of the Moscow and St. Petersburg slums. The people waiting for the North Avenue bus looked as if they had just arrived from Ellis Island. Still, there was plenty of work. An immigrant would come to Chicago, get a job in a factory, and keep it for the rest of his life. He would speak some English, some Polish, some Hungarian, and some Italian because

From the *Washington Post*, Sunday August 18, 1996, C1.

these are the people he worked with. Once, you could say, he knew what he was, to what culture he belonged. Now he was no longer sure.

He worked all the time. The immigrants often had that gray, weary look of people working long hours and weekends, but they had no complaints about that. The neighborhoods smelled of steaks and fried chicken, where in the old country all you could smell was turnips and cabbage.

The city had an air of prosperity with all the banks, office buildings, and modern apartment houses along the lake, and yet it didn't feel like a big city. After eight o'clock the Loop was dark except for a few movie houses and seedy bars. Hardly anyone was to be found on the streets on weeknights. Perhaps a few farmboys and drunken soldiers loitering outside the Greyhound bus station while the El passed overhead with a face or two pressed to its window, peeking into the dark. In winter it was even worse. There could be a bone-chilling wind blowing off the lake. At least working around the clock kept you warm.

Chicago gave me a better sense of what America was than some small town would have. Its mixture of being, at the same time, very modern and progressive and very provincial is our national specialty. Add to that the realization that so much of our prosperity depends on cheap labor. Immigrants and blacks kept Chicago humming.

I liked the anarchy of the city. There were dives and strip-joints a few blocks away from the monumental Art Institute and the ritzy hotels. Chicago was the garage sale of all the contradictions America could contain. Some rusty water-tower on the top of an old warehouse would look as beautiful as some architectural wonder along the lakeshore. Every notion one had of aesthetics had to be revised if one were to appreciate the city. My greatest teachers, in both art and literature, were the streets I roamed.

Everybody I knew all of a sudden wanted to get educated. If you had to work for a living, as many did, it was night school, of course.

My father was an optimist. He always felt like the money would fall out of the blue sky. He bought the American Dream. It just hadn't been delivered yet. So when I realized soon enough that my parents didn't have the means to put me through school, I attended the University of Chicago at night and worked during the day at the *Chicago Sun-Times*.

Children of immigrants, sons and daughters of blue-collar workers all set out to better themselves. The world of art, literature, philosophy, and sciences opened before us. I wanted to know everything instantly. Anytime I heard a name of a writer or a new idea, I would think: "Oh, God, I'm completely ignorant! I better run to the library and look it up."

The public library was the best place in town. Incredibly, they'd let you take those thick art books home so you could sit in your kitchen, eat your hot dogs and beans, and study the paintings of Giotto and Rembrandt. I took full opportunity of the library's beneficence. I read riding to work: I read while pretending to shuffle papers on my desk; I read in bed and fell asleep with the lights still on.

By the time I arrived for the night classes the next day, I was dead tired. The classes were large, lively. There would always be one or two older students arguing with the teacher, saying things like: "Just because it's written in the book, it doesn't mean it's true." No matter how exhausted everybody happened to be, we all perked up watching the professor squirm.

Older people remembered the Haymarket Riots and other labor unrest. Today everybody behaves as if it was the rich who decided on their own to give their employees the forty-hour week with decent pay. Back then people knew how long it took to make the greedy share a portion of their profits.

Weary or not, I was flying high. I found a small basement apartment on Dearborn, between Goethe and Schiller, in a building now torn down. It had a fancy address, but my place was a rat-infested dump in a crummy old tenement. The Oak Street beach, however, was only a few blocks away. I could go swimming any time I wanted. In local bars, I met budding writers and poets. I even met the famous novelist Nelson Algren at some party.

The second time I bumped into him, I was carrying a volume of Robert Lowell's poetry. "Forget that," he told me. "A kid like you, just off the boat . . . Go read Whitman, read Sandburg and Vachel Lindsey."

I took his advice. I wrote poems like this:

> When I see a cockroach,
> I do not grow violent like the others,
> I stop as if a sign of recognition
> Had passed between us . . .

The literary scene in Chicago was small. One met the same faces, it seems. We'd be squeezed in a room, dark except for a couple of lit candles stuck in Chianti bottles, Charlie Parker and Stan Getz on the cheap, portable record player. The women were dressed in black. Their hair fell down to their shoulders and over their eyes so they gave one the impression they were playing peekaboo all the time. Parisian existentialism had finally come to the Midwest. We were reading Sartre and Camus and quoting them to each other between puffs of cigarette smoke. There'd be a bottle of bad whiskey or rum that tasted like something someone stole from their grandmother's medicine cabinet, but otherwise not much to eat or drink, since everybody was broke.

In the literary crowd, there were many socialists and even a few ex-communists. In those days, much more so than today, radical intellectuals came from working-class backgrounds. They worked with their hands, or they were officials in some union. Jewish, German, Irish fellows who all had plenty of advice for a young poet like me. Beware of the Eastern literary establishment, they told me. You'll end up writing sonnets about Orpheus and Eurydice when you should be writing poems about old ladies who sweep the downtown offices at night.

They had a point. When you're young, and even more so when you're an immigrant, you are looking for role models. You want to blend quickly. I was all ready to put on English tweeds with leather elbow patches and smoke a pipe, but they wouldn't let me: "Remember where you came from, kid," they reminded me again and again.

There's no question they had me figured out. Thanks to them, I failed in my natural impulse to become a phony.

One of the great temptations for an immigrant is to go native the whole way, start eating canned soup, white bread, and Jell-O and hide one's passion for sausages smothered in onions and peppers and crackling in fat. I read Emerson and Thoreau and other New England writers and loved them, but I knew my identity was different. I was already a concoction of Yugoslav, American, Jewish, Irish, and Italian ingredients—and the stew wasn't ready yet. There were more things to add to the pot. More identities. More images to cook.

Here I am on the midnight El riding to work or coming back after a long day. It's winter. It's bitter cold. Every time the door opens, we shiver, our teeth chatter. When it shuts, the heat turned on high and the closely pressed bodies make it even worse. It's hard to keep my eyes open. I'm asleep standing up. If I don't watch it, I'll miss my stop and wake up at the end of the line. I'll be halfway to Iowa. It'll be two o'clock in the morning and I'll be the only one on the open platform pacing back and forth to keep warm, muttering to myself at first, then shouting, shouting at the top of my lungs:

"What a life! What a city! What a country!" And I'm leaving out the cuss words.

NIGHT SKY
To Linda Connor

This Saturday night, the sky is a great Pythagorean jukebox sparkling
in a corner of a darkened night club.

> The black wax is spinning.
> Tarantula nebula.
> It's one of the golden oldies.
> The mystics among us will hear the music.

Written for *On the Music of the Spheres*, a limited edition book of Linda Connor's
photographs of the night sky, and published by the Whitney Museum in 1996.

The star map hanging down over the blackboard in my grade school classroom remains where it was forty-seven years ago. The trees are bare and it's still raining. Everyone is bent over their work and I alone am daydreaming while watching a small insect crawl over the map on its way to the Dog Star.

He wants to be one of its fleas is what I think.

A large family of circus performers. There go the bear and the lion who sheds golden tears. The carrot-haired Venus and the winged-horse Pegasus come next. The show has started. There are dwarfs, too, I'm told. The acrobats and the fire-eaters have sequins sewn to their black suits.

How do we win the love of Betelgeuse? The trumpets, the drums, and the voice of the master of ceremonies are much too far away.

Even the encyclopedia entry about the sky is full of poetry:

"During spring evenings," it says, "Orion is still above the horizon; Leo is high up with Virgo to the East; Capella is descending in the northwest and Vega is rising in the northeast. In the west, Aldebaran and the Pleiades are still visible."

And—I want to write in the margin: There goes my grandmother, the one the neighbors call the witch, riding a white goat while clutching the Holy Bible to her breast.

The cow alone in the fields, does it raise its heavy head to gaze at the stars?

How about daddy longlegs, the pair of fireflies, the lone cricket?

The night sky loves only the solitary ones. To the one sitting in a corner with his face to the wall, it offers its own secret invitation on the breath of night wind.

When he finds himself in the desert or on the mountaintop, he will want immediately to confide himself to the sky.

Oh the things we would all say to the stars in the sky if we found ourselves alone in a lifeboat at sea.

It's the Death Mask of the Universe we are staring at.

There are candles burning in its eye-pits and in its huge gaping mouth.

Where is the ear, dark as the bottom of a coffee cup, where all our prayers went in?

Where's the other ear where they all went out?

Where am I? That's my first question.

—SAMUEL BECKETT, *THE UNNAMABLE*

I'm nothing; a mere drop in the ocean.

My existence is a matter of complete indifference to you, Cassiopeia.

Cities burning, empires falling, someone addressing the crowd from the gallows with a noose already around his neck are all equally of no importance to you.

Perhaps the ecstasy of hearing your beautiful name on our lips is all that you know?

And then, more likely, you don't even know about that.

If the photographers are soul-thieves, whose soul is being stolen in a photograph of the night sky?

The soul of the last one to go to bed and the soul of the first one to rise in the morning, perhaps?

Photography is a black art like alchemy. It turns matter into spirit and spirit into matter.

Still, there are moments when looking at a photograph of a night sky we have a hunch what the word *soul* means, what the word *infinity* encompasses.

And then, friends, there are those clear summer nights when Time, our killer, goes to take a long siesta in the star-strewn meadows.

The old clock on the wall that ticks even more loudly after midnight, because its two hands are afraid of each other in the dark, is quiet for once.

No one can find the key to wind it up.

If you want to know the correct time, look deep into the eyes of a black cat.

The ambition of Byzantine church architecture is to invite the sky in and make it welcome between the walls of the humblest of its churches. The interiors of their domes, therefore, resemble a planetarium. The holy icon of the Mother of God here below is like a saucer of milk set out for the stars in the sky to drink at midnight.

The heaven in Byzantine frescoes has the appearance and the smell of a burning candle about to be put out by the galactic wind.

The levitating archangels and saints have the awestruck faces of children riding a Ferris wheel.

The lazy light of the stars is trying to calm our jitters.

Hush, it says, the moment the night falls.

In my lifelong insomnia, I even tried counting Greek and Egyptian gods like sheep.

Psst, I told them, when their stone-steps in the sky got to be too loud.

After taking a good look at the sky through a telescope at the planetarium, my mother concluded, "The whole creation is an absurdity! A practical joke."

Large numbers gave her a headache. For her, the commonplace claim that the universe is infinite was a comic rather than a tragic proposition.

I, too, rejoice in the craziness of it all. For me, the sky full of stars is the unbeliever's paradise.

I was put under a spell one night on a high hill.

—GUILLAUME IX OF AQUITAINE

No sooner had I started my reverie than I was light-years from the earth, a tightrope walker on his way to the confetti palace.

I was the galactic Marco Polo.

I rode a unicycle with its wheel on fire.

I saw the stars go down to catch a brief glimpse of themselves in lakes and rivers.

The solitude of the timeless sparkling in the deep black water.

If not for the dog barking after me tonight, none of us would know we were here.

My private interview with the Infinite Universe went something like this:

So, this is the brightly lit gambling casino of the imagination?

The bets are constantly being made and the roulette wheels, as far as I can see, turn unattended?

(Did I imagine it, or did it really shrug its shoulders in reply?)

A worldwide chain of firecracker supply stores is what this is.

The owner wears a black cape and has a huge black moustache like a famous hypnotist.

His daughters are writing secret love notes in Arabic script to a mysterious someone.

"Call me in the evening," one note says.

Love: the volume of one of the distant radio galaxies turned down real, real low.

from

THE METAPHYSICIAN IN THE DARK

IN PRAISE OF FOLLY

Folly is in poor repute even among the greatest fools.

—ERASMUS

1.

It's almost the year 2000. All the New York City hotel rooms and fine restaurants are already booked for New Year's Eve. The astrologers are busy predicting the future, and so are the Pentagon and the CIA. Ancient Babylonian princesses and Egyptian priests are sending daily messages through the mouths of housewives in Texas and New Jersey. Many strange occurrences are due to take place, we are told weekly in supermarket tabloids: A huge monument to Elvis Presley will be sighted on Mars. Doctors will bring Abraham Lincoln back to life for ninety-nine seconds. Vintage red wines will be made from plastic cups discarded in fast-food restaurants. With a single wire inserted in the ear, we'll be able to tape our dreams the way we tape TV programs on our VCR.

But what about poetry? What will the poets be doing in the next century? You do not have to be a Nostradamus to predict that the poets will be doing exactly what they've been doing for the last three

From *Georgia Review* 52, no. 4 (Winter 1998).

thousand years: howling and kicking about how nobody ever appreciates them.

Here is a thought I had recently while strolling in New York. Out of the blue, so to speak, I remembered Sappho. I had spent the afternoon in a bookstore turning the pages of new books of poetry, and it suddenly occurred to me that if she were miraculously to come back from the dead and were to see this crowd and this traffic, she'd of course be terrified, but if a few of the contemporary lyric poems I had just read were translated for her, she'd be on familiar ground. Astonishing! I thought. I'm an almost three-thousand-year-old poet, and didn't know it! The kind of poetry I write today has its origins in what she started doing back then.

Here then is the story of my life:

When I was still a snot-nosed kid, my name was Ovid, Horace, Catullus, Sextus Propertius, and Martial. My specialty was mixing the serious with the trivial, the frivolous with the high-minded. I was a holy terror. I wrote lines like these:

> When she's on her chaise-longue,
> Make haste to find a footstool
> For those dainty feet of hers,
> Help her on and off with the slippers.

"Better a metropolitan city were sacked," Robert Burton wrote, "a royal army overcome, an invincible armada sunk and twenty thousand kings should perish, than her little finger ache." That was my plan, too. I had nothing to do with sundry windbags who wrote odes to every two-bit tyrant who came along, tabulated their conquests, glorified their slaughter of the barbarians, and praised their incomparable wisdom in peace and war. I poked fun at the rich and the powerful, gossiping about their wives and daughters milking cocks while their husbands' and daddies' backs were turned. I didn't even spare the gods. I turned them into a lot of brawling, drunken, revengeful, senile wife swappers.

I myself roamed the streets of Rome frequently inebriated. I fell in and out of love a thousand times, never failing to tell the whole world about my new love's incomparable virtues and perversities. Then, I got into trouble. The emperor packed me off to permanent exile in a godforsaken hellhole at the farthest reaches of the empire. His guardians of virtue took the opportunity to warn the populace against lyric poetry—which is nothing more, they said, than a call to debauchery and a brazen mockery of everything ever held sacred.

Of course, nobody bothered the official eulogists-for-hire, who were busy protecting the solemnities of state and church from ridicule. It was the lyric poem, with its exaltation of intimacy, that had been suspect ever since Sappho started the craze by elevating individual destiny over the fate of the tribe, preferring to savor Anactoria's "lovely step, her sparkling glance and her face," rather than "gaze on all the troops in Lydia in their chariots and glittering armor."

It's true. It was the love of that kind of irreverence, as much as anything else, that started me in poetry. The itch to make fun of authority, to break taboos, to celebrate the naked body, to claim that one has seen an angel in the same breath as one shouts that there's no God, and so forth. The discovery that the tragic and the comic are always entwined made me roll on the floor with happiness. Seduction, too, was always on my mind: if you take off your shirt, my love, and let my tongue get acquainted with yours, I'll praise your beauty in my poems and your name will live forever. It worked, too. Much of lyric poetry is nothing more than a huge, centuries-old effort to remind our immortal souls of the existence of our genital organs.

In the so-called Dark Ages, when mud was everywhere up to the knees, the common folk made their bed for the night on the dirt floor, cozy and blissful in one big embrace with their pigs and sheep; hens perched on the rafters over their heads; and only the dogs slept with one of their eyes open, on the lookout for roaming poets. For centuries, not only yokels but also ladies and gents had little to amuse themselves with but a few strains of Gregorian chant and the daily earful of a lot of

bad cussing about the hard life and the weather. I was a lone, bummed-
out, lice-ridden monk, reduced to roving the countryside and begging
every night for a few crumbs and a bit of straw to sleep on in some
rich man's drafty castle. There, in gratitude for the hospitality, I would
offer a gamut of racy love poems, pious legends of saints' lives, drinking songs, funeral laments, faithful-wife poems, and sly satires on the
ways of kings and popes. At the same time, I had to be extra careful to
make the murderous and drunken company at the table laugh and even
shed a tear at how hungry and cold, how skinny and forlorn I looked
now that—*oh the sweet voice of the woodland nightingale*—I'd even lost
my cloak and breeches at dice!

> I turn to you in misery and tears
> As turns the stag, when his strength gives out.

You get the idea? Oh, the guises I had—more aliases than all
the con artists of the world put together. I was that petty felon Vil-
lon, who almost ended up strung by his neck; Guillaume IX, Duke of
Aquitaine, who wrote his poems while he snored away in the saddle;
Shakespeare, who some scholars tell you was not really called that but
something else; Signor Dante, who gave us a first-class tour of hell to
prepare us for the horrors of the twentieth century; and so many others. My fondest incarnation remains Thomas Bastard, who lived from
1566 to 1618 and whose life and career my anthology of Elizabethan
verse describes, more or less, thus:

> A country clergyman who made pitiably small headway in life,
> Bastard published his book in 1598. It was much ridiculed. Bas-
> tard died, touched in his wits, in debtors' prison in Dorchester.

My life was like the history of costumes. One season I wore a
powdered wig, rode in a glass coach, and scribbled sonnets on the cuff

of my shirt between duels, taking time out to praise classical measures and restraint; next I was a wild-haired revolutionary shouting encouragement to the crowd while standing on some real or imaginary barricade, assuring my listeners that we poets are nothing less than the unacknowledged legislators of the world.

Some nerve, you must be saying to yourself. Ha-ha! Just wait till I tell you about my American adventures.

2.

No sooner had Columbus sailed back to Spain than I started scribbling poems. It must have been the climate in the New World—hot and humid in the south, bleak and cold in the north—that for years kept me from getting a decent poem written in this vast land of mystery. How many still remember that the first explorers and settlers expected to run into the Chinese over the next horizon? The Frenchman Nicollet even went and provided himself in Paris with a robe of Chinese damask embroidered with birds and flowers, in order to be properly attired while crossing the prairie and finally sitting down to sip tea and schmooze with some old mandarin. In any case, it took me years of sleepwalking before I could open my eyes and see where I truly was.

Forget about El Dorado and New Jerusalem. Forget about the devil in the forest and the comely witches stripping to frolic naked around his campfire. Forget about Oriental spices and jewels. Here were grim little towns with factory walls blackened by age. Here were crowded tenements with men and women huddled against the weather, lying on their sides, knees drawn up, their heads touching the roach-infested floor. Here were seedy rooming houses populated by an assortment of loners, eccentrics, bad poets, and a dozen other kinds of losers.

How quickly the New World got old for me. Some days it felt

like being buried alive. I was weary, resigned like Bartleby to staring at walls. Yet on other days the windows were wide open, the sun was shining, America still remained to be truly discovered.

The poet is the eye and tongue of every living and every inanimate thing, I told everyone I met. Poetry is nothing less than a divinely appointed medium. God himself doesn't speak prose, but communicates with us through hints, omens, and not-yet-perceived resemblances in objects lying around us. Unfortunately, American life storms about us daily, but is slow to find a tongue. I looked in vain, I shouted like a street preacher, for the poet whom I describe.

It didn't take long. I grew a white beard and made the announcement that Americans, of all people at any time upon the earth, have probably the fullest poetical nature, and that the United States themselves are essentially the greatest poem.

How do you like that? I said to myself.

This is what you shall do, I wrote. Love the earth, the sun, and the animals, despise riches, give alms to everyone who asks, stand up for the stupid and crazy, reexamine everything you have been told in school and church or any book, hate tyrants, and dismiss whatever insults your soul. Do these things, and your very flesh shall be a great poem.

I tell you, I felt right at home in America.

All truths wait in all things to be discovered, I proclaimed. The number of unknown heroes is equal to the number of greatest heroes known, and I will name them all. The cow with its head bowed and munching the grass surpasses any statue.

I went on to make a poem of things overlooked, slighted, and forbidden. Still and all, my exuberant praise of all matters sexual was a permanent scandal in a country founded by the followers of Calvin.

At the very same time I was saying all that, however, I had a secret other, someone reserved and suspicious in the face of my utopian grandeur and self-confident rhetoric. We live in a magic prison, a haunted house, a dark labyrinth, an inscrutable forest, my other said; we are trapped in a finite infinite, an uncertain certainty, caught in a maze of oxymorons and paradoxes in a universe whose chief characteristic is its ambiguity. That other America came with a large graveyard. In it, the poet is a recluse, a secret blasphemer, and a heroic failure at best.

What my two sides had in common was an inability to submit to bounds and limits. They both aimed to join heaven and earth in their poems. What an ideal pickle to find oneself in, especially as an immigrant: Poetry as the place where fundamental epistemological, metaphysical, and aesthetic questions can be raised and answered. Poetry as the process through which ideas are tested, dramatized, made both a personal and a cosmic issue. I liked that. The poet's struggle may be solitary, but it is an exemplary struggle nevertheless.

American poetry's dizzying ambition to answer all the major philosophical and theological questions is unparalleled. Grand inquisitors, philosopher kings, totalitarian cops of all stripes would have plenty to do with me after a pronouncement like the following: "The poet—when he is writing—is a priest; the poem is a temple; epiphanies and communion take place within it."

Spiritual adventurer is the name of the game, folks. In America I bragged that I was starting from scratch, naked, without history and often without any religious belief, climbing an imaginary ladder up to heaven to find out for myself what all the fuss is about. I made American literature into a great paradox factory. On one hand, I desired to embody and express rare visionary states, and on the other, I wished to give my readers a hard and dry look at everyday reality. Literalists of the imagination—that's what I wanted us to be. Finding a place for the genuine in this artifice we call poetry (which I myself admitted disliking) was my great project. My most original achievement may very well have been my odd insistence that the only way to tell human beings about angels is to show them a blade of grass.

Ah, the three-thousand-year-old poet! You've got to see the night-mares I get from all the bad poems I've written. A day doesn't go by without some professor wagging her finger at me. Why, only recently I was described as a self-pitying little fascist, peddling his phallocen-tric, petit bourgeois claptrap. Twenty centuries of ridicule, my friends! Pedants poring over my poems, then teaching them to the young in such a way that the children are guaranteed to hate poetry for the rest of their lives. Some mornings, when the weather is damp, I get a sore neck, as if I were still Sir Walter Raleigh, convicted on charges of blasphemy and sedition, awaiting the executioner's ax in the Tower of London.

Here's my view of these long centuries:

One century's no worse than the other, if you ask me. A break in the clouds once in a while, an afternoon nap in the shade in the arms of your one and only, maybe a kiss or two, and that's about it. Sooner or later, the meal gets eaten, and we're left with just some chicken bones on our plate. The rest of the time it's plagues, wars, famines, persecutions, exile, and hundreds of other calamities and miseries that rule the day.

I suppose, dear readers, you think I am exaggerating? You imag-ine yourselves, of course, in a palazzo attended and closely fussed over by numerous servants while you argue with princes and highborn floo-zies about the paintings of Titian and the metaphysics of Campanella's *City of the Sun*. Don't make me laugh. All I see is open sewers in a street, reeking with the stench of horse and human excrement, while nearby a twelve-year-old witch is being burned at the stake by the Inquisition.

The true poets always know the score. Happiness, love, and the vision of the Almighty and his angels come and go. The moment we taste a morsel of bliss, begin to savor it, and lick our lips—oops! Our house catches fire, someone runs off with our wife, or we break our leg. Poetry is best, therefore, when it finds itself at the heart of the human comedy; there's no more reliable reporter of what it means to be in this pickle. My view is that poetry is inevitable, irreplaceable, and necessary as daily bread. Even if we were to find ourselves living in the crummiest country in the world, in an age of unparalleled vileness and stupidity, we'd find that poetry still got written.

I know what troubles you: all the hyperbole poets are prone to, all that monkey talk and bizarre imagery we are forever hustling. Poets allege that the only way to tell the truth is to lie plenty. They put trust in their metaphors and in their wildest flights of the imagination. Poetry, they argue, is the only place where an incorrigible liar can have an honest existence, providing he or she lies really well.

My dear reader, *don't you see?*

Life would be perfectly pointless if I, the poet, didn't come and tell you—in so many ingenious ways—that all your amours, all your secret sufferings and fond memories, are potentially significant, deeply important, and even intelligible, and that you, when all's said and done, dear reader, really have no cause to fret about anything, as long as I'm here, night and day, doing the worrying for you.

THE DEVIL IS A POET

Last May, on my first trip to Lisbon, I finally had the opportunity to see Bosch's *Temptation of St. Anthony*. On a rainy weekday morning, the Museu Nacional de Arte Antigua, a converted seventeenth-century palace, appeared closed. After my friend and I paid the admission in the dim lobby, we encountered no one, except for an occasional guard dozing off on his or her feet. It was so quiet in the museum that every time we stopped before a painting, we could hear ourselves breathe. The palace houses the largest collection of fifteenth- and sixteenth-century Portuguese paintings in the world, muddy with age and badly in need of cleaning. We made our lengthy tour among what were mostly religious paintings, admiring a few works here and there, lingering for a while in the applied-arts wing before the marvelous Japanese screen showing a Portuguese delegation disembarking in Nagasaki in the sixteenth century, but finally we had to ask one of the women attendants as to the whereabouts of Bosch.

We crossed several cavernous rooms, the martyrs being tormented in the paintings seemingly as surprised by our sudden appearance as we were by theirs, and just as we began to suspect that we had misunderstood the directions we were given, there was the altarpiece, far larger than we had expected it to be. The triptych was set up and slightly elevated on a kind of platform, well lit, newly cleaned, its reds, blues, and yellows bright and rich, the details vivid, the whole spectacle simply breathtaking. For a painting to still be able to shock after almost five centuries is no small accomplishment. How many other works of art can do that? We stood before it absolutely stunned, overwhelmed and supremely happy, thinking, There cannot be any other world but this. Surprisingly, all that feverish activity, with its myriad of grotesque particulars in all three panels, gave the impression of coherence and purpose. Of course, I had read enough about Bosch previously to know that the theological and philosophical meaning of this and most of his other paintings has remained elusive despite numerous attempts to solve their mystery; nevertheless, I could not escape the feeling that in this painting everything fits together and makes sense in some still unknown way.

Since not much is known about Bosch except for the years of his life—ca. 1450–1516, in the town of 's-Hertogenbosch in the Netherlands—speculations have ranged widely about the originality of his art. The sources of his iconography and his ideas have been sought in heretical and doomsday sects, alchemical practices, medieval diableries, astrology, and, most persuasively in my view, in bestiaries, fantastic travel books, and folklore. He has been called a mystic, a moralist, a satirist, a schizophrenic, and even a realist. The Black Plague, the pillage and massacres of the Hundred Years' War, witch burnings, as well as many of the horrors of our century, came to mind at first seeing the triptych. The extraordinary thing about Bosch is that his vision is somehow both old and modern. I was reminded of Rimbaud's poem "Alchemy of the Verb":

> I accustomed myself to simple hallucinations. I would see quite clearly a mosque in place of a factory, a school of drummers made up of angels, carriages on the roads in the sky, a drawing room at the bottom of a lake; monsters, mysteries; a vaudeville billboard conjured up horrors in my path.

Wherever imagination has reigned supreme in art and literature since Goya and Blake, Bosch suggests himself as a predecessor.

All these and other musings, of course, came to me later. Facing the painting, I was simply trying to orient myself. The temptation of St. Anthony, I recalled, took place in the Egyptian desert, but what I saw before me was a mixture of various kinds of landscapes with buildings from different historical periods. These ruined towers, tombs, and palaces looked like the stage set of some lost opera co-written by the Marquis de Sade. Temptation of holy men was a standard subject in Bosch's day, but while the tradition counted on a few devils, he made the whole of creation one huge hybrid creature, a demon, as it were, composed of human, animal, vegetable, and inanimate parts.

Exaggeration and distortion of features have always been the staple of comic image making, but Bosch did something else. He was a visionary collagist. He painted as if one could only get at reality by first chopping up everything and then reassembling it again. Like Lautréamont, who wrote in a poem, "beautiful as the encounter of a sewing machine and an umbrella on a dissecting table," he plays the game of joining seemingly unjoinable realities, making the results seem inevitable and leaving us to reconsider the meaning of representation. One of his earliest commentators, Fray Jose de Siguenza, said in 1605, "The difference, which, to my mind, exists between the pictures of this man and those of all others is that the others try to paint man as he appears on the outside, while he alone had the audacity to paint him as he is on the inside." In other words, the Spaniard regarded Bosch's grotesqueries as a form of naturalism.

In the meantime, there is the actual painting to feast one's eyes on. Its sky is thick with odd flying contraptions worthy of a Mad Max movie. Instead of brooms, human beings and devils are riding on fishes, birds, and sailing ships as if this were the most normal thing to do. One demon is doing a handstand on a flying scythe. A stork has a mast of a ship attached to its tail. St. Anthony is saying a prayer on a bullfrog, while next to him an incubus waves a branch with a few dry leaves left on it as if to whip him and make him go faster.

It's much worse down below. A village is on fire, the smoke darkening a portion of the sky. An army, presumably responsible for this, is trotting off merrily, their leader on a white horse. A great solemn allegorical procession of grotesque creatures winds across all three panels. They are dressed as men and women of rank who at first appear to be wearing carnival masks until one notices that their body parts belong to other species. Tree trunks, branches, even an earthen pot and many other unlikely items make up the rest of their bodies. One man wears an owl on his head, another an apple. Inside each being there are multiple monsters hiding, devouring each other or struggling to come out. Cruelty, folly, and lechery reign in every nook and cranny.

What caught my attention right off was the chapel in the central panel, in which Jesus stands with his face turned toward us, apparently distracted from his prayer by the tumult outside. Incredibly, he has been praying to himself crucified on the cross. Next door, there's what looks like a Venetian palazzo. In a tent on its roof a monk and a woman are guzzling wine while over their shoulders a naked woman is diving from the parapet into the canal, and another fat monk, already undressed and with a towel over his shoulders, is cautiously descending the steep steps, watched from inside the palace by a big, old cow and a large bird carrying a tall ladder.

A kind of exhilaration came over me the more I studied the painting. As with the best images in Fellini's and Pasolini's films, or some outrageous comparison in a poem by Russell Edson or James Tate, I was delighted. There's no joy like the one a truly outrageous image on the verge of blasphemy gives. In Bosch, wickedness and innocence are constantly rubbing shoulders. To paint a true picture of the world, he seems to be saying, one needs to include both what people see with eyes open and what they see when they shut their eyes. He does not tell us which is which. For him, the visible and the invisible belong in the same landscape.

It took me a while to begin to pay attention to the saintly hermit and his story. In the left wing we see him helped on his way by three companions, one of whom is Hieronymus himself. St. Anthony is weak from battling the fiends. They're crossing a small bridge, underneath which a monk and a demonic creature are reading—a letter or perhaps a set of instructions about the next round of temptations. A birdlike messenger with a funnel on his head and skates on his feet is delivering a further missive. Over the saint's bowed head, a fish on wheels carts a church steeple. A giant on all fours, right out of *Gulliver's Travels,* with a cloak of grass over his shoulders and an arrow sticking out of his forehead, stares dumbfounded at the goings-on in the sky. Up his rear end, in a small house almost crushed by his weight, there's the entrance to a brothel with a woman peeking out of the window on the lookout for customers.

I was also interested in the fellow with the black stovepipe hat and red robes casually lounging in the central panel with his back to us, who resembles the conjuror in Bosch's famous painting *The Conjurer.* Is he the director of this *theatrum mundi?* He calmly observes a pig-headed priest reading from a blue prayer book as if auditioning for a part, while a dead woman with a hollow tree for a bonnet and clutching a living child in her arms waits her turn. Does he himself understand what he has created, or is he as perplexed as we are? Behind his back, a huge tomatolike fruit has cracked open with ripeness. A horse-headed demon strumming a harp leads the way out of it, riding on a plucked goose that wears boots, inside whose severed neck another animal-like face is peeking out.

Each one of us is a synthesis of the real and unreal. We all wear a guise. Even within our own minds, we make constant efforts to conceal ourselves from ourselves, only to be repeatedly found out. Bosch did not need Freud and Jung to tell him that our inner lives are grotesque and scandalous. He also knew something they did fully appreciate. The world inside us is comic. Bosch's paintings cannot be understood without appreciating their riotous humor.

Satan pulled every trick out of his infernal bag, and still the saint went on praying. He saw himself surrounded by a swarm of night-marish creatures and harems of naked women, and his composure did not leave him. Finally, Satan dispatched the saint's own wife. In the right-wing panel we see her play bawdy peek-a-boo at the entrance to a hollow tree draped over with a red cloth which a drunken demon is drawing back. The saint is as calm as the sunlit meadow at the edge of the woods next to the burning village, or that deer grazing on the roof of the ruin in the central panel. These are the serene corners of life oblivious to tragedy that Auden spoke of in his great poem "Musée des Beaux Arts." Bosch, too, knew that truth. In *The Ascent to Calvary*, painted on the exterior of the right wing of the triptych, we see Christ collapsing under the weight of his cross while a small boy sitting on his father's shoulders is offering an apple to one of the men who has been mistreating our Lord. Again and again Bosch insists that where there is evil, there's also innocence. Nobody ever saw them in such close prox-imity. That's what makes his paintings so terrifying.

Bosch's initial purpose was probably didactic. Temptation was an occasion to conjure up deadly sins and warn against them, but his imagination subverted the original impulse. I suspect he ended up by enjoying the "demonic beauty" of his creations. Even more subver-sively, his habit of juxtaposing fantastic with realistic detail gave his paintings a far more ambiguous view of creation and humankind. An art that was supposed to be crystal clear to the faithful ended up being an art rich in unsavory innuendoes. Every artist's imagination holds up a mirror to reality, both the outer and the inner, but how those two realities will finally mingle in the reflection, the owner of the mirror may not even suspect. That is because the devils inside us are all poets, and so, luckily, are the angels.

Out on the street the weather had cleared, so we decided to walk until we found a place to have lunch. Lisbon is a large, bustling city of many hills with breathtaking views of the river Tejo, which flows into the Atlantic a few miles beyond the harbor. What gives the city its distinct character is the maze of old neighborhoods with narrow,

cobbled streets, their houses covered with tiles and painted bright colors. A blind man came around the corner and collided with me, giving
me a good whack with his white cane. I wish I could say he resembled
St. Anthony, but he did not. At the restaurant, a tall, lean, and bearded
waiter who served us dried linguiça, grilled squid, and chicken and eel
stew with shrimp looked vaguely familiar, but we could not place him.
We mentioned Vasco da Gama and a few other old navigators, and let
it go at that. Late that night, I woke, sat up in bed, and saw the whole
painting clearly, and in its central panel the sharp profile of the "conjurer" in red had the pointy beard of our waiter.

THE POWER OF AMBIGUITY

On Eva Hesse, untitled, ca. 1961, black and brown ink wash

There are works of art that can be confidently described as minor and of marginal importance, perhaps even to the artist in question, that for reasons far from clear, one can't get enough of. In my own case, I have often been drawn to minimalist works, from Joseph Cornell to Agnes Martin, where the paucity or the almost complete absence of narrative, or even of formal complexities, is an invitation to a kind of poetic reverie. I suppose this is like saying I prefer empty rooms to overdesigned, cluttered interiors, spaces where a single chair or an empty birdcage can do wonders for the imagination. Empty space makes us discover our inwardness. In such rooms one has the feeling that time has stopped, that one's solitude and that of the remaining object are two actors in a metaphysical theater.

This work is one of the series of semiabstract, untitled ink washes on paper that Eva Hesse composed in 1960 and 1961. They are like Symbolist poems. Instead of words and images, smudges, erasures, chance drippings, scribbles, tangled and incomplete forms, contrasts of shadow and light tease our imaginations. If they had titles, of course, it would be another story. The title is like a caption to a news photo; it conditions our response as it tells us what we are supposed to be seeing. The

From *ArtForum* (Summer 1999).

naming of the subject matter is already an interpretation. The delightful uncertainty and the free play of associations the untitled work gives rise to are curtailed for the sake of easy identification.

The ink wash I'm enchanted with appears at first glance less of a problem. The silhouettes of two tall buildings and perhaps even a third one are visible through a small window across a stretch of what very likely could be Central Park in puddles of shadow. It's the brown darkness of an overcast evening with clouds racing and traces of dying light lingering on in the west. There is an air of decrepitude about the scene. Here is the laundry of sundown hung out to dry, as it were, the day's washing, wind-beaten and made grimy by the fumes of the city.

No sooner have I said that than I begin to have my doubts. This window does not really look like a window. It's more like a bamboo picture frame. I have seen such frames on mirrors in people's hallways and in photographs on side tables in a living room where someone once young and handsome is surrounded by exotic knickknacks and memorabilia. How strange to find one enclosing what presumably is an urban scene—unless what we are seeing here is a reflection in a mirror? The point is, it doesn't quite make sense. The frame inside the frame is tilted as if held in someone's unsteady hands. The artist's strategy unsettles our expectations and makes strange what was ordinary only a moment ago.

The more I look at the piece, however, the more I experience its power, the power of its ambiguity. The trap it sets for the imagination is no different from the one found in the sediment on the bottom of a fortune-teller's coffee cup. Blurry outlines, partial views, bizarre cropping elicit a suggestive magic. This drawing is, indeed, like a Symbolist poem. I'm thinking of Mallarmé or Hart Crane at their most hermetic. The secret of that art is not in what you put in, but in how much you leave out. The "poetic" and the "lyrical" states, the Symbolists knew, are beyond exegesis. For instance, when Crane in "To Brooklyn Bridge" describes the lit windows at night as "The city's fiery parcels all undone," the spark of that image transcends any paraphrase. Crane writes: "As a poet I may be possibly more interested in the so-called illogical impingements of the connotations of words on the consciousness (and their combinations and interplay of metaphor on this basis) than I am interested in the preservation of their logically rigid significations at the cost of limiting my subject matter and perception involved in the poem."

Opacities of the evening, a city that appears in ruins, a scene out of a dream, memory of a momentary glance, remains of an old sadness without a cause, the enigma of the real, and the threatening unreality that always hovers over the real. There are times when the world wears the colors and the shadows of our inner life, when reality and imagination appear to be in cahoots. "The imagination is not a State: it is the Human Existence itself," Blake wrote. Hesse may think she is drawing a cityscape, while in truth she is dipping into the ink of her own inwardness.

The simplest test for the strength of any work of art is how long one can bear to look at it. This work passes that test for me. I experience in it the shudder of two different selves coming together. I know why Hesse stopped when she did. I picture her pausing with her brush, staring at the drawing, beginning to fall under its spell herself, then for a brief moment fancying someone else seeing what she sees. Being a poet, I know what she was after. I, too, wish to make contact with some unknown person's inner life. Our mutual hope is to bequeath a phrase or an image to the dreamers so that we may live on in their reverie. Because she has done that to me, I have no choice but to revisit this little work, again and again.

BUSTER KEATON

Only recently, with their issue on videotape, have all the films of Buster Keaton become widely available. It's likely one may have seen "The General" (1926) in some college course, or caught a couple of shorts at some museum retrospective of silent comedy, but such opportunities were rare and for most moviegoers in this country nonexistent. When Keaton's name came up, people who knew who he was would often say how much they preferred his laid-back stoicism to Chaplin's sentimentality, admitting in the same breath that, regretfully, they had not seen one of his films in a long time.

I first heard about Buster Keaton from my grandmother, who was also of the opinion that he was the funniest of the silent-movie comedians. This didn't make much sense to me at the time since she described him as a man who never smiled, who always stayed dead serious while she and the rest of the audience screamed with delight. I remember trying to imagine his looks from what she told me, going so far as to stand in front of a mirror with a deadpan expression until I could bear it no longer and would burst out laughing. In the early post–World War II days in Belgrade, there was still a movie theater showing silent films. My grandmother took me to see Chaplin, Harold Lloyd, the cross-eyed Ben Turpin, but for some reason we never saw Keaton.

From *Writers at the Movies*, ed. Jim Shepard (New York: HarperCollins, 2000).

Is that him? I would occasionally nudge her and whisper when some unfamiliar, somber face appeared on the screen. Weary of my interruptions, which disrupted her passionate absorption in films, one day upon returning home she produced a pile of old illustrated magazines. She made for herself her customary cup of chamomile tea and started thumbing through the dusty issues, allowing me to do the same after she was through. I remember a black-and-white photograph of a sea of top hats at some king's or queen's funeral; another of a man lying in a pool of blood in the street; and the face of a beautiful woman in a low-cut party dress watching me intently from a table in an elegant restaurant, her breasts partly exposed. My grandmother never found Keaton. It took me another seven years to actually see a film of his. By the time I did, my grandmother was dead, the year was 1953, and I was living in Paris.

Most probably, I was playing hooky that afternoon, sneaking into a cinema when I should've been in class, but there was Buster Keaton finally on the screen, wearing a porkpie hat and standing on the sidewalk at the end of a long breadline. The line keeps moving, but for some reason the two fellows standing in front of him do not budge. They are clothing-store dummies, but Buster does not realize that. He takes a pin out of his lapel and pricks one of the slowpokes, but there is no reaction; meanwhile the line up ahead grows smaller and smaller as each man is handed a loaf of bread. Then Buster has an idea. He pricks himself to see if the pin works. At that moment the store owner comes out, sticks his hand out to check for rain, and takes the two fully dressed dummies under his arms and carries them inside.

A few other gags have remained vivid in my memory from that first viewing of Keaton's shorts. In the one called "Cops" (1922), Buster buys an old horse and a wagon. The horse is deaf and doesn't hear his commands, so he puts a headset over the horse's ears, sits in the driver's seat, and tries to telephone the horse. In another scene, he pats the same horse on the head, and the horse's false teeth fall out. In the short called "The Playhouse" (1921), Keaton plays all the roles. He's the customer buying the ticket, the conductor of the orchestra and all his musicians, the nine tap dancers, the stagehands, and everyone in the audience, both the grown-ups and the children.

As for the appearance of Buster himself, everything about him was at odds. He was both strange looking and perfectly ordinary. His expression never changed, but his eyes were eloquent, intelligent and sad at the same time. He was of small stature, compact and capable of sudden astonishing acrobatic feats. Keaton, who was born in 1895 in a theatrical boardinghouse in Piqua, Kansas, started in vaudeville when he was three years old. His father, the son of a miller in Oklahoma, had left his parents to join a medicine show. That's where he met his future wife. Her father was coproprietor of one such show. For the next twenty years, they toured nationally, often in the company of famous performers of the day, such as Harry Houdini. Eventually, the Three Keatons, as they were called, developed a vaudeville comic act that consisted of acrobatic horseplay centered on the idea of a hyper child and his distraught parents. Buster hurled things at his pop, swatted him with flyswatters and brooms while his father swung him around the stage by means of a suitcase handle strapped to the boy's back. What looked like an improvised roughhouse was really a carefully planned series of stunts. The point is worth emphasizing, since it was with such and similar acts in vaudeville that silent-film comedy stagecraft originated.

The first principle of Keaton's comic personae is endless curiosity. Reality is a complicated machine running in mysterious ways whose working he's trying to understand. If he doesn't crack a smile, it's because he is too preoccupied. He is full of indecision, and yet he appears full of purpose. "A comic Sisyphus," Daniel Mowes called him. "OUR HERO CAME FROM *NOWHERE*," a caption in "High Sign" (1920) says, continuing: "HE WASN'T GOING *ANYWHERE* AND GOT KICKED OFF *SOMEWHERE*." Bedeviled by endless obstacles, Buster is your average slow-thinking fellow, seeking a hidden logic in an illogical world.

"Making a funny picture," he himself said, "is like assembling a watch; you have to be 'sober' to make it tick."

In the meantime, my mother, brother, and I were on the move again. We left Paris for New York. A few years later I was back in France as an American soldier. It turned out that they were still showing Keaton films in small cinemas on the Left Bank. That's when I saw most of the shorts and a few of the full-length films like "The General" and "The Navigator" (1924). Since there always seemed to be a Keaton festival in Paris, a day came when I took my children to see the films. They loved them and made me see the gags with new eyes, since they often noticed comic subtleties I had missed.

"A good comedy can be written on a postcard," Keaton said. A comic story told silently, that even a child could enjoy, we should add. Is it the silence of the image that frees the comic imagination? Of course. Think of cartoons. In silent films we can't hear the waves, the wind in the leaves, the cars screeching to a halt, the guns going off, so we fill in the sound. For instance, in Keaton's full-length film "Seven Chances" (1926), a man learns that his grandfather is leaving him seven million dollars providing he is married before seven o'clock in the evening on his twenty-seventh birthday, which just happens to be that day. He proposes to every woman he knows and is rebuffed, and places an ad in the afternoon paper, explaining his predicament and promising to be in church at five that afternoon. Several hundred prospective brides, old and young, show up wearing bridal gowns, one of them even arriving on roller skates. The prospective bridegroom runs for his life, and the brides stampede after him through busy downtown Los Angeles. All of us who saw the movie can still hear the sound of their feet.

In an essay entitled "How to Tell a Story," Mark Twain makes the following observations:

> To string incongruities and absurdities together in a wandering and sometime purposeless way, and seem innocently unaware

that they are absurdities, is the basis of American art. Another feature is the slurring of the point. A third is the dropping of a studied remark apparently without knowing it, as if one were thinking aloud. The fourth and the last is the pause.

Twain explains what he means:

> The pause is an exceedingly important feature in any kind of story, and a frequently recurring feature, too. It is a dainty thing, and delicate, and also uncertain and treacherous; for it must be exactly the right length—no more and no less—or it fails of its purpose and makes trouble. If the pause is too short, the important point is passed and the audience have had the time to divine that a surprise is intended—and then you can't surprise them, of course.

Comedy is about timing, faultless timing. It's not so much what the story is about, but the way it is told, with its twists and surprises, that makes it humorous. Keaton draws a hook with chalk on the wall and hangs his coat on it. A brat in the theater drops his half-sucked lollipop from the balcony on an elegant lady in a box who picks it up and uses it as a lorgnette. The hangman uses a blindfold intended for the victim to polish the medal on his jacket. The shorts, especially, are full of such wild inventions. No other silent-film comic star was as ingenious.

Among hundreds of examples from Keaton's films, one of my favorites comes from the short "Cops." At the annual New York City policemen's parade, Buster and his horse and wagon find themselves in the midst of the marching cops. Buster wants to light a cigarette, and is searching his pockets for matches, when a bomb thrown by an anarchist from a rooftop lands next to him on the seat with its short fuse already sizzling. There's a pause, "an inspiring pause," as Twain says, building itself to a deep hush. When it has reached its proper

duration, Buster picks up the bomb absentmindedly, lights his cigarette with it as if this were the most normal thing to do, and throws it
back over his head.

The short "Cops" is paradigmatic Keaton. Again, the plot is sim-
plicity itself. In the opening scene we see Buster behind bars. The bars
turn out to belong to the garden gate of the house of a girl he is in love
with. "I WON'T MARRY YOU TILL YOU BECOME A BUSINESSMAN," she
tells him. Off he goes, through a series of adventures, first with a fat
police detective in a rush to grab a taxi, the contents of whose wallet
end up in Buster's hands. Next, he is conned by a stranger who sells
him a load of furniture on the sidewalk, pretending he is a starving
man being evicted. The actual owner of the furniture and his family
are simply moving to another location. When Buster starts to load the
goods into the wagon he has just bought, the owner mistakes him for
the moving man they've been expecting. His trip across town through
the busy traffic culminates when he finds himself at the head of the
police parade passing the flag-draped reviewing stand where the chief
of police, the mayor, and the young woman he met at the garden gate
are watching in astonishment. Still, the crowd is cheering, and he
thinks it's for him. After he tosses the anarchist's bomb and it explodes,
all hell breaks loose. "GET SOME COPS TO PROTECT OUR POLICEMEN,"
the mayor orders the chief of police. People run for cover, the streets
empty, the entire police force takes after the diminutive hero.

What an irony! Starting with love and his desire to better himself
and impress the girl he adores, all he gets in return is endless trouble. It's the comic asymmetry between his extravagant hope and the
outcome that makes the plot here. The early part of the movie, with
its quick shuffle of gags, gives the misleading impression of a series
of small triumphs over unfavorable circumstances. Just when Buster
thinks he has his bad luck finally conquered, disaster strikes again.
The full force of law and order, as it were, descends on his head. Innocent as he is, he is being pursued by hundreds of policemen. Whatever
he attempts to do, all his stunts and clever evasions, come to nothing

because he cannot outrun his destiny. After a long chase, he ends up, unwittingly, at the very door of a police precinct. The cops are converging on him from all sides like angry hornets, blurring the entrance in their frenzy to lay their nightsticks on him, but incredibly Buster crawls between the legs of the last cop, he himself now dressed in a policeman's uniform. Suddenly alone on the street, he pulls a key out of his pocket, locks the precinct's door from the outside, and throws the key into a nearby trashcan. At that moment, the girl he is smitten with struts by. He looks soulfully at her, but she lifts her nose even higher and walks on. Buster hesitates for a moment, then goes to the trashcan and retrieves the key. "No guise can protect him now that his heart has been trampled on," Gabriella Oldham says in her magnificent study of Keaton's shorts. At the end of the film, we see him unlocking the door and being pulled by hundreds of policemen's hands into the darkness of the building.

What makes Keaton unforgettable is the composure and dignity he maintains in the face of what amounts to a deluge of misfortune in this and his other films. It's more than anyone can bear, we think. Still, since it's the American Dream Buster is pursuing, we anticipate a happy ending, or at least the hero having the last laugh. That's rarely the case. Keaton's films, despite their laughs, have a melancholy air. When a lone tombstone with Buster's porkpie hat resting on it accompanies THE END in "Cops," we are disconcerted. The images of him running down the wide, empty avenue, of his feeble attempt to disguise himself by holding his clip-on tie under his nose to simulate a mustache and goatee, are equally poignant. Let's see if we can make our fate laugh, is his hope. Comedy at such a high level says more about the predicament of the ordinary individual in the world than tragedy does. If you seek true seriousness and you suspect that it is inseparable from laughter, then Buster Keaton ought to be your favorite philosopher.

I have in mind the history of murder. Massacre of the innocent is a nearly universal historical experience, and perhaps never more so than in the last hundred years. Deranged leaders with huge armies and brutal secret police out to kill, gas, and imprison every one of us for the sake of some version of a glorious future, while being idealized and cheered by their followers, is what we have had to live through. "It takes a great ideal to produce a great crime," the historian Martin Malia writes. The problem for those constructing heaven on earth is that there is always an individual, a class of people, or a national, ethnic, or religious group standing in the way. Communism alone killed between 80 and 100 million people. It is also worth remembering the millions of displaced people, all those made destitute for life as a result of these ideological bloodbaths. Is poetry a holiday from such realities? It certainly can be. There are many examples of poets who, judging by their work, never read a newspaper in their lives. Still, a poet who consistently ignores the evils and injustices that are part of his or her own times is living in a fool's paradise.

History written by historians, as we know, speculates about the causes and meanings of cataclysmic events and the motives of the statesmen involved in them. Foucault says: "We want historians to confirm

A version of this essay appeared in *The Uncertain Certainty* (Ann Arbor: University of Michigan Press, 1986).

our belief that the present rests upon profound intentions and immutable necessities. But the true historical sense confirms our existence among countless lost events without a landmark or a point of reference." This is where the poets come in. In place of the historian's broad sweep, the poet gives us a kind of reverse history of what in the great scheme of things are often regarded as "unimportant" events, the image of a dead cat, say, lying in the rubble of a bombed city, rather than the rationale for that air campaign. Poetry succeeds at times in conveying the pain of individuals caught in the wheels of history. One of the most terrifying lines of twentieth-century poetry is by the Italian poet Salvatore Quasimodo, who speaks of "the black howl of the mother gone to meet her son crucified on a telephone pole." The individual who is paying for the intellectual vanity, fascination with power, and love of violence of some monster on the world's stage is the one that I care about. Perhaps only in lyric poetry can that mother's howl be heard as loudly as it ought to be.

Nearly everyone who made history in the last century believed that the mass killing of the innocent was permissible. This is true not only of the Nazis and the Communists, whose savageries were perpetrated in the name of an idea, but also of the democratic countries that in their many bombing campaigns, unintentionally and often intentionally, slaughtered hundreds of thousands. We Americans often fought evil with evil, and while we did so, many innocents caught in between paid the price. No matter what politicians and military men tell us, bombing has always been a form of collective punishment. Theoreticians of air power from Giulio Douhet to Curtis LeMay have never concealed that purpose. They argue that in war there must not be any differentiation between military personnel and civilians. With the help of new technologies, total war and mass terror became a reality for many human beings in the last hundred years. Bombs falling from the sky, armies slaughtering each other, civilians fleeing for their lives, the orphan factories working around the clock—that's what the poet has to think about or ignore.

In the days of mounted cavalries, foot soldiers, and cannons dragged by horses, the civilian population had to worry about a long siege, eventual conquest with accompanying pillage and rape, and an occasional burning of a city, but those things were not in themselves primary objects of military action. The first bombs were dropped in the mid-nineteenth century from balloons, dirigibles, and other such lighter-than-air vessels. Actually, it was in the war of 1849 that Austrians attempted to drop thirty-pound bombs on Venice using paper balloons. In the absence of photos, one imagines a bird's-eye postcard view of the city with its canals, boats, churches, palazzos, and piazzas. The sky is blue, the gulls are flying, and the streets are teeming with humanity as if it were carnival time. A red and white balloon drifts dreamily over the highest steeples, is about to drop its single explosive device, when an unexpected gust of wind sweeps it out of range and far off into the blue Adriatic. Nowadays, whether conventional or nuclear bombs are being utilized, everyone expects to be a sitting duck. Mass terror on a scale impossible to imagine in previous centuries is a real possibility, an option carefully studied by every military power in the world.

If not for the invention of photography and eventually television, our image of war would still come from paintings of historical scenes and illustrations for daily newspapers. Even the burning villages and firing squads in such illustrations, if you have ever seen them, have an idyllic air about them. We end up being more interested in the artist's skill in rendering the event than in the horror of what is taking place. Unhappily for warmongers everywhere, however, the fate of soldiers and civilians in wartime has been amply documented. To thumb through a book of old news photos of battlefield carnage, or watch documentary footage of an air raid on Berlin in progress, is a deeply sobering experience. Here's a row of burnt and still smoldering buildings of which only the outside walls remain. Rubble lies in the streets. The sky is black except for dragons of flames and swirling smoke. Most probably there are people buried under the rubble. We can't hear their voices, but we know for certain that they are there. I remember a photo of a small girl running toward a camera in a bombed city somewhere in China. No one else is in sight. There are thousands of such haunting images from the many wars fought in the last century. After almost a hundred years of bombing, it takes a staggering insensitivity and insouciance not to acknowledge what a bombing raid does in an urban area and who its true victims are.

Given the shocking number of casualties in bombings of cities, there are good reasons no one wishes to dwell on them much, except someone like me who had the unenviable luck of being bombed by both the Nazis and the Allies. Here are some appalling figures: 40,000 dead in the Blitz; another 40,000 dead in Hamburg in 1943; 100,000 in Dresden in 1945; 100,000 in Tokyo in 1945, plus Hiroshima and Nagasaki, where another 135,000 perished. And the list goes on. There's Berlin, and many other German and Japanese cities, and more recently Hanoi, where an estimated 65,000 died, and finally Baghdad. As John Kenneth Galbraith pointed out in an article in the *New York Times*, the ordinary citizens of Germany, Japan, Korea, Vietnam, and Iraq were far more in fear of our bombers than of their own oppressive governments, and why wouldn't they be? In Germany alone, 593,000 German civilians were killed and over 3.3 million homes destroyed. In Japan, without counting the victims of the atomic bombs, over 300,000 people perished just in 1945. Are deaths of enemy noncombatants truly of so little consequence? The answer—judging by the long, cruel history of the twentieth century's bombings—is a resounding yes. It is also worth remembering that the bombing of civilians is rarely punished as a crime. These air campaigns are based on the ridiculous premise that the dictator cares about the welfare of his own people and will not permit the destruction of his country to continue. Of course, if he really did give a damn he would not be a dictator. What happens, instead, is that the two warring sides become allies against the civilians in the middle. This may sound like an outrageous assertion to someone who has never had bombs drop on his or her head from a few thousand feet, but I speak from experience. That's exactly how it feels on the ground.

In modern warfare, it has become much safer to be in the military than to be a noncombatant.

Of course, there's nothing reliable about any one of these rounded-off figures of casualties. Bombing history plays games with numbers to conceal the fate of individuals. The deaths of women and children are an embarrassment. All religious and secular theories of "just war," from St. Augustine to the United Nations Charter, caution against their indiscriminate slaughter. Consequently, the numbers vary widely, depending on the source and the agenda of the historian, when they are not entirely omitted from history books. Even when they do appear, they are as incomprehensible as astronomical distances or the speed of light. A figure like 100,000 conveys horror on an abstract level. It is a rough estimate since no one really knows for sure. It is easily forgotten, easily altered. A number like 100,001, on the other hand, would be far more alarming. That lone, additional individual would restore the reality to the thousands of casualties. When one adds to these figures the sum total of people who were bombed and somehow survived, the numbers become truly unimaginable.

My own story belongs with those of these anonymous multitudes. Here's a little poem based on a few images of the bombing of Belgrade in 1941 from a World War II documentary.

Cameo Appearances

I had a small, nonspeaking part
In a bloody epic. I was one of the
Bombed and fleeing humanity.
In the distance the great leader
Crowed like a rooster from a balcony,
Or was it a great actor
Impersonating the great leader.

That's me, I said to the kiddies.
I'm squeezed between the man
With two bandaged hands raised
And the old woman with her mouth open
As if she were showing us a tooth

That hurts badly. The hundred times
I rewound the tape, not once
Could they catch sight of me
In that huge gray crowd,
That was like any other gray crowd.

Trot off to bed, I said finally.
I know I was there. One take
Is all they had time for.
We ran and the planes grazed our hair,
And then they were no more
As we stood dazed in the burning city,
But, of course, they didn't film that.

The beauties of Nature, the mysteries of the Supreme Being, and the torments of love are still with us, but a shadow lies over them. "God is afraid of man . . . man is a monster, and history has proved it," says Cioran. Some of us are who we are because of that kind of thinking. For example, I remember a night during the Vietnam War. I had returned home late after a swell evening on the town and happened to turn on a TV channel where they were presenting a summary of that day's action on the battlefield. I was already undressed and sipping a beer when they showed a helicopter strafing some small running figures who were supposedly Vietcong and were more likely just poor peasants caught in the cross fire. I could see the bodies twitch and jump as they were hit by a swarm of bullets. It occurred to me that this had been filmed only hours ago and here I was in my bedroom, tired but no longer sleepy, feeling the monstrosity of watching someone's horror from the comfort of my bedroom as if it were a spectator sport.

Can one be indifferent to the fate of the blameless and go about as if it doesn't matter? Yes, there have been more than a few fine poets in the history of poetry who had no ethical feelings or interest in other people's sufferings. There is always religion available, of course, or some theory of realpolitik to explain away the awful reality and ease one's conscience. What if one doesn't buy any of these theories—as I do not? Well, then one just writes poems as someone who sees and feels deeply, but who even after a lifetime does not understand the world.

THE ROMANCE OF SAUSAGES

Even their names are poetry to me: chorizo, merguez, rosette, boudin noir, kielbasa, luganega, cotechino, zampone, chipolata, linguiça, weisswurst—to name just a few. Whose mouth has not watered in a well-stocked butcher shop or fancy food market at the sight of many varieties of sausages, fresh and smoked, stuffed with pork, beef, lamb, liver, veal, venison, poultry, and seasoned with herbs, garlic, pepper, and spices too numerous to count? Until about ten years ago, there was a small store specializing in regional French sausages on Rue Delambre in Montparnasse, that famous little street where at one time Isadora Duncan lived, Man Ray had his first studio, and Hemingway met Scott Fitzgerald in a bar called Dingo's. Each time I entered that shop, I experienced a surge of emotions as if I were about to lose control of myself and make a scene. I'd point to one kind of sausage, change my mind and point to another, then ask for them both. After they were already expertly wrapped and I was on my way out, I often rushed back and bought a couple more varieties. My visits were a year apart, but the owners remembered me well and approached me each time with a smile of recognition and a touch of apprehension.

"They are bad for you," some of my friends warn me when I confess to them my sin, as if all that stands between eternal life and me

From "The Poetry of Sausages," in *Food and Wine*, June 2000.

is one nicely grilled, richly seasoned andouillette. Sad to say, there are people who regard lovers of sausages as living in a kind of nutritional Dark Ages, ignorant of cholesterol counts and caloric intake. For them all those Italians, Greeks, Hungarians, North Africans, Chinese, Germans, and Portuguese frying, grilling, boiling, and poaching happily are living terribly misguided lives. They have the highest esteem for native cuisines, but sausages are where they draw the line. Don't you know the disgusting things they put in them? they say to me incredulously after I appear unconvinced. Of course, I know. Some of the oldest and wisest cultures on earth eat them, is my defense. In France there's even an organization called the A.A.A.A.—the Amicable Association of Appreciators of Authentic Pork Tripe Sausages. A group of upright citizens, I imagine, who regard the sausage "made with pig's intestines filled with strips of choice innards mixed with pork fat and seasonings" to be the one and only ideal. In Finland, there is a similar society, whose members meet once a week to conduct what they call "sausage tests" while sitting naked in a sauna.

A sausage served in a restaurant of distinction can be an unforgettable occasion. An impeccably attired and dignified waiter has just uncovered a plate on which lies a lone wild-boar sausage next to a sprig of parsley. It is a joy to behold, and the first nibble doesn't disappoint, and yet, something is not quite right. A sausage feels more at home at a carnival or in a steamy kitchen. Sausages are sociable. A hot Tunisian lamb sausage will get along just fine with a potato from Idaho. A good-looking chicken leg, tentacles of a squid, and green peas from the garden are equally swell company. Portuguese, who love to combine odd ingredients in their cuisine, make a stew of pork, linguiça, and little neck clams. Sausages are the true multiculturalists. A large, mixed, and rowdy company makes eating them even more memorable.

My old buddy Bob Williams, in Hayward, California, used to make Italian sausage and peppers to perfection. He'd invite five or six people, give us a few bottles of good Zinfandel and even better Chianti, and take his time with the food. Finally he'd pour some olive oil in a frying pan in the kitchen just so our noses would know something was happening. Then, in due time, the onions would go in so the excitement could really begin. Before putting in the sausages, he'd bring them out to us so we could feast our eyes on them and grow hungry in anticipation. Supposedly, a Neapolitan guy in Oakland who didn't speak a word of English made them from an old family recipe. I never believed this story entirely, but such stories seem to be obligatory among cooks who serve sausages. There's always some ethnic in a small grocery store or a luncheonette in some outlying suburb or inner ghetto who sells the best sausage you ever tasted.

Indeed, by now Bob's sausages are beginning to send tantalizing smells our way, and everyone is rushing to pull up a chair to the table. Even a couple of elegant women who by their appearance eat nothing but baby vegetables are fighting for the bread in an unseemly hurry. Bob is carrying in a basket of freshly picked hot peppers from the garden for us to munch on, so that we can grow red in the face, gasp with astonishment at the wallop they pack, and gulp wine like water while listening to the sausages make their cheerful music on the stove. Since this is a confession, let me admit it: Italian sausages can be a big disappointment. They tend to be overdone, the peppers burnt, the onions likewise. It's all about timing, faultless timing. The accumulated experience of the cook in an inspired moment creates a small masterpiece in a frying pan impossible to repeat exactly.

In a country where almost everyone is continuously on a diet, the sight of so many sausages arriving on the table is always a shock. Despite his cherubic appearance and his broad smile, Bob makes me think of the devil in some medieval miniature dangling a tempting morsel before a saint kneeling in prayer. "Oh, how wonderful, but not for me!" a few of the company protest, quickly following that solemn announcement with, "Well, perhaps, maybe, just a tiny, little taste," as they reach with their forks. No one is waiting to be served. There's not enough bread, and the sausages are vanishing before our eyes as if they are part of a magic act. A bit of grease has fallen on a pale yellow silk blouse, but its owner doesn't care. She's laughing with her mouth full. A sudden, horrible realization is on everyone's mind: *I love sausages. I'll kill for another sausage.* "Keep them coming," we are shouting to Bob, who is back in the kitchen, and he's more than happy to oblige.

It all depends on how one looks at it. It's either a blessing or a curse to be a poet in the Holy Land, a place with so much history, so much myth and religion. As far as Yehuda Amichai was concerned, it was like being ground between two grindstones, or like living next door to God. Every time he opened his eyes, the biblical past was there. Where once miracles were performed and prophets fell down struck by some vision, there were now traffic jams and crowded beaches. Tradition for an American poet is something one seeks in the library. For Amichai in Jerusalem, it came with his cup of morning coffee and the first look out of the window.

"Lovely is the world rising early to evil," he writes in an early poem, because there's that too. The endless cycle of wars, massacres of the innocent, and the inevitable despair that comes with it. What is amazing about Amichai is how levelheaded he stayed to the very end, balancing his philosophical gloom against a lust for life. Was there a greater love poet in the last century? I can't think of one. "A psalmist," Anthony Hecht called him. Even when he played the role of an amused observer of human folly, he praised left and right. His visions of happiness have a modest, human scale. White shirts and undershirts on the laundry line mean for now there is peace and quiet here.

From *Tin House* 2, no. 3 (2000).

Even when he was a young poet, he wrote about death. First-generation Israeli, born in Germany in 1924, immigrated in 1936, there was something unsettled in him, as if his parents' migration had not yet quieted in him. His subject was always himself, poetry as an ongoing journal of one's reaction to the world. Memory and forgetting were his constant preoccupation. Everything came down to that. The miracle that someone remembers, the unthinkable horror that we all forget. Amichai was a wise man who wanted to remind us of our hearts. The clarity of his poems is a testimony to his humility before the immense task. He wrote lyric poems because there are moments in every life that must not be lost. Who will remember the rememberers? he asked. We, who read and love his poems, will.

STARGAZING IN THE CINEMA:
ON JOSEPH CORNELL

Joseph Cornell, who died in 1972, has turned out to be one of the most admired American artists of the last fifty years. While he was certainly known in the New York art world by the late 1940s, and his name and an occasional reproduction of his work may have been seen in a book devoted to Surrealist art, his fame and wealth never approached that of a great many of his contemporaries. The boxes now on display in this country's biggest museums could still be bought for as little as $250 in the early 1950s.

In the last decade, however, the proliferation of books and essays about him has produced a vast bibliography that equals and most often surpasses those on other artists of his generation. In addition to numerous introductions to museum and gallery exhibition catalogs, a new biography, three book-length monographs, as well as a selection from his diaries, letters, and files, have been published. What is striking about almost everything written about Cornell is that it tends to be unusually fine. He seems to bring out the best in art historians and critics, as this study of his "cinematic imagination" by Jodi Hauptman confirms. Cornell went about making art in such a novel way while employing such unlikely materials that making sense of what he did requires

Review of *Joseph Cornell: Stargazing in the Cinema*, by Jodi Hauptman. From the *New York Review of Books*, April 27, 2000.

some of the originality and the imagination that went into his art.

Cornell, who could neither paint, draw, sculpt, nor hold a movie camera, is famous above all for his small, glass-fronted shadow boxes with their puzzling assemblages of found objects, and less so for his collages and short films. In addition to hundreds of works of art, he left behind a vast archive of files, memorabilia, and source material on his various projects, all stored now at the Smithsonian, which the authors of these recent studies have gone over for clues. As Deborah Solomon writes in her recent biography: "It is often said of artists that they live in fear of being misunderstood. Cornell, by contrast, lived in fear of being understood." [1] Like Edgar Allan Poe and Emily Dickinson before him, Cornell was a lover of secrets and mysteries. He himself described his boxes as being like forgotten games, the abandoned games of a childhood rich in ambiguities. The art world being what it is today, Cornell's independence of mind appears worthy of emulation.

"A gourmet art by a man who ate junk food" is how Robert Motherwell described his work. Even to people who saw him fairly often he was a complete enigma. They remember him as drab looking, always preoccupied, speaking in monologues, oblivious to other people, an eccentric and a loner. Unmarried and with no sexual experience till the very last years of his life, he lived with his mother and an invalid brother who suffered from cerebral palsy in a small house on Utopia Parkway in Queens, whose basement he had turned into his studio. He ate little, never touched alcohol or set foot in the famous bars the painters and writers then frequented. He made appearances at art shows and gallery openings, greeting acquaintances and making a speedy departure. Cornell, who roamed the streets of Manhattan for almost fifty years, was usually to be found at home in Queens by eight o'clock in the evening. Except for time spent at boarding school in Massachusetts, this strange man never traveled beyond the five boroughs and their environs.

Joseph Cornell was born in Nyack on the Hudson River on December 24, 1903, a descendant of some of the oldest New York

Dutch families. His father was employed for many years in woolen manufacturing, starting as a salesman and advancing to the position of a textile designer. By all accounts, he was a cheerful man in love with theater, music, and with a taste for the good life. Cornell's mother was an avid reader who even wrote a movie scenario in her youth. They had four children, of whom Joseph was the oldest. In 1917 the family's luck suddenly changed. The father died of leukemia and left them with large debts. Mrs. Cornell tried to make ends meet, baking cakes and knitting sweaters, but for many years afterward, the family struggled, living one step above poverty. Nonetheless, with the help of her husband's former boss, Cornell's mother succeeded in sending her son to Phillips Academy at Andover for four years.

Joseph was a poor student. He took courses in French language and literature and for one year was most likely a classmate of Walker Evans, another inveterate collector of images. However, he failed to fulfill the course requirements and left school without receiving a diploma. Back in New York, he went to work immediately in order to help the family, now living in Bayside, Queens. Through his father's old connections in the trade, he got work as a salesman for a textile company with offices on Madison Square. From 1921 to 1931, he made the rounds from one manufacturer to another offering his samples. Killing time between appointments, Cornell browsed in used book stores along Fourth Avenue between Union Square and the Bowery and in hundreds of junk shops from Fourteenth Street to Times Square. These were the places where the contents of many attics and immigrant suitcases ended up. One could discover just about anything on their dim shelves and in their dusty bins, something valuable or nearly worthless brought to America as a souvenir or an heirloom from St. Petersburg, Paris, Shanghai, or any other place on the face of the earth.

Long before he started making his boxes, Cornell was already a connoisseur of ephemera, bringing home to Queens old books, movie magazines, silent-film postcards, nineteenth-century toys, engravings, theatrical memorabilia, dolls, maps, and much else that anyone else would regard as nothing but trash. It's rare to encounter a young scavenger, but that's what he certainly was, obsessive and with no idea what he was going to do with his hoard. The inventory of one of his early boxes gives the idea:

Object. 1941. Box construction with velvet-paneled exterior sides, brass-ring grip, and paint-spattered glass front. Contains 3 paper parrot silhouettes, mounted on wood backings, paper cutout of 2 parakeets, corks, miniature fork and spoon, pine cone and bark, and dried leaf fronds. Back and sides of interior covered with collage of German book fragments, baby photo, paper clock face, etc. Column at left covered with collage of German book fragments with penny candy embedded in it.[2]

In November of 1931, after seeing a show of Surrealist art at the Julien Levy Gallery, he was so intrigued by some Max Ernst collages made with nineteenth-century engraved illustrations that, supposedly, he went home to Utopia Parkway and late that night, after his mother and brother had gone to sleep, made his first black-and-white collages on the kitchen table out of the old books and prints he had previously collected. One Saturday afternoon soon after, he stopped by the gallery and showed Levy three small collages he had done. Levy's surprised reaction was that these were works of Ernst he might have misplaced—or so he claims in his memoirs. Regardless of whatever truly happened that day, Cornell returned to the gallery promptly with some boxes—not the shadow boxes he's famous for and which he would not begin making till five years later, but round pill-boxes he had bought in a drugstore and emptied. Cornell replaced their original contents with tiny shells, sequins, rhinestones, beads, ground red glass, black thread, and scraps of blue paper, while often retaining the original label of the product. SURE CURE FOR THAT TIRED FEELING, one of them announces. The result of this frenzied creative activity was that

Levy, that same winter, not only decided to include some of Cornell's work in a new Surrealist exhibition at his gallery, but also asked him to design the cover for the catalog. These works in the show, for want of a better name, were simply called *Surrealist Toys*.

Despite the continual association of Cornell with the Surrealists, and the influence of Ernst and Duchamp on his work, which he readily acknowledged, it would be wrong to regard him as one. Mary Baker Eddy rather than André Breton was his true spiritual guide. He had converted to Christian Science at the age of twenty-three and remained a devoted practitioner all his life, making daily visits to its reading rooms and pondering its theology. There was too much black magic in Surrealism, he said. The movement's hatred of religion, explicit sexuality, black humor, and admiration for Freud and Marx were anathema to him. He was the "authentic Romantic soul," Dore Ashton aptly noted.[3] Nostalgia for happier times and for purer lost loves was still congenial to him; so was the accompanying outpouring of sentimentality, on which the Surrealists, like the rest of the Modernists, gagged. What makes Cornell so interesting and makes him difficult to categorize as an artist is that he is a tangle of antithetical aesthetic positions. Whatever the case may be, the discovery of the collage technique gave him an unexpected opportunity to "objectify" whatever impulse lay hidden behind his maniacal collecting. It also provided him with a poetics an urban wanderer such as himself could put immediately to use. Both Baudelaire and Emerson believed in the mystic religion of universal analogy, but while they sought its manifestations in nature, Cornell found his "forest of symbols" in the city. Somewhere on the island of Manhattan, there were, he believed, a few objects, dispersed in unknown locations, that rightly belonged together despite being seemingly incompatible in appearance. Starting with paper collages and eventually making them three-dimensional with the help of various kinds of boxes, Cornell gradually left behind his early influences and struck out on his own. It is worth pointing out that Cornell worked in the absence of any previous idea of beauty. A kind of flea-market democracy is present in his work. "The question is not what you look at, but what you see," Thoreau wrote somewhere in his journals. There was no separation in Cornell's mind between high and low culture. Is there another serious artist who loved both Vermeer and Barbie dolls? He shuffled trinkets within his boxes for months and years on end until he found an image that pleased him, without previous knowledge about what that image would turn out to be.

"Joseph's mind worked by association and by passionate identification with specific things, and a very acute feeling of connection between specific things, but I don't think by intellectual theory," Donald Windham wrote.[4] Fetishism far more than Surrealism is the hidden logic that brings together a threaded needle, a doll's forearm, a mirror fragment, a plastic lobster, a thimble, a yellow bead, and a dollhouse knife. Cornell saved mementos of the places and people he met while roaming the city. He writes repeatedly in his diaries of "intangible visitations," "little coincidences," "sublime moments," and of objects found shortly after such encounters that helped him preserve their memory.

A box, in that sense, is a place where the inner and the outer realities meet on a small stage. What gives the viewer an additional delight are the titles of the pieces themselves: *Soap Bubble Set, L'Égypte de Mlle Cléo de Mérode, Pharmacy, Museum, Taglioni's Jewel Casket, Hôtel du Nord, The Life of King Ludwig of Bavaria,* and more intriguingly *Penny Arcade Portrait of Lauren Bacall.* There may not be any obvious connection between the artwork and the label, but our imagination before long finds one. The boxes actually make me think of poems at their most hermetic. To engage imaginatively with one of them is like contemplating the maze of metaphors on some Symbolist poet's chessboard. The ideal box is like an unsolvable chess problem in which only a few figures remain after a long intricate game whose solution now seems both within the next move or two and forever beyond reach.

The years between 1932 and 1945 were a period of wide-ranging and hectic activity for Cornell. In addition to experimenting with different types of boxes and collages, he freelanced as a designer for *Vogue, House and Garden,* and *Dance Index.* The editors of these magazines knew of his vast image library and went to him when they needed movie and theater memorabilia. As his father did before him, he stopped being a salesman, and after a brief period of selling refrigerators door-to-door, he was hired as a designer by a textile studio. Most important, he met Marcel Duchamp, who became a lifelong friend and a booster. Cornell had his first one-man exhibition at the Julien Levy Gallery in 1932 and continued to show there and elsewhere repeatedly, in the company of the Surrealists, for the rest of the decade. He wrote a film script in 1933, *Monsieur Phot,* a movie not intended to be made but only imagined, and created his first collage movie in 1936.

Cornell's *Rose Hobart* is an example of what he called "tapestry in action." It was pieced together by cutting up found footage of a sixteen-millimeter print of an early talkie, *East of Borneo.* Using scissors and tape, he cut the film into segments, which he then spliced out of sequence. What was originally a seventy-seven-minute feature became after Cornell's editing a plotless nineteen-minute film devoted solely to its actress. The original movie is a hackneyed jungle drama about a certain Linda, played by an actress named Rose Hobart, who travels to the ends of the earth, the fictional principality of Maradu in Indonesia, to find and bring home her drunken husband, who is a court physician to the Sorbonne-educated and dapper reigning prince. Linda resists the attempts at seduction by the spooky monarch, whose fate, it turns out, is mysteriously tied to the island's active volcano. In the movie's final scene, Linda shoots the prince as he opens the curtain to reveal the erupting volcano, and the husband-doctor, realizing the great love his wife bears him, miraculously recovers his sanity that very moment.

As Hauptman describes it in her book:

> Rose Hobart's performance in *East of Borneo* consists of anxious and twitchy movements of the body and rapidly changing facial

expressions. In collating frames of the actress, Cornell seeks not to smooth out her jarring behavior but to emphasize her frenetic actions through disjunctive editing. Reveling in these joints, breaks, and splices (each of which presents another face of the actress), the artist constructs *Rose Hobart* of mismatches, awkward juxtapositions, and temporal discontinuities.

The entire effect, despite claims for the film as a work of genius by avant-garde filmmakers, strikes me as uninspired. Cornell lacks the feel for suspense or for comic timing of someone like Buster Keaton, who used montage years before him in the silent film *Sherlock, Jr.* Of course, in his own mind, Cornell imagined he was purifying the original film, rescuing and immortalizing the beauty of Hobart. It doesn't work for me. The sure touch and the impeccable aesthetic discernment of his boxes and collages are missing, not just from this movie but from all his films.

The premiere of the film took place at Levy's gallery in December of 1936 shortly after the opening of the MOMA exhibition "Fantastic Art, Dada, Surrealism." Salvador Dalí was in the audience with several other European artists when Cornell projected the film through a piece of tinted blue glass, while slowing the speed down to that of a silent movie—about two-thirds the pace of the original talkie. In place of the original sound track, he played a scratchy record with a bouncy Brazilian beat that he had picked up in a junk shop. Halfway through the film, Dalí jumped out of his chair, lunged for Cornell's throat, and had to be restrained. He went on shrieking that Cornell had stolen the idea for the film right out of his head. The cinema collage was undoubtedly an idea Dalí had been mulling over and already toying with in *Un Chien Andalou* and *L'Âge d'Or*, the Surrealist films he had made with Luis Buñuel a few years earlier.

Hauptman's book is a study of six of Cornell's "portrait-homages," and there's no question that she is onto something. She says, "It was Cornell's interest in motion pictures, in fact, that in many ways guided his artistic production." He kept archives on movie stars, divas, and ballet dancers both living and dead, as well as on unknown little girls (his "nymphs") whose pictures he had seen in art books and magazines. These files remind me of the ones J. Edgar Hoover kept on figures in public life. They consist of publicity photos, pictures and articles from newspapers and magazines, and his copious notes. Women obsessed this man who pretended that he had no interest in any kind of sex. We have lost sight of what poets from the days of Ovid and Catullus, and until recently, readily acknowledged. The dream of seduction, as much as anything else, is the motive for art. Poets, if truth were told, have spent more time thinking about what's under someone's skirt or inside someone's pants than about God.

Standing outside Manhattan's Hollywood Movie Theater, at Broadway and Fifty-first Street, one day in 1944, Cornell found himself hypnotized by the sight of a poster of Lauren Bacall looking out at him from behind glass and through the mist of light rain, Hauptman reports. "Memoried glances" is what he called such encounters. How to give them a second life was one of his chief aesthetic problems. Described by journalists as a combination of Marlene Dietrich, Katharine Hepburn, and Bette Davis, with overtones of Mae West and Jean Harlow, Bacall, they said, radiated as much sex as the law would allow. The movie *To Have and Have Not* (1944), costarring Humphrey Bogart, was made when she was only nineteen. Cornell saw something in her face that reminded him of his favorite stars of the silent pictures, whom he preferred to those of the present. He saw the film five or six times and started collecting material on the actress. What he was after, he explained, was not an actual scene but what one remembers from the film, more of a romantic afterglow. In that sense, *Penny Arcade Portrait of Lauren Bacall* is as much a self-portrait as it is a portrait of the actress.

The box construction he made for her, now in the Art Institute of Chicago, is worth describing in detail. It stands 20½ inches high. The interior has a Masonite panel partially stained blue. There are seven circular openings across the top covered with glass and just below them five horizontal openings containing five postcard views of the New York skyline behind blue glass panes. Below them are another five circular openings, each with parallel threads coiling around small gears. The center compartment frames the recessed black-and-white photograph of Bacall behind a blue glass pane bisected by lines of blue paint. On both sides of the center compartment, there is a single vertical compartment, each containing two columns of eight wood cubes painted blue or with a pasted-on photo of Bacall: two identical ones as a grown-up, five identical ones as a child, and four identical ones of her cocker spaniel. Beneath the central compartment are three additional small compartments, the ones on the left and right with Bacall and the middle one containing a mirror. All three are behind blue glass. A small red wood ball, when dropped from the top, travels through the labyrinthine interior by a series of hidden glass runways, past the actress's face, bringing it to life momentarily, and into the mirrored compartment across the bottom of the box before exiting through the hinged door.

Hauptman's chapter on the portrait of Bacall is both insightful and great fun. She tells of early amusement arcades in New York, with their shooting galleries, punching bags, and machines that read fortunes and tested lung capacity, and gives the history and explanation of devices called kinetoscopes and mutoscopes, which offered miniature spectacles and short narratives for the viewer: "Soon these coin-operated cabinets, filled with spools and gears that either threaded the images on celluloid in front of a light source (kinetoscope) or rapidly flipped individual cards past a peephole (mutoscope) . . . became the most popular amusement in the arcade." They were known as "Automatic Vaudeville" or "Penny Dreadfuls" and ran anywhere from sixteen to sixty seconds, ranging in subject matter from travelogues and newsreels to titles like "French High Kickers" and "Peeping Jimmie."

Lauren Bacall's portrait recalls the boundless ingenuity of these contraptions, which worked with coin, plunger, or brightly colored pinballs. "Looking into Cornell's boxes rehearses the voyeurism experienced in the cinema, and the cuts of both his collages and his visual/textual projects bear strong resemblance to filmmakers' editing strategies," Hauptman writes. Strangely, Cornell, though a filmmaker himself, preferred stills to motion pictures. The large central photograph of Bacall dominates the box and recalls the experience of a close-up in a movie. It gives the illusion of getting "close" while dramatizing both the intimacy and the unreachability of the person on the screen. "The eye of the camera," Cornell explained, is able "to ensnare the subtleties and legendary loveliness of . . . [the actress's] world." Time stops, as it were, and pure absorption takes over without the distraction of the story. What the artist wanted us to experience is Bacall's "innocence." He hoped to create a different image of her, moving away from the slinky, sultry, sexy look propagated by publicity agents to a shiny, clean look, "fumigated of Hollywood booze, cigarette smoke and slow-motion mugging." What the rest of us actually experience peeking inside this box, I would guess, is anything but that.

While Hauptman makes scattered attempts to enlist the help of psychoanalytic literature and literary theory, she is most persuasive when she follows her own hunches in unraveling the hidden verbal and visual threads of these homages. "Preserving and protecting examples of evanescent femininity," as she points out, was what drove Cornell. Nevertheless, as she herself demonstrates incidentally, works of art even when conceived out of the seamiest of motives have a way of transcending the artist's intentions. It is not easy to account for the exquisite taste and elegance of so many of his box constructions. One of his goddesses was chance. She taught him how to open himself to the unknown. He obeyed her, and he also cheated on her. Luckily, he let her lead him often enough to small, unimportant things whose beauty is as much a surprise to us as it was to him. She is the collaborator whose intimate biography it is not easy to write.

Cornell grew up with the movies, as Hauptman's book reminds

us. What she says about Cornell is true of other artists as well as of poets and fiction writers. Yes, we all saw a lot of movies, but one wouldn't know it from reading most literary and art criticism. We fell in love, not just with some actor or actress, but with fleeting scenes that stayed with us for the rest of our lives. Boxed in the darkness of the movie theater, watching the projected light turn miraculously into an image on the screen, longing to be up there with the strange men and women who in that moment seem more real than our own lives—how familiar all that is. Cornell continues to be fascinating because he was able to incorporate an aspect of our experience of the modern American city rarely found in the work of other poets and artists. His one supreme insight was that the transcendental and the immutable could be found anywhere—in what is most banal, commonplace, and overlooked. Anyone who has been captivated by one of his boxes would have to agree that he was right.

Notes

1. Deborah Solomon, *Utopia Parkway: The Life and Work of Joseph Cornell* (New York: Farrar, Straus, and Giroux, 1997), 336.

2. *Joseph Cornell,* ed. Kynaston McShine (New York: Museum of Modern Art, 1980), 289.

3. Dore Ashton, *A Joseph Cornell Album* (New York: Viking, 1974), 10.

4. Donald Windham, "Things That Cannot Be Said: A Reminiscence," in *Joseph Cornell Collages, 1931–1972* (Los Angeles: Corcoran Gallery, 1978), 11–13.

LITERATURE AND THE GODS:
ROBERTO CALASSO

Everything, in the world, exists to end up in a book.

—MALLARMÉ

The surprising durability of ancient Greek myths in an age when Homer, Ovid, and other classics are no longer taught in our schools is astonishing and not easy to explain. In this country, we have never been very good at history, barely troubling to remember our own in much detail, and the same is true of the literary past, which is gradually being expunged from the curriculum. When it comes to pagan myths, most of the champions of progress take it for granted that they have nothing to say to us anymore. How wrong they are. This year, for example, saw the publication of *Gods and Mortals,* an anthology of modern poems based on classical myths.[1] Out of 323 poems in the book, roughly one-fourth are the work of contemporary American poets. When it comes to being out of sync with reigning intellectual fashions, poets get the prize every time.

As for the anthology itself, the structure is thematic, so one finds poems on almost every figure in mythology, with Orpheus and Eurydice and the wanderings and homecoming of Odysseus seem-

Review of *Literature and the Gods,* by Roberto Calasso, trans. Tim Parks. From the *New York Review of Books,* September 20, 2001.

ing to be the favorites. Poets who have vastly different and frequently unreconcilable ideas of poetry, such as, for example, Joseph Brodsky and Gregory Corso, Robert Creeley and Richard Wilbur, Lucille Clifton and Jorie Graham, are to be found reflecting on some god or mortal hero. To paraphrase Charles Olson, myth is a bed in which human beings continue to make love to the gods.

What is it in these stories that the poets find indispensable? The answer has to be that they still feed their imagination. What Ezra Pound said long ago still appears to be true today: "No apter metaphor having been found for certain emotional colours, I assert that gods exist." Here's a poem of his from 1912 commemorating that discovery:

The Return

See, they return; ah, see the tentative
Movements, and the slow feet,
The trouble in the pace and the uncertain
Wavering!
See, they return, one, and by one,
With fear, as half-awakened;
As if the snow should hesitate
And murmur in the wind,
         and half turn back;
These were the "Wing'd-with-Awe,"
         Inviolable,

Gods of the wingèd shoe!
With them the silver hounds,
         sniffing the trace of air!

Haie! Haie!
         These were the swift to harry;
These the keen-scented;

These were the souls of blood.

Slow on the leash,
                    pallid the leash-men![2]

Even in our days of technology and globalization, it may be that the world we live in is too complex a place to explain with just one god. We need Eros, Apollo, Dionysus, Narcissus, and the rest of their tribe to make sense of things. For poets, there is also an additional motive. The big headache for over a hundred years has been how to find a larger setting for one's personal experience. Without some sort of common belief, theology, mythology—or what have you—how is one supposed to figure out what it all means? The only option remaining, or so it seems, is for each one of us to start from scratch and construct our own cosmology as we lie in bed at night. A poet who backtracks into myth is longing for a community that no longer exists. Or if it still does, it is a community of solitary readers and insomniac philosophers who are unknown to one another.

The Italian writer Roberto Calasso's book of essays *Literature and the Gods*, based on Weidenfeld Lectures he gave at Oxford, takes up this very subject of what we mean when we talk about gods. It discusses such figures as Hölderlin, Baudelaire, Nietzsche, Nabokov, Leopardi, Lautréamont, and Mallarmé and makes keen observations on several others. What is startling about Calasso's brief survey of the renewed interest in myth and pagan deities in Western literature is how recent it is in some countries. In eighteenth-century France, Greek myths were called childish fables, Shakespeare was seen as barbaric, and biblical tales were regarded as nothing more than priestly indoctrination to suffocate any potentially free spirit and enlightened mind. While the gods were never entirely lost sight of, supplying a bit of rhetorical dazzle and moral allegory in occasional poems and plays, only in painting, Calasso argues, did they run free over the centuries:

Thanks to its wordless nature, which allows it to be immoral without coming out and saying as much, the painted image was able to restore the gods to their glamorous and terrifying apparitions as simulacra. Hence a long and uninterrupted banquet of the gods runs parallel with Western history from Botticelli and Giovanni Bellini, through Guido Reni and Bernini, Poussin and Rembrandt (*The Rape of Persephone* would itself suffice), Saraceni and Furini and Dossi, right through to Tiepolo.

With the Romantics, the world of the Greeks returns as a lost paradise and an aesthetic ideal. Speaking about gods became acceptable again. There's hardly a European poet in the nineteenth century who did not mention them. Their reasons were often superficial: they wanted to sound noble, exotic, pagan, erotic, erudite, or poetic. According to Calasso, the attraction of these antique fables for someone like Leopardi was that they were the mysterious remnants of a world where reason hadn't yet been able to unleash the full effects of its lethal power, "a power that 'renders all objects to which it turns its attention small and vile and empty, destroys the great and the beautiful and even, as it were, existence itself.'"

This attitude, as Leopardi himself realized, was absurd. Pretending to be ancient Romans or Greeks while concealing the fact that they were modern Europeans made some of the poets look silly. In France, among the Parnassians and Symbolists, that silliness had a use: it sheltered one against the vulgarity of the shopkeeper. "Everything can be at home in this century but poetry," Leopardi wrote, a sentiment far removed from what Emerson and Whitman were saying a few years later; for them, in America at least, this was the golden age for poets.

*

"Difficult are the gods for men to see," the ancient *Hymn to Demeter* already complains. Before they became literary clichés, the pagan deities lived the quiet lives of exiles in our midst, revealing their true nature only to a select few. The more modern literature tried to be absolutely original, the more it rummaged in the unconscious, the more it came face to face with them. Once again Orpheus picked up his lute, Venus seduced mortal men, Sisyphus shouldered his rock, and Odysseus dallied with Calypso. As Calasso points out—and there's no disputing him—perhaps only to Hölderlin among the poets did the gods show themselves in their full radiance. Yet their supreme mystery has always been close. "Whatever else it might be, the divine is certainly the thing that imposes with maximum intensity the sensation of being alive," Calasso writes. Where we find ourselves fully awake, divinities make their appearance. Emily Dickinson used the word "awe" to describe that experience in which the entire familiar world loses its normal significance and leaves one speechless in the presence of something one can no longer name. For us moderns, these cannot be the same gods as of old. Calasso writes:

> They are no longer made up of just the one family, however complicated, residing in their vast homes on the slopes of a single mountain. No, now they are multitudes, a teeming crowd in an endless metropolis. It hardly matters that their names are often exotic and unpronounceable, like the names one reads on the doorbells of families of immigrants. The power of their stories is still at work. Yet there is something new and unusual about the situation: this composite tribe of gods now lives *only* in its stories and scattered idols. The way of cult and ritual is barred, either because there is no longer a group of devotees who carry out the ritual gestures, or because even when someone does perform these gestures they stop short. The statues of Shiva and Vishnu still drip with offerings, but Varuna is a

remote and shapeless entity to the Indian of today, while Prajapati is only to be found in books. [Varuna was the supreme
lord of the cosmos, the keeper of divine order. Prajapati was
the lord of creation.] And this, one might say, has become the
natural condition of the gods: to appear in books—and often
in books that few will ever open. Is this the prelude to extinc-
tion? Only to the superficial observer. For in the meantime all
the powers of the cult of the gods have migrated into a single,
immobile and solitary act: that of reading.

The effect of such solitary acts of piety and devotion of the
few, as Calasso has amply shown, ought not to be underestimated.
Two of his previously translated books, *The Marriage of Cadmus and
Harmony* (1993) and *Ka* (1998), are formidably ambitious attempts
to retell the stories of Greek and Indian mythology, untangle their
many variants, and meditate on their meaning. "Stories," he writes
about the Greeks, "never live alone: they are the branches of a family
that we have to trace back, and forward." It is the same with India:
"So many things happening, so many stories one inside the other,
with every link hiding yet more stories." Calasso serves as our guide
in the maze.

Both of these books have been extravagantly praised, and
deservedly so. In the ambition of the undertaking and wealth of material, they are comparable to Ovid's *Metamorphoses* or *The Thousand
and One Nights*, except the end result is very different. What Calasso
has done is original and difficult to classify. The stories not only reassemble the ancient myths into a new synthesis, but also include literary, philosophical, and historical commentary. Still, despite their
extraordinary erudition and insight into the minds of these two cultures, these are not scholarly studies. They are powerful works of the
imagination in their own right that will most likely inspire future gen-
erations of mythographers and poets.

Calasso refreshes our memory of how violent the myths are.

Murder, rape, incest, and acts of unbelievable cruelty are matters of course. It is a world in which innocents suffer, justice is infrequent, and when it does come, it often comes too late. The trouble with too many poems on classical myths is that they are often no more than a pretext for lyric posturing, an evocation of the beauty of the bygone world and its ill-fated heroes and heroines at the expense of the harsher vision of the original. The perennial challenge in recounting myth, it seems to me, is how to make believable a pretty girl who is half fish and whose song mesmerizes sailors.

Calasso is a consummate storyteller, mixing drama, gossip, and even passages of poetry. He brings to life the ancient soap operas with their large cast of divine and human characters and keeps us entertained. Like all good stories and poems, the myths have many layers of meaning, which Calasso's cunningly told narratives manage to preserve. Did ideas come first and the myths come afterward in order to illustrate them, or did the Greeks discover them as they listened to the stories? Here is an example of what I have in mind, from Calasso's re-creation of the myth of Persephone, the goddess of fertility who was carried off into the underworld by Hades (Pluto). In the Eleusinian mysteries she appears under the name Kore:

> It was a place where dogs would lose their quarry's trail, so violent was the scent of the flowers. A stream cut deep through the grass of a meadow that rose at the edge to fall sheer in a rocky ravine into the very navel of Sicily. And here, near Henna, Kore was carried off. When the earth split open and Hades' chariot appeared, drawn by four horses abreast, Kore was looking at a narcissus. She was looking at the act of looking. She was about to pick it. And, at that very moment, she was herself plucked away by the invisible toward the invisible.

What fascinates Calasso is that moment of heightened consciousness. Kore sees herself reaching for a narcissus, just as Hades snatches her away to be his bride. Interestingly, Calasso writes that her name doesn't just mean "girl" but "pupil" of the eyes. In the myth she turns away from the beautiful flower, their eyes meet, and she sees her pupil reflected in his. If, as Socrates claims, and Calasso points out, the Delphic maxim "Know Thyself" can be understood as "Look at Thyself," this marvelous story of the double gaze conveys a magnificent insight. As our consciousness divides to observe itself—observation for which looking at a narcissus is an evident metaphor—that invisible other watching within us is no other than our death, as it were. In other words, and this strikes me as both true and astonishing, we come to our self-knowledge through the eye of our mortality, since, obviously, if we were going to be around forever such experiences would not be so precious.

The Greeks, as Calasso demonstrates, had more in mind. For them, this moment is not just about self-knowledge but also about aesthetics. Our precarious life, fleeting and irreplaceable, has another dimension. That which exists once and only once is beautiful, the myths keep telling us. It is precisely because we are mortal beings that things have a significance and an intense presence at times. To come to understand that was a momentous discovery for literature. What has lyric poetry been for almost three thousand years, one can ask, but an aesthetic justification of mortality?

"The first enemy of the aesthetic was meaning," Calasso writes in *The Marriage of Cadmus and Harmony*. In the aesthetic experience the meaning is there, but it doesn't impose itself. What dominates is a presence of someone or something one does not wish to name just then. The search for meaning takes one away from what is there before one's eyes. Once again, Calasso is calling attention to the moment of heightened consciousness, its self-sufficiency and the wordless understanding that comes with it. Like a "pure light of midsummer," such is the presence of the god Dionysus, according to the poet Pindar. Perfection always keeps something hidden, says Calasso. And to conceal with light was always the Greeks' specialty.

*

If our own classic myths still resonate imaginatively and philosophically for us, what about the ones from India? At first reading *Ka*, one
is overwhelmed by the unfamiliarity of the names, the oddness of the
stories, and their endlessly metamorphosing divinities. We are likely to
be baffled by the plurality of viewpoints, clashing metaphysical ideas,
and the difficulty of drawing a distinction between different traditions
and schools of thought. Once again, Calasso's prose, in Tim Parks's
masterful translation, casts its narrative spell. Eventually one begins
to situate oneself in an exotic universe. As in Greece, the enigma of
consciousness—that light capable of seeing what it illuminates—is at
the center of cosmic mystery, as it was understood by the Aryans (or
Aryas) who invaded India around 1500 B.C.:

> Just as some claim that every true philosopher thinks but one
> thought, the same can be said of a civilization: from the begin-
> ning the Aryas thought, and India has ever continued to think,
> the thought that dazzled us *ṛṣis:* the simple fact of being con-
> scious. There is not a shape, not an event, not an individual in
> its history that cannot, in a certain number of steps, be taken
> back to that thought, just as Yājñavlkya demonstrated that the
> three thousand, three hundred and six gods could all be taken
> back to a single word: *brahman.*

Here is an Indian myth that reads like a sequel to the Greek one about
Kore and Hades:

> The Person in the Eye is not born alone, cannot exist alone. The
> first couple were the two Persons in the Eye. In the right eye
> was Death. In the left eye his companion. Or again: in the right
> eye was Indra [the warrior god and thunder god of the Vedas].
> In the left eye his partner Indrānī. It was for these two that the

gods made that division between the eyes: the nose. Behind the barrier of the nose two lovers hide, as though separated by a mountain. To meet, to touch, they must go down together into the cavity that opens up in the heart. That is their bedroom. There they twine in coitus. Seen from outside, the eyes of the sleepers are hidden by the eyelids as though by a curtain around a bed. Meanwhile, in the heart's cavity, Indra and Indrānī are one inside the other. This is the supreme beatitude.

What is truly extraordinary, as Calasso convincingly shows in *Literature and the Gods*, is that in the guise of what he calls "absolute literature" some of the mythic Indian ideas seem to reappear in the West. He is not talking about direct influence of Indian thought or mythology, which was largely unknown in the nineteenth century, but of an authentic independent discovery by Western poets of similar perceptions. Of course, before any of that was possible, poetry had to free itself from the obligation to be socially relevant. Poets were now saying that poetry is like music, a language that cannot be paraphrased into another language. It is a knowledge that refuses to be subject to any other knowledge, in touch with the nameless origins of everything, the home of even the gods themselves.

One gets a better idea of what Calasso has in mind from his lecture on Isidore Ducasse, the nineteenth-century French poet who wrote under the name of Comte de Lautréamont. *Les Chants de Maldoror*, that notorious work of macabre humor and hallucinatory erotic imagery, was written, as he says, "on the principle that *anything* and *everything* must be the object of sarcasm," not just the posturing of his contemporaries with their sniveling self-pity and romantic melancholy, but even those who raged against it like Baudelaire. Before he died at the age of twenty-four in 1870, Ducasse lived entirely in books. He drew all his material from them, freely stole passages from classics and rewrote them reversing their meanings. The word *"chants"* in the title makes one expect a book of songs, perhaps a French equivalent of *Song of Myself.* Instead, we find an anti-Whitman who exults in mixing up genres. As his translator Alexis Lykiard notes, in Ducasse we get prose poetry, poetic prose, the gothic fantasy, the serial novel, horror and humor, authorial interventions, disruptions of space and time, stories within stories, plagiarism, techniques of collage, changes of style as frequent as his hero Maldoror's own metamorphoses, and an elliptical rather than linear structure.

Rimbaud is undoubtedly a better poet, and his *Illuminations* and *A Season in Hell* have been far more influential works, but they lack Ducasse's poisonous air of mockery. For him, writers are stooges, and so is every literary propriety. He thought, Calasso writes, that "literature is a continuum of words to be interfered with as one pleases, by transforming every sign into its opposite, if that's what we want." Previously, even the most rebellious literature stayed in touch with some version of the real world. Ducasse got rid of all that. "Any literature that challenges the eternal truths is condemned to feed only on itself," he wrote. And he did just that.

The two finest essays in Calasso's new book are on Stéphane Mallarmé. In the century of exact sciences, confident positivism in philosophy, and naturalism and realism in literature, Mallarmé cultivated obscure inner states and spoke approvingly of an art consecrated to fictions. In a piece based on a lecture given at Oxford and Cambridge Universities in 1894, he writes:

> Description conceals the fullness and intrinsic virtues of monuments, the sea and the human face; *evocation, allusion* or *suggestion*, though somewhat casual terms, point to what may be a very decisive trend in literature, one which both limits and sets free; for the special charm of the art lies not in the handful of dust, so to speak, not in the containing of any reality through description, in a book or a text, but in freeing from

it the spirit, that volatile dispersion which is the musicality of nothing.[3]

Here modern literature and ancient myths meet. Without knowing the Vedic texts and with only a superficial acquaintance with Buddhism, Mallarmé was trying to give a name to a process at the heart of old esoteric traditions. It kept eluding him, but he made great poetry out of his attempt to do so. "There must be something occult in the ground of everyone," is how he described it in a letter. "I firmly believe in something hidden away, a closed and secret signifier, that inhabits the ordinary." "Yes, I *know*," he writes in another letter, "we are nothing but vain forms of matter—yet sublime too when you think that we invented God and our own souls." About Mallarmé, Calasso writes that never had poetry been so magnificently superimposed upon the most mysterious and elementary fact of all, the very medium in which every quality and every likeness appear, and which is called consciousness. What draws him to Mallarmé is the poet's recognition of that truth, which Calasso himself has chased after in all his books. For Mallarmé and Calasso, as for Heidegger, thinking of Being is the only way to deal with poetry.[4] In their different ways they also have a longing for the absolute and are ready to go for broke. For them, the game of being and nothingness is the supreme game, the only one worth playing.

"There is a very strong and very ancient emotion," Calasso writes, "that is rarely mentioned or recognized: it is the anguish we feel for the absence of idols. If the eye has no image on which to rest, if there's nothing to mediate between the mental phantasm and that which simply is, then a subtle despondency creeps in." The oldest dream ever recorded, it turns out, is told by a woman, the overseer of a palace in Mesopotamia, who in her dream enters the temple and finds that the statues have vanished and so have the people who worshiped them.

For Calasso, literature is the guardian of every such space haunted by phantoms: "For whatever they may be, the gods manifest themselves above all as mental events. Yet, contrary to the modern illusion, it is the psychic powers that are fragments of the gods, not the gods that are fragments of the psychic powers." Before they could come back, literature had to find again that place, inscribed in the very ground of our being, where they have always made their presence known.

Mallarmé has been both an ideal and a dead end for poets. His greatness, Octavio Paz wrote, "lies not just in his attempt to create a language that would be the magic double of the universe—the Work conceived as a Cosmos—but above all in the consciousness of the impossibility of transforming that language into theater, into a dialogue with man."[5] Once there's nothing left but a few cryptic words for the initiates, what started out as a new understanding of aesthetics has turned into mysticism. A poem cannot be pure: it is a marriage of contradictions, reverence and blasphemy, asceticism and sensuality. As much as I admire Calasso's uncompromising search for the heart of the poetic, I'm not convinced that such a search is the best way to go about writing poetry. The most attractive and puzzling aspect of the long history of poetry is that no conception of the poem is final.

Literature is never the product of a single agent, Calasso tells us. There are always at least three actors: the hand that writes, the voice that speaks, the god who watches over and compels. They could be called the I, the Self, and the Divine. The relationship between them is constantly changing as they take turns viewing themselves and the world. Mallarmé, Calasso says, gave notice that having left by society's front door, literature was back through a cosmic window, having absorbed in the meantime nothing less than everything. Calasso concludes his study by saying that we still draw sustenance from this "daring fiction." We undoubtedly do, while reminding ourselves that the search for the absolute doesn't always take place in such a rarefied atmosphere, but has to contend with everything else human beings do, from tossing and turning all night with a toothache to falling in love with someone who doesn't care whether you exist. The best critique of absolute literature is to be found in Calasso's three books on myth, where that crowning paradox is never forgotten. Besides, as he himself has told us, the gods get bored with men who have no stories to tell.

Notes

1. *Gods and Mortals: Modern Poems on Classical Myths*, ed. Nina Kossman (New York: Oxford University Press, 2001).
2. Ezra Pound, *Selected Poems* (New York: New Directions, 1949), 24.
3. *Symbolism: An Anthology*, ed. and trans. T. G. West (New York: Methuen, 1980), 8.
4. For Calasso's reflections on Heidegger, Kafka, Flaubert, Nietzsche, Marx, Freud, Walter Benjamin, and Karl Kraus, among others, see the collection of his essays *Forty-nine Steps*, trans. John Shepley (Minneapolis: University of Minnesota Press, 1998).
5. Octavio Paz, *The Bow and the Lyre*, trans. Ruth L. C. Simms (New York: McGraw-Hill, 1975).

from

MEMORY PIANO

SAUL STEINBERG

He drew a labyrinth and himself in it.

He drew a left hand drawing the right hand while the right hand drew the left hand at the same time.

He drew a man crossing himself out with a pen.

He drew the letter *E* sitting at a table and eating the letter *A*.

He drew a fat baby about to smash the globe with a hammer.

He drew two rabbits embracing inside a dragon's mouth.

He drew a man drinking champagne out of a woman's high heel shoe with a straw.

He drew a crowd of question marks facing soldiers with their guns pointed at them.

He drew Sisyphus pushing a huge question mark up the hill.

He drew the line of the horizon to hang and dry a pair of mended socks, a shirt, and a dishrag.

A man removed his nose as if it were a pair of wire-rimmed eyeglasses.

A cat sipped a martini with a goldfish floating in it.

A woman came into the room wielding a flyswatter like an ax.

Don Quixote charged a large pineapple with his spear.

From *Journal of the Poetry Society of America* 58 (Spring/Summer 2002).

A large man with a bow and arrow shot at a speech balloon over his head full of ornate, illegible writing.

A man carried a huge heroic portrait of himself down the sidewalk.

A woman carried a vase in place of her head with a single red rose in it.

A small dog at the zoo pulled at the leash in order to bark at a lion's cage.

An old man raised a doll-like little girl so she could get a closer look at the moon.

Another man took a stern look at a blank canvas in a museum.

At a county fair there were shooting galleries called: Mondrian, Rimbaud, Rasputin, Kierkegaard, Fear & Trembling, etc.

He made a thumbprint on a sheet of paper then drew a shirt and a tie to go along with it.

He drew sixteen identical landscapes stretching to the empty horizon. Small indistinct figures, identically dressed in black, stood in groups or apart from each other.

A man held at the end of a string a winged angel who looked like himself.

The sphinx in the desert resembled someone's mother-in-law.

A portly businessman rode a horse, carrying a sword and a shield. His wife tagged behind, mounted on a donkey and wearing a pillbox hat, clutching a purse. Up ahead, they could see the sign for a MOTEL.

A knight chased a dragon down a steep hill while a huge boulder rolled after him.

An old married couple: the husband was the Jack-in-the-Box who popped up smiling while his wife stood contentedly by his side.

A portly lady dressed like Queen Victoria swung a cat-o'-nine-tails.

When a certain man opened his mouth to speak, a huge scribble came out of his mouth.

In an old school picture, with all the faces equally blurred, a blue arrow pointed to one face.

A bust of a woman sat on a TV table with wheels. On her head she had rabbit ears and from her back one could see a long cord plugged into an electric outlet.

A small dog sat on a carpet on which a huge lion had been embroidered.

He drew a cat with a raised saber standing proudly over a big fish.

He drew an American toothpick, then a French toothpick, and finally a Greek toothpick.

He drew a dinner plate with a rubber ball on it and a hammer placed on one side and a pair of pliers and a screwdriver on the other.

Saint George riding on his horse attacked a dragon no bigger than a toad in the grass.

Blind Justice with a sword in one hand and the scale in the other met a veiled Bedouin woman in the desert.

Uncle Sam was a matador. He waved an American flag in front of a huge Thanksgiving turkey.

A boy was being scolded by his mother after having cut off a peacock's tail with scissors.

The Peace Dove flew over our heads with a carving knife in its beak.

Here was a street of snarling, barking dogs and beat-up old cars with their hoods raised and their trunks open.

A man carried his exact double over his shoulders.

A large man on wheels had an opening on his back and a ladder down which ten of his lookalikes were descending.

Two men dressed to look like Uncle Sam watched with surprise a third man passing on the street who also looked like Uncle Sam.

A little girl sat on a seesaw with a pot of flowers sitting opposite her.

Uncle Sam and the Statue of Liberty were street musicians. He played the violin and she a toy drum while two ants danced at their feet.

Hotel Emperor was nothing but an enlarged photograph of a chest of drawers with many windows and a door drawn on it.

Then there was something called the *SHEPHERD FACTORY* where Romanian, Irish, Calabrian, and Sardinian shepherds were being manufactured.

In all of the drawings he made of me, I looked like a provincial Eastern European intellectual. I worked in the town hall shuffling yellowed, ink-stained land deeds and birth certificates and in my free time composed political manifestos and love poems to the widow of the local funeral parlor director.

THE SINGING SIMICS

I once broke a blood vessel in my mouth singing opera. I had had a huge molar extracted, had gone to work the following day, and just as I was putting on my coat to go home, I heard that one of my coworkers was going to hear *The Magic Flute* that night at the Met. To give him a sample of the great music he was about to hear, I started singing the big "Queen of the Night" aria. At the end of a coloratura passage, I hit a note so high all the dogs being walked in Washington Square Park two blocks away must have jumped. All of a sudden, something popped like a bubble gum where the tooth had been pulled out. My mouth was full of blood. I ran into the bathroom and stuck some paper towel on the wound thinking, no sweat, it'll stop. Since I lived only six blocks from the office, I waited to get home before I checked my mouth again. The moment I removed the wad of paper the blood started gushing. Somewhat alarmed, I stuck more paper towels between my teeth and went in search of a dentist in the neighborhood. I rang a lot of bells, but since it was Friday night no one came to my aid. Then I did something very peculiar. I went to the movies with my mouth clenched hard, figuring, I'm no bleeder, this is bound to stop sooner or later. I saw *High Sierra* with Bogart and Ida Lupino, which I had never seen before. I always liked her soulful, intelligent acting and she had me captivated. After the

From the *Harvard Review* (Fall, 2003).

show, I went home, removed the wad, and the blood filled my mouth again. Now I was really scared. I put a fresh wad in and caught a taxi. It took me to the New York University Hospital, but for some reason which I now forget, they couldn't take me. With my mouth closed I could not argue, so I took their advice and set off for the Bellevue Hospital, which was only a few blocks away. However, I had forgotten to ask in which direction. First Avenue was dark and empty, so I could see myself being mugged to top off a perfect evening. Somehow I got to the emergency room where they took my name and told me to take a seat. The waiting room was packed with people stricken with various emergencies. There were at least two pregnant women in labor pains, a young fellow with blood on his face, and dozens of others looking equally miserable. I was there for hours, or so it seemed, before I saw the doctor. He put in a couple of stitches and that was that. I was so overwhelmed with gratitude, and not knowing how to repay them at that moment, I grabbed and kissed the nurse's hand on the way out.

Come to think of it, in our family we were always getting in trouble on account of singing. In the late 1950s and early 1960s my uncle Boris and I went often to the opera. At the old Met on Fortieth Street standing room tickets were sold an hour before the performance. There'd be a long line because they cost only a dollar, but if you came early enough you usually got in. The amazing thing about it was that once you were inside you stood next to some of the best seats in the house, brushing shoulders with men in tuxedos and women in evening gowns. Boris was a tall, balding fellow, an aspiring tenor who had quit a high-paying job in a trucking company to take lessons from an ex-voice teacher from the Juilliard School of Music. He was extremely opinionated about every aspect of the performance and put on quite a show himself. Like other standees, we tried to position ourselves as close as possible to the stage, then if someone did not turn up or left early we'd take their seats. The only problem was that every time the lead tenor struck up an aria, Boris sang along. Sotto voce, or so he imagined, but lots of people heard him and tried to quiet him down. He protested loudly. He was merely demonstrating to me how the role was supposed to be sung and he didn't care to be interrupted. A couple of times an usher was summoned. Once the wife of one of the tenors singing who happened to be sitting close by came over to argue with Boris about the merits of her husband's performance. The opera was in progress, the short, bowlegged tenor and the hefty diva were swearing eternal love on the stage, and that woman in the audience was about to punch Boris. On another occasion, he was so annoyed with the tenor in *Cavalleria Rusticana* that he made a move to climb on the stage and show the poor fool and the whole house what grand opera was supposed to be like. Boris had a voice to wake up the dead, everyone agreed. Unfortunately, he had a bad ear, which his friends and family kept secret from him. After the opera was over, he sang in the street and on the subway on the way home. I recall the astonished faces of sleepy passengers on some downtown local opening their eyes wide to find in their midst Andrea Chénier himself, the great French Romantic poet and innocent victim of revolutionary justice dying on the guillotine and singing with his last breath:

> Come un bel di di maggio
> che con bacio di vento
> e carezza di raggio
> si spegne in firmamento,
> col bacio io d'una rima,
> carezza di poesia,
> salgo l'estrema cima
> dell'esistenza mia.

It didn't help that I kept laughing while Chénier told everyone between sobs how, kissed by rhyme and caressed by poetry, he climbed the final peak of his existence. Who let these two lunatics loose? the grumpy passengers asked themselves as they exchanged glances.

My mother, too, liked to give impromptu performances in public.

She had studied singing in Paris with a famous voice teacher, had taught singing for many years in a Belgrade conservatory and then in Chicago. In her old age, she told every stranger she met the story of her life, interspersed with vocal accompaniment. Short and stocky, armed with an umbrella, she'd stand in line at the dry cleaners and belt out an aria. She would do the same in a supermarket or in a dentist's waiting room. It embarrassed the hell out of me. Like her father, the much-decorated First World War hero, she was a lifelong hypochondriac who made almost nightly trips in an ambulance to the hospital where she entertained the emergency room staff with her vast repertoire. She had a small, well-trained voice that stayed youthful even into her eighties. Finally, some tone-deaf doctor got fed up with her and sent her to a psychiatrist. She broke into song there too. Eventually, I received a phone call from the shrink who begged me to come by and give him some basic information about my mother because he couldn't make heads or tails of what she was saying when she was not singing. Mozart was the love of her life, so what she gave him were genuine bel canto renditions in original Italian with many hand-gestures and eye rolls. I'm Zerlina, she would say, batting her eyelashes. Don't waste your time, I told the psychiatrist when I saw him. He was a young fellow and determined to get to the bottom of her imaginary maladies, or so he assured me. No sooner had we started rummaging in her dark closets than we heard my mother's voice in the waiting room. That afternoon she was the countess in *The Marriage of Figaro:*

> Porgi amor, qualche ristoro
> Al mio duolo, a' miei sospir!

"What is she saying?" the shrink pressed me.

"I think it means, Grant, O love, some sweet elixir to heal my pain, to soothe my sighs," I told him. And that was the last I ever saw or heard of him.

Did my mother like the way Boris sang? Of course not. Her

favorite singer in the family was my father. The two of them had met in a music school when they were in their early twenties. After graduation, they gave a recital together, sang lieder, old Italian art songs, and operatic arias. My father never sang professionally, only when he had too much to drink. He'd sit with a wineglass in his hand and start off softly. He was a handsome man with a pretty tenor voice and he knew how to deliver a song and make the lyrics vivid and poignant. I never heard anybody complain about him. He had the most incredible musical ear I ever encountered. He could harmonize with the hum of the refrigerator. Give him Johnny Cash or Billie Holiday on the radio and he'd immediately find a way to fit in. Otherwise he didn't try to show off. Now and then, at the end of a fine meal in a restaurant, he couldn't resist it, but he'd make it intimate, just for you and him and perhaps for that beautiful woman sitting alone at the next table.

Given that kind of competition, I never opened my mouth in public except for that one time, although I know lots of songs and arias. Once in a while in the shower, I'll sing Otello's "Esultate" or Figaro's "Se vuol ballare, signor contino," and then I remember Boris and my parents and stop right there with the soap stinging my eyes.

TSVETAEVA
The Tragic Life

When it comes to the Russian poetry of the last century, Osip Mandelstam, Anna Akhmatova, and Boris Pasternak are reasonably familiar
names, but not Marina Tsvetaeva, who is their equal. Because she is
extraordinarily difficult to translate, her work is almost unknown, and
even when it becomes available it makes little impression. She seems
foreign and beyond reach with her elliptical syntax and her unusually
tangled metaphors. There's also the sheer volume and range of her
writing. One of her long poems, for instance, celebrates Lindbergh's
transatlantic flight, while others derive their plots from fairy tales. She
has hundreds of poems, a number of near epic length in addition to a
fair amount of prose, including memoirs, diaries, and letters, as well as
several plays in verse. Not everything she wrote is, of course, first-rate,
but a lot is. Is she as good as Eliot or Pound? one may ask for the sake
of comparison. She is as good as they are and may have more tricks up
her sleeve as a poet.

Her life makes for an unusually gripping story, which several
fine biographies of the poet published in the last twenty years have
recounted in great detail. Tragic lives, of course, cannot be compared

Review of *Earthly Signs: Moscow Diaries, 1917–1922*, by Marina Tsvetaeva, trans.
Jamey Gambrell; and *Milestones*, trans. Robin Kemball. From the *New York Review
of Books*, February 13, 2003.

in their degree of awfulness. Even in normal times one can't be sure how much the mess people make of their lives is due to failings of character and strings of bad luck, and how much to the circumstances in which they found themselves. When it comes to men and women who lived through decades of wars, revolutions, and exile, it gets harder to know whom or what to blame. As Tsvetaeva said in a poem, "I fear that for such misfortune the whole of / Racine and the whole of Shakespeare is not enough! . . ." [1]

Marina Tsvetaeva was born in 1892 in Moscow and grew up in an atmosphere of culture and refinement. Her father was a classical philologist who taught at Moscow University and was the founder of one of the city's important museums. Marina's mother was an accomplished pianist who wanted her daughter to be a musician. In 1902, on the advice of her doctors after being diagnosed with tuberculosis, she withdrew Marina and her younger sister from school and traveled to Italy in search of a cure. In 1905 the family returned to Russia, where the mother died a year later. Marina attended school in both Russia and Paris, where she started writing poetry and translating from French. A collection of her poems, *Evening Album,* was published in 1910 and well received. Her verses were romantic and sentimental, as was to be expected from an adolescent, but she also was said to have brought in this connection a new and bold intimacy to Russian poetry.

In 1912 Tsvetaeva married Sergei Efron, who came from a well-known family of encyclopedia publishers and political radicals. He was younger than she was. That same year she brought out her second book of poems, *The Magic Lantern,* and gave birth to a daughter, Ariadna (Alya). Money from her family made the newlyweds well-off. They bought a house in Moscow and spent their summers on the Crimean coast. The marriage, however, was not a success. Tsvetaeva had affairs with the poets Sofia Parnok and Osip Mandelstam. In April of 1917, her second daughter, Irina, was born and Efron, wanting most likely to get away from the awkward situation at home, volunteered for the Imperial Army. The October Revolution caught Tsvetaeva in the Crimea. She returned to revolutionary Moscow in late November, while her husband was joining the White Army to fight the Bolsheviks. For the next three years she had no word of him.

Tsvetaeva found herself alone at twenty-five, nearly destitute with no means to support herself and her two small children. She survived with the help of friendly neighbors and by selling her belongings. Here's a description from the prose collection *Earthly Signs* of her life in Moscow:

> I get up—the upper window is barely gray—cold—puddles—saw-dust—buckets—pitchers—rags—children's dresses and shirts everywhere. I split wood. Start the fire. In icy water I wash the potatoes, which I boil in the samovar. (For a long time I made soup in it, but I once got it so clogged up with millet that for months I had to take the cover off and spoon water from the top—it's an antique samovar, with an ornate spigot that wouldn't unscrew, wouldn't yield to knitting needles or nails. Finally, someone—somehow—blew it out.) I stoke the samovar with hot coals I take right from the stove. I live and sleep in one and the same frightfully shrunken, brown flannel dress, sewn in Alexandrov in the spring of 1917 when I wasn't there. It's all covered with burn holes from falling coals and cigarettes. The sleeves, once gathered with elastic, are rolled up and fastened with a safety pin.

A thief once broke into Tsvetaeva's flat and was horror-struck by the poverty he found. She asked him to sit down and talked to him. When he got up to leave he offered her money. Nevertheless, in her diary after one such dark moment, she makes a surprising remark:

> I didn't write down the most important thing: the gaiety, the
> keenness of thought, the bursts of joy at the slightest success,
> the passionate directedness of my entire being.

Despite the never-ending hardship, this was a productive period for
her. She wrote long verse dramas and dozens of short lyrics. She also
filled her notebooks with what she saw and heard as she took trips to
the provinces in quest of food. Some of these comments are included
in *Earthly Signs,* a marvelous selection from her diaries and essays in
an exceptionally fine translation by Jamey Gambrell. They give us a
view of the times not very different from that found in Isaac Babel's
stories. Tsvetaeva is an excellent reporter. Despite what historians may
pretend, in revolutionary times stealing is more important than ideas.
While the leaders of the revolution promise the moon, murder and
looting are the only reality the powerless know.

Tsvetaeva's autobiographical writings and her essays are filled
with memorable descriptions and beautifully turned phrases. "The
heart: it is a musical, rather than a physical organ," she says, for example. Or: "Death is frightening only to the body. The soul can't conceive
of it. Therefore, in suicide, the body—is the only hero." Her views on
everything from the behavior of human beings to the nature of poetry
are shrewd and original. None of that sharpness of insight was much in
evidence in her own life where she made one mistake after another. In
the winter of 1919–20, unable to feed her children, she placed them in
an orphanage. The older one, Alya, became ill, and Tsvetaeva brought
her back home and nursed her to health. In February her younger
daughter, who was not yet three years old, died of starvation in the
same orphanage. Overcome by guilt for what amounted to her neglect
of the child, she only very rarely mentioned her again.

"I am an inexhaustible source of heresy," Tsvetaeva declared.
"Not *knowing* a single one, I profess all of them. Perhaps I even create them." She didn't like Chekhov with his sense of proportion; she

always took sides. One of the funniest memoirs in *Earthly Signs* contains her description of a poetry reading with eight other women at which she read poems in praise of the White Army to an audience consisting mostly of Red Army soldiers. The duty of poetry, she believed, was to take the side of the defeated. She also found the word "poetess" applied to herself to be insulting. There are more essential distinctions in poetry, she said, than belonging to the male or female sex. Her courage and independence are remarkable when one remembers that other decent people had to grovel and that most of the other poets—even those who changed their minds later—were welcoming the Revolution. For a long time they could not accept that all that suffering was for nothing.

While Tsvetaeva's early poetry was admired by her contemporaries, the same cannot be said of her work in the 1920s. This is how her former lover Mandelstam described her poems: "The sorriest thing in Moscow is Marina Tsvetaeva's amateurish embroidery in praise of the Mother of God." Complaining about women's poetry in general and about her specifically, he went on to say that hers is a kind of verse that offends both ear and historical sense.[2] Leon Trotsky, in his once widely read and revered *Literature and Revolution* (1923), agreed, calling it a narrow poetry encompassing the poetess herself; a certain gentleman in a derby hat or military spurs; and finally God, who performs the duties of a doctor specializing in female complaints. In émigré literary circles, it was usually the same story. "She enters literature wearing curlers and a bathrobe as though she were headed for the bathroom," a critic wrote.[3]

Jamey Gambrell sums up well the difficulties of Tsvetaeva's work in her concise and extremely perceptive introduction to *Earthly Signs*:

> Tsvetaeva is not easy reading, even for educated native speakers of Russian. She confronts readers with a Joycean profusion of idioms and styles, ranging from the metaphorical speech of fairy tales and the circumlocutions of peasant dialect to a high

literary diction steeped in Greek and Roman myths, the classics, and German Romanticism. She used almost all the classic Russian meters, adding her own innovations, and she made original use of Russian folk rhythms. Her subject matter draws on an equally diverse range of literary, historical, and folkloric sources. As Voloshin once said, ten poets coexisted in Tsvetaeva.

The linguistic density of her poems can be compared to that of Gerald Manley Hopkins, except that she has many more voices. In a letter to Rilke, with whom she had an epistolary romance, she writes:

> I am not a Russian poet and am always astonished to be taken for one and looked upon in this light. The reason one becomes a poet (if it were even possible to become one, if one were not one before all else!) is to avoid being French, Russian, etc., in order to be everything.

A bit later in that same letter, however, she says: "Yet every language has something that belongs to it alone, that *is* it." [4] Tsvetaeva is the poet of that *it*. "In an almost biblical sense," Gambrell writes, "the Word is the vehicle of creation; engendering both subject and emotion, it is the incarnation of the spirit."

To be a poet of the ear and make sound more important than sight is to make oneself virtually untranslatable. None of the translations of her poetry that I've read—and there are a great many of them—are able to convey her full verbal power, though some, like the ones by Nina Kossman and Michael M. Naydan, come close. In translation she is too often made to appear painfully awkward and dull when she is nothing of the sort. Here's how Robin Kemball renders one of her poems in *Milestones:*

Poem Number 31

A wild old hag told me plainly
Bent like a yoke in her frenzy:
—Not yours to lie idly dreaming,
Not yours to be bleaching linen,
Yours to reign—in some lost outstation,
Yours to kiss, my dearie—a raven.

I went white as a cloud as I listened:
Bring out the white burial vestment,
The black foal's no more for whipping,
The cathedral pope's no more for tippling,
Lay me peacefully under the apple tree,
With no prayers, no incense to cradle me.

A low bow is the thanks I say for
The advice and imperial favor,
For those pockets of yours, so empty,
For your prisoners' songs in plenty,
For the shame half-shared with sedition,—
For your love, for the fierce love you've given.

When the bell tolls from the cathedral—
I'll be dragged away by the devils.
As we sank our glasses together,
I was saying, and I'll tell the Creator—
That I loved you, my sturdy youngling,
Beyond fame and beyond the sunshine.

This doesn't sound like the great poet I've been praising. Unfortunately, this is the impression one gets from *Milestones,* a collection of mostly short lyric poems written in 1916. Many of the translations, even when they partially succeed, are marred by an unfortunate, unidiomatic choice of words and phrases. Tsvetaeva translating her poems into French herself did not do much better. She took greater liberties than Kemball does, transposing and changing the tonality of the poems, not only using different words but also changing images in the hope of preserving the essential, claiming that in another language one has to write something new. This seems like sensible advice, except the translations she made were no good. Still, in my view, taking freedoms now and then is the only way to proceed with translations of her poems and, with luck, pull off the impossible.

In May 1922, Tsvetaeva left Russia with her daughter to rejoin her husband, who was then living in Prague. She got as far as Berlin, where, while waiting to be reunited with Efron, she had an affair with her publisher. After two months in Berlin, the family moved to a village on the outskirts of Prague, where they lived for the next two and a half years. Her son, Georgy (known as Mur), was born in 1925. The years in Czechoslovakia were comparatively happy. There were stipends for Russian émigré students and intellectuals generously provided by the government. Tsvetaeva was also writing. Some of her long poems were written at this time, including *The Swain* and *The Pied Piper* (both of which are based on fairy tales), and two of the very best, *Poem of the Mountain* and *Poem of the End*, were both inspired by another infatuation. In a letter that her husband wrote at that time, he describes what it was like living with her:

> Marina is a woman of passions. . . . Plunging headfirst into her hurricanes has become essential for her, the breath of life. It no longer matters who it is that arouses these hurricanes. Nearly always (now as before)—or rather always—everything is based on self-deception. A man is invented and the hurricane begins. If the insignificance and narrowness of the hurricane's arouser is quickly revealed, then Marina gives way to a hurricane of despair. A state which facilitates the appearance of a new arouser. The important thing is not *what* but *how*. Not the essence or the source but the rhythm, the insane rhythm.

Today—despair; tomorrow—ecstasy, love, complete self-abandon; and the following day—despair once again. And all this with a penetrating, cold (maybe even cynically Voltairean) mind. Yesterday's arousers are wittily and cruelly ridiculed (nearly always justly). Everything is entered in the book. Everything is coolly and mathematically cast into a formula. A huge stove, whose fires need wood, wood, and more wood. Unwanted ashes are thrown out, and the quality of the wood is not so important. For the time being the stove draws well—everything is converted to flame. Poor wood is burnt up more quickly, good wood takes longer.

It goes without saying that it's a long time since I've been any use for the fire.

Her own explanation in a letter doesn't contradict her husband's:

I am not made for [this] life. With me, everything is a conflagration. I can be engaged in ten relationships at a time (fine "relationships," these!), and assure each one from the deepest depth that he is the only one. But I cannot tolerate the slightest turning of the head away from me. I HURT, do you understand? I am a person skinned alive, while all the rest of you have armor. You all have art, social issues, friendships, diversions, families, duty, while I, in the depth, have NOTHING. It all falls off like the skin and under the skin there is living flesh or fire—I'm Psyche. I do not fit into any form, not even the simplest form of my poems.[5]

Almost all of the poems that make up her greatest single collection, *After Russia*, were written at that time. Here is a poem from that book which is one of the first I ever read of hers and which I have never forgotten. It comes from *The Penguin Book of Russian Verse,* published in 1962 in what the editor calls "plain prose translation," which I still prefer to several other versions in verse:

An Attempt at Jealousy

What is your life like with another woman? Simpler, isn't it? A
    stroke of the oar! Did the memory of me,
a floating island (in the sky, not on the waters), soon recede, like a
    coastline? . . .
Souls, O Souls, you will be sisters, not lovers!
What is your life like with an ordinary woman? Without the
    divine? Now that you have dethroned your queen and have
    yourself renounced the throne,
what is your life like? How do you busy yourself? How are you
    shivering? How do you get up [from your bed]? How do you
    manage to pay the price for immortal triviality, poor fellow?
"I've had enough of convulsions and palpitations—I'll rent a
    house!" What is your life like with a woman like any other,
    you, my chosen one?
Is the food more congenial and eatable? Don't complain if you get
    sick of it! What is your life like with a semblance—you who
    have trodden upon Sinai?
What is your life like with a stranger, a woman of this world?
    Tell me point-blank: do you love her? Does shame, like Zeus's
    reins, not lash your brow?
What is your life like? How is your health? How do you sing?
    How do you cope with the festering wound of immortal
    conscience, poor fellow?
What is your life like with a market commodity? The price is
    steep, isn't it! After the marble of Carrara what is your life like
    with a piece of crumbling plaster of Paris?
(God was hewn out of a block, and has been smashed to bits!)

What is your life like with one of a hundred thousand
women—you who have known Lilith?

Have you satisfied your hunger with the new market commodity?
Now that magic has lost its power over you, . . . what is your
life like with a woman of this earth, without either of you using
a sixth sense?

Well, cross your heart: are you happy? No? In a pit without depth
what is your life like, my beloved? Harder than my life with
another man, or just the same?

In November 1925, the family moved to Paris in the hope that
Tsvetaeva would have more contact with writers. Her first public reading was a triumph she never managed to repeat. After being initially
well received by the Russian community, relations eventually soured
over the years for both literary and political reasons. Soviet literature
was anathema to the émigrés, but not to her. She praised Communist
poets like Mayakovsky in public. In the meantime, the family lived in
poverty. Her husband had no profession, no practical skill, and no wish
to get a regular job. Only Russian politics interested him. In the 1930s
he became involved with an organization called the Union for Return-
ees to the Soviet Union, which was widely and correctly believed to
be a front for the Soviet secret service. After his political views took a
Stalinist turn, Tsvetaeva, who had supported the family with her writing and with financial help from her rich friends, found herself more
and more ostracized because of her husband's activities.

At home, the atmosphere was tense. Efron talked about going
back to Russia and expiating his guilt for having fought with the
Whites in the Civil War. The children took their father's side. Her
daughter started working for a French Communist magazine and
began moving in pro-Soviet circles. Tsvetaeva with her experience of
communism had fewer illusions. It must be remembered that this was
the time of Stalin's Great Terror. Going back was almost as crazy as
for a Jew to return to Hitler's Germany. Efron, she told people, saw

what he wanted to see and closed his eyes to what was really happening in Russia. Even after her daughter left for Moscow in 1937, she was reluctant to follow. Then, life became impossible for her in France. Her husband was interrogated by the French police in connection with the murder of a Soviet spy who had refused to return home.

In September of 1937, before they could ask him any more questions, Efron fled to the Soviet Union. Later investigations established that he worked for the NKVD and participated in several assassinations, including that of Trotsky's son. Not even Tsvetaeva's closest friends could believe that she knew nothing of her husband's intelligence work. People avoided her. She was excluded from literary gatherings and was no longer published. She survived with the help of a small stipend provided to her by the Soviet embassy while waiting to receive permission to return. Her loyalty to her husband and children, all of whom wanted to return, overrode any reservations she had. On June 12, 1939, she and her son finally departed. In her last letter before sailing from Le Havre, she wrote to a Czech friend: "Goodbye! What comes now is no longer difficult, what comes now is fate."

In Moscow she learned that her sister was in the camps. Barely two months after Tsvetaeva's return, her daughter was arrested and accused of spying for Western powers, and shortly after so was her husband. Efron was most likely shot soon after, while her daughter spent some seventeen years in the camps and in exile in Siberia. Tsvetaeva was never to see them again. She had no money and no place to live. Old friends were afraid to have anything to do with a wife of an "enemy of the people" and an ex-émigré. As a writer, for the Communists she did not exist. If she wasn't standing in some prison line to leave a parcel for her husband and daughter, she was looking for work. She did some translating which brought a little money, and even put together a collection of poems, but it was rejected by the publisher with the explanation that her poems had nothing to say to the Soviet people. Pasternak did what he could to help, but it wasn't much. When Germany invaded Russia in June 1941 and the bomb-ing raids over Moscow increased, her panic grew. She managed to be evacuated to Elabuga, a small town on the Toima and Kama rivers. Tsvetaeva rented a room in Elabuga from a local couple, and went to a larger town nearby, where a number of writers had already been settled, and tried to get a permit to move there. She even applied for a job as a dishwasher in the writers' cafeteria.

There was reason to hope that she would get permission, but by this time she herself was beyond hope. On August 31, while her son and her landlords were out, she hanged herself in the entrance way of her room. She left three notes, two of them pleading to friends to take care of her son and the last one to him: "Forgive me," she wrote,

> but it would only have gotten worse. I am seriously ill, this is no longer me. I love you madly. Understand that I couldn't live any more. Tell Papa and Alya—if you see them—that I loved them to the last minute, and explain that I had reached a dead end.

Tsvetaeva was buried in an unmarked grave in Elabuga's cemetery. Mur was drafted into the army in 1943 and was killed in combat in July of 1944.

One of her biographers, Victoria Schweitzer, writes:

> When she was removed from the noose and taken to the morgue, the undertaker found a tiny (1x2 cm) blue moroc-cobound notebook in one of the pockets of her apron. There was a very slim pencil attached to the notebook, but to all intents and purposes the notebook was too small to write in. The undertaker kept this notebook, kept it for more than forty years, and on his deathbed asked for it to be given back

to Tsvetaeva's relatives. In it, like a message from the other world, was one word in Tsvetaeva's handwriting: Mordovia.

This was the name of the Soviet republic in the Urals where her daughter Alya had been sent to a camp.

"God, do not judge! You were never a woman on this earth," she once wrote.

Notes

1. Victoria Schweitzer, *Tsvetaeva* (New York: Farrar, Straus and Giroux, 1992), 275.
2. Simon Karlinsky, *Marina Tsvetaeva: The Woman, Her World, and Her Poetry* (Cambridge: Cambridge University Press, 1985), 128–29.
3. Ibid., 157.
4. Boris Pasternak, Marina Tsvetaeva, and Rainer Maria Rilke, *Letters: Summer 1926* (New York: New York Review Books, 2001), 221.
5. Karlinsky, *Marina Tsvetaeva*, 135.

ADAM'S UMBRELLA

The first visual record of police interrogation we have comes from a Seventh Dynasty tomb in Egypt, two thousand years before Christ. The image shows a man being held by three others while the fourth one beats him with a bamboo stick and the fifth, who appears to be the one in charge, supervises the procedure. The sight is disheartening, Borislav Pekić comments. In four thousand years not much has changed. Prisoners still get beaten. And that's not the worst that happens to them, of course. There have been many refinements since the pharaohs in methods of inducing physical and mental pain. We must give credit to the Holy Inquisition, which contributed more than any other institution to the development of the role of the interrogator. The inquisitors' techniques of persuasion were especially admired by modern totalitarian states where ideological heresy likewise came to be regarded as a capital crime.

Only educated people conversant with nuances of doctrine and with a talent for abstract speculation could count on becoming inquisitors. Their task was no longer to bash heads and extract fingernails but to have the prisoner comprehend the nature of his transgression and make a public confession. Today, in the name of the war

---

Review of *How to Quiet a Vampire*, by Borislav Pekić, trans. Stephen M. Dickey and Bogdan Rakić. From the *New York Review of Books*, June 24, 2004.

on terror, ill-treatment and torture in all their ancient and modern varieties are again being used more or less openly by some countries, including the United States. These practices, surprisingly, have the approval of a number of distinguished law professors and opinion makers who argue that to defeat evil we may have to do the unthinkable now and then.

Were he alive today, Borislav Pekić would not have been persuaded. His interest in the abuse and torture of prisoners comes from firsthand experience. Unlike his better-known Serbian contemporaries, the novelists Danilo Kis and Aleksandar Tisma, who also wrote extensively about imprisonment, Pekić actually spent time in jail as a political prisoner under the Communists. Born in 1930, he was arrested in 1948 in Belgrade while still in high school, and accused of organizing a conspiracy against the state. He did not deny his guilt. The secret student organization of which he was one of the founders planned to engage in sabotage in addition to proselytizing for democratic reforms.

This was an act of bravery akin to starting in Nazi Germany an association to combat the spread of anti-Semitism. He was interrogated, treated roughly, and made to sign a statement in which he admitted plotting against the state because, supposedly, he and his friends could not bear the freedom and happiness his fellow citizens now enjoyed. In other words, he was made to realize that rather than having fought for liberty as he had previously told himself, he had been a mortal enemy of that liberty. He served five years out of a fifteen-year sentence.

Exactly how he was made to confess the opposite of what he believed, Pekić describes in *Godine Koje su Pojeli Skakavci* (Years Eaten by Locusts), a three-volume memoir, still to be translated, of his time in prison, published in 1991, a year before his death. As much as he dwells on his own predicament, he is even more interested in the stories of his fellow prisoners and his jailers. Prison turned out to be a pivotal experience in his life. When he was arrested, he was an upper-middle-class boy whose father, ironically, had been a high police official before the war. After his pardon in 1953, Pekić was an outcast in a state where one's political past and unquestioning loyalty to the Party were decisive factors in getting ahead. The best thing a man like him could do under the circumstances was to become invisible. That, however, was never to be Pekić's talent. The day he was to be set free, he refused to leave the prison until the fountain pen that was confiscated at his arrest six years before was returned to him. The officials showed him a large stash of fountain pens and implored him to select the one he liked best, but he continued to insist that his own be given back to him.

After his release, Pekić studied psychology in Belgrade, and then between 1958 and 1964, he worked in the film industry writing numerous screenplays and publishing a few literary works under a pseudonym. His novel *The Time of Miracles* (*Vreme Cuda*) came out in 1965 when he was already thirty-five years old.[1] It turned out to be a success with both the critics and the reading public. The book is made up of stories based on Christ's miracles in the New Testament. Pekić reimagines the events from the point of view of those on whom the miracles were performed by a passing stranger who did not ask for their consent or care much what happened to them afterward. In place of traditional narrative and theology, he offers his own counter-parables as a corrective. What interests him, as it does in his other books, is the gap between some religious or political doctrine and the actual outcome for a particular person.

The Time of Miracles is a blasphemous book with scenes and images that could have come from Gnostic gospels and the canvases of Hieronymus Bosch. The story of resurrection is also given a twist. A disciple, greedy for salvation, begs Jesus to let him carry the cross so that he may save his own soul. Jesus, who never refuses anyone in spiritual need, lets him take up the cross while he himself vanishes in the crowd. The Roman centurions in their drunkenness do not notice the switch and crucify the wrong man.

The Houses of Belgrade (*Hodocasce Arsenija Njegovana*, 1970), Pekić's next novel, has a far more conventional narrative.[2] It tells the story of a well-to-do house builder and landlord who shuts himself inside his apartment on March 27, 1941, the day street demonstrations in Belgrade overthrew the government, which had signed a nonaggression pact with Hitler, and who doesn't emerge from it until June 3, 1968, when once more he discovers that the streets are full of protesting students. As the novel opens, Pekić's hero, an elderly man in failing health, is composing a commentary on his life. He lives on memories of the houses he built, which he observes through binoculars from his top-floor window. During the Allied bombing in 1944, he at first refuses to go down into the cellar, insisting on remaining at his window and trying to ascertain if any of his houses are being hit.

"How does one tell a story that is outdated, pointless, incomprehensible, perhaps risky and yet touching?" Pekić asks himself in one of his essays.[3] Arsenie Negovan, his hero, is a member of what in Serbia turned out to be a quickly emerging and as quickly declining class of urban merchants and professionals whose fates were sealed by the Second World War and communism. *The Houses of Belgrade* is an elegy for that lost world, a world to which Pekić's own family belonged. Arsenie Negovan was a builder in a country in which cities are forever being reduced to ruins by some foreign invader or, as in the case of Sarajevo and Vukovar, by home-grown lunatics.

In 1971, Pekić moved with his family to London where, except for a few extended visits to his homeland, he lived in self-imposed exile until his death. These were extremely prolific years for him. In addition to the books already mentioned, he published novels, plays, books of science fiction, and several works of nonfiction. His novel in seven volumes, *Golden Fleece* (*Zlatno Runo*, 1978–86), is regarded as his masterpiece. In 1990, Pekić participated in the founding of the Democratic Party in Serbia, to which both the recently assassinated premier, Zoran Djindjic, and the present one, Vojislav Kostunica, also belonged, before they became enemies. He also took part in the first demonstrations against the Milosevic regime.

The last things he wrote were newspaper articles and speeches and their theme was the democratic future of Serbia. Rereading the pieces today, I'm struck by his willingness to forgive his old enemies and by his rosy outlook. Like other moderate nationalists, he did not foresee what tragedies lay ahead, since, more than the others, he believed in compromise. Serious consideration of other people's views and a genuine attempt to understand them was the essence of democracy for Pekić. Without compromise, he wrote, there can be no normal life for us. He knew how difficult finding the middle ground politically had always been for Serbs; nevertheless, he hoped that for once they might come to their senses, seize the opportunity, and act wisely.

How to Quiet a Vampire, well translated by Stephen M. Dickey and Bogdan Rakić, is a book without a trace of optimism. First published in 1977, it is the story of a former SS officer, Konrad Rutkowski, now a professor of medieval history at the University of Heidelberg, who like thousands of other Germans vacations on the Dalmatian coast, in his case in the town of D. where twenty-two years before, during the Second World War, he served as a Gestapo officer. His wife, whose idea it was to take the trip, has no knowledge that this is the place where he was briefly posted, and so remains oblivious of her husband's inner turmoil. Rutkowski's efforts to both renounce and justify his past are detailed in twenty-six letters which he writes to his brother-in-law back in Germany, who also happens to be a professor of history. Pekić, writing as the narrator, depicts himself as the scholarly editor of the letters who provides a preface, numerous footnotes, and several additional documents and commentaries at the end of the book. In his introduction, he characterizes the writing as a mixture of personal confession and a historico-philosophical essay. These elements, of course, are present in Pekić's other fiction. He was always as interested in ideas as in his characters and his plots.

The former Gestapo officer, Professor Rutkowski, uses the letters to conduct a bitter polemic with the European intellectual tradition of which he proudly considers himself to be a descendant. He ascribes to it the great share of the blame for his personal tragedy as well as the moral ruin of Germany. The content of each letter is consequently associated with a different European philosophical school and a work of a particular philosopher. *The Meditations* of letter 1 belong to Marcus Aurelius; *Matter and Memory* of letter 2 to Henri Bergson; *Thus Spake Zarathustra* of letter 3 to Nietzsche, and so forth. By the last letter, Leibniz, Descartes, Freud, Schopenhauer, Berdyaev, Hegel, Spengler, Husserl, Erasmus, Plato, Hume, Abelard, Heidegger, Jaspers, Sartre, Saint Augustine, Camus, Marx, and Wittgenstein have all been alluded to. In his view, these are the real culprits for the delusions and violence of the twentieth century. He writes to his brother-in-law:

> Although you've never read Wittgenstein, you worship him. Although you didn't understand Hegel, you worship him, too. The same goes for Kant, Schopenhauer, and Nietzsche. You owe this not only to your status as an academic, but also to your conviction that Ideas, especially philosophical ones, are a necessary corrective to the disgusting lives we're sometimes forced to lead. The idea that philosophy could inspire one such life, organize it, and defend it as ideal seems blasphemous to you. I assure you, however, that something just like that is what's going on. Your naive conviction (we'll see how naive it really is) that thinking philosophically means secluding oneself from reality and absolving oneself of all responsibility in connection with it—and that such seclusion is the condition *sine qua non* of every unbiased philosophical view—stems from an insidious wish, camouflaged in a general independence of the intellect, to disavow any responsibility for this world, whereby your harmlessness acquires a completely different meaning. . . . The thought that logical speculations could be connected in any way with beatings and the mutilation of people's souls seems to you to be a monstrous injustice—not against the people but against the speculations.

On a mundane level, Rutkowski's story goes like this. He was born in 1916 in a region of Yugoslavia called Banat, formerly a part of the Austro-Hungarian Empire, where his German ancestors settled in the fifteenth century. His father was a moderately well-off farmer. Rutkowski studied medieval history at the University of Heidelberg between 1934 and 1938 and received his doctorate there in 1940. The subject of his thesis was German-Polish relations before the Reformation. He returned home and began teaching grammar school in a town near Belgrade. When the war came, he failed to respond to the mobilization call to the Yugoslav army and soon after the arrival of German troops in April of 1941, became a member of the SS and eventually a Gestapo officer.

He carried out his police duties in Belgrade, except for temporary assignments in D. on the Adriatic coast and later in a town in Slovenia. Following both of these periods of service, he spent time in military hospitals suffering from extreme nervous exhaustion. When the war ended, he was subject to criminal proceedings by the Allied military authorities and sentenced to what was then known as work rehabilitation, following which he spent two years without steady employment until his former professor at Heidelberg brought him as a lecturer to the university and his academic career flourished.

The special operation in D. with which his letters are concerned occurs in 1943, when, following the capitulation of Italy, which had been occupying the Dalmatian coast, the German army and police moved into the region. Rutkowski is a member of a small unit led by an old Nazi Party member and experienced Gestapo investigator, a certain Standartenführer Steinbrecher, whose mission is to take over the police station and the duties the Italians performed until recently. As they are moving into their new quarters, Steinbrecher lectures Rutkowski on the complexities of police work in an occupied state. His ideas are terrifying. He sounds to me like a brilliant follower of the philosopher Carl Schmitt, who took his antiliberal philosophy of the state to its logical conclusions. In Steinbrecher's view, as in Schmitt's, a strong, healthy state must have perpetual adversaries. Enemies are the bolts that hold the machinery of the state together. Mutual suspicion, the covert desire of human beings to snitch on each other, ought to be encouraged. Since universal spying and denunciation are going to be the rule in the future, there'll always be plenty of work for cops to do. Police will only become unnecessary if every human being on earth becomes a policeman.

Even the famous incident in the Garden of Eden ought to be studied for what it can teach us about running a state. Forbidding the fruit to be taken from one tree, fruit completely indistinguishable from the fruit in any other tree, could have had as its goal only the enthronement of prohibition as such to test its effects on people. Plucking fruit from that tree in particular proved that this was not a matter of an ordinary theft, but a premeditated act violating divine order and thus an act of rebellion. According to Steinbrecher, the original sin was the first political crime. The craving to violate the prohibition and to disturb the established order, the conspiracy of a particular man and woman with that as its goal (abetment and solicitation), the participation of the serpent as an agent provocateur and probable informer, make it so. Finally one person, God, appears in every legal guise—as legislator, investigator, prosecutor, judge, and even the one who administers punishment in the end. Vishinsky, Stalin's infamous prosecutor in the 1930s who argued that there is no difference between the intention and the crime, would have agreed with that view. Adam and Eve should have confessed and asked for forgiveness long before they reached for the apple in the tree.

A few days after they move to D., the Germans discover in the cellar of the police station a middle-aged prisoner left behind by the Italians. The file clerk Adam Trpković, they find, was arrested for failing to salute the flag while passing the town hall and was subsequently forgotten by the Italians, who left in a hurry. He has survived by eating tangerines intended for the black market that were also in the cellar. To the great astonishment of the Germans, he still has with him his umbrella. They don't know what to do with him. They want to let him go, but the presence of that umbrella puzzles them and creates bureaucratic difficulties when it comes to filling out the forms for his official release. How are they to account for it? They can't. As one would expect, once Steinbrecher learns of the situation, he has a different view. Why shouldn't we begin our police work with him? he asks, even though he is ready to agree that the file clerk is an insignificant nobody. Nonetheless, he's a member of an enemy nation, and that is a sufficient reason to take a further look into his background. Rutkowski has no comment, but he's horrified. Despite all evidence to the contrary, he still holds on to the belief that their duty is to learn the truth. His commanding officer sets him straight:

> The truth? My foot! What are we, a bunch of goddamned philosophers or something? We make truths, Obersturmführer Rutkowski! We don't learn them, we make them! That's a creative endeavor, not an investigative one. We're artists, my dear sir. . . . I'd say poets.

Rutkowski pretends to himself that he can find a way to help the clerk. For Pekić, he has the intellectual's special ability to ignore evil by explaining it away. His unhappiness comes from his dim awareness that he is a hypocrite. In the end, he does nothing to help the innocent man. He who acts, he consoles himself, has no time for balances and scales. Rutkowski needs his "although," "maybe," and "on the other hand" to conceal his cowardice from himself. Steinbrecher, suspecting his ambivalence, assigns him to be the one who questions the clerk. He even provides him with the transcript of one of his own prized interrogations for guidance. The full text, included in the appendix of the novel, is worth studying closely for the way in which an extraordinarily logical mind can be an instrument of iniquity.

"A man can dodge even bullets, but not logic," Pekić writes. The task of the interrogator is to make the prisoner accept reason in place of reality and assume full responsibility for probable events that in truth never happened. Reality is a sin against reason for which the prisoner has to pay with his life. Chance is illogical; therefore it cannot and must not exist. In principle, it is always possible to show that it is more logical for something to have happened than not. One may say that philosophically it is necessary that everything be intentional; otherwise there can be no meaning. Because no such thing as coincidence can exist, there are also no mitigating circumstances. All circumstances in which one finds oneself are by their very nature aggravating. When our mothers warned us that someone who lies will also steal, that a thief will also commit murder, and that a murderer will end up on the gallows, they were giving expression to a view that a policeman of Steinbrecher's school can only confirm from his practice.

The clerk he is questioning through the night is not cooperating with Rutkowski. He barely replies, doesn't appreciate that his interrogator is suffering morally for his sake, and appears resigned to his fate. Even more infuriatingly, he is still clutching his ridiculous umbrella which no one, for some unknown, superstitious reason, dares to take away from him. How the memory of the clerk, Adam Trpković, comes to haunt Rutkowski and becomes his vampire is the story of the letters. Writing to his brother-in-law in the hope that words can cancel deeds, he seeks a compromise between suicide and apathy. In truth, his letters for the most part are a labored attempt to dodge responsibility and give a different explanation for his gutlessness.

"Can you recognize in Steinbrecher's linguistic jeremiad the semantic longings of Rudolph Carnap?" he writes to his brother-in-law, who, unknown to him, hasn't even bothered to read the letters. Pekić calls *How to Quiet a Vampire* "a sotie," deriving the term from satirical popular plays in France in the fifteenth and sixteenth centuries, in which a company of *sots*, fools, exchanged badinage on contemporary persons and events. It is a grim comedy about what happens to philosophical ideas when they end up in a police cellar. "Knowledge is the prerequisite for all evil," Steinbrecher says. Ignorance can be wicked when it gets the chance, but crime on a large scale comes from the learned. Pekić reminds us that respected scientists were asked for technical assistance to solve the problem of how to burn the most human bodies in the shortest time with the lowest expenditure in death camps. Rutkowski, as much as he denies it, is an intellectual monster himself. Once he comes to that realization, his solution to how to get rid of his remorse is equally hideous. He writes in the next to the last letter:

> The problem wasn't finding the key to my past—which was what I was passionately trying to do in my letters—but to find the one to my future. Tomorrow is what makes me human; yesterday is what makes me a corpse. The mistake was reviving something I should have taken long ago and buried forever. Our problem is not how to revive, but how to quiet our vampires. The past is a vampire and the real question is how to quiet it forever. We don't have a third option. Either we drive a stake through the vampire's heart or our blood is soon completely sucked dry. In order to achieve the former, we must for once begin with the excretion of the poisonous spirit of intellectual analysis from our lives.

For a short book, *How to Quiet a Vampire* has a complicated plot which I've barely sketched out. On one level, it is a psychological study of a descent into madness of an intellectual who in his ideas gradually begins to turn into an apologist for a brutal authoritarian state with its martyrs of destruction and saints of demolition. The story of the file clerk also takes many unexpected turns. He appears to Rutkowski as a ghost and perhaps even as the devil himself; his execution by hanging turns out to be a kind of mock crucifixion and resurrection. In my opinion, the realistic and fantastic aspects of the narrative are not as well intermixed as they are in Bulgakov's *Master and Margarita*, which undoubtedly was one of Pekić's models. He strives to inflate the clerk and the guilt-ridden professor of history into even more universal symbols after it has become unnecessary to do so. Leaving some of the subplots and commentaries out—and that includes most of the appendix—would have made a brilliant novel into a great one.

For Pekić, history is not to be understood as created by Hitler, Stalin, and all the countless lesser-known executioners who do their killing. Rutkowski and Adam Trpković are more revealing of the history of our time: the one who supposedly knows better, but closes his eyes, and the one who pays with his life for that negligence. There was nothing suspicious about this wretch, nothing incomprehensible except his umbrella, Rutkowski writes. Nevertheless, Steinbrecher orders that the clerk be hung with it. "Do you sense the advantage of farce over all other forms of human humiliation?" he tells Rutkowski. "Farce kills truth, destroys faith, ridicules every feat of heroism. Can someone be a hero in his underwear while holding an umbrella?" Not even Achilles could have managed that, Steinbrecher says. The reader of *How to Quiet a Vampire* will disagree. The funny little man who carries an umbrella in one hand while holding on to his shorts with the other as he is being led to the gallows is the only true hero in a tragic farce.

Northwestern University Press should be commended for its series Writings from an Unbound Europe, in which Pekić's novels and dozens of other first-rate works of fiction in translation from the former Communist countries of Eastern Europe have appeared and continue to appear.

Notes

1. Trans. by Lovett F. Edwards (Evanston: Northwestern University Press, 1994).
2. Trans. by Bernard Johnson (Evanston: Northwestern University Press, 1994).
3. Borislav Pekić, *Odmor od Istorije* (Belgrade: BIGZ, 1993), 175.

from

THE RENEGADE

THE RENEGADE

As the curtain goes up, I'm sitting naked on the potty in my grand-father's backyard in a little village in Serbia. The year is 1940. I look happy. It's a nice summer day full of sunlight, although Hitler has already occupied most of Europe. I have no idea, of course, that he and Stalin are hatching an elaborate plot to make me an American poet. I love the neighbor's dog, whose name is Toza. I run after him carrying my potty in my hand, wanting to pull his tail, but he won't let me.

What would I not give today to have a photograph of Toza! He was a country mutt full of burrs and fleas, and in his wise and sad eyes, if we had known how to read them, we would have found the story of mine and my parents' lives.

I had a great-uncle of whom nothing is known. I don't even know his name, if I ever did. He came to America in the 1920s and never wrote home. Got rich, my relatives said. How do you know that? I asked. Nobody knew how they knew. They had heard rumors. Then the people who'd heard the rumors died. Today there's no one left to ask. My great-uncle was like one of those ants who, coming upon a line of marching ants, turns and goes in the opposite direction for reasons of his own.

First published in the *New York Review of Books* (2007).

Ants being ants, this is not supposed to happen, but it sometimes does, and no one knows why.

This mythical great uncle interests me because I resemble him a bit. I, too, came to America and, for long stretches of time, forgot where I came from or had no contact with my compatriots. I never understood the big deal they make about being born in one place rather than another when there are so many nice places in the world to call home. As it is, I was born in Belgrade in 1938 and spent fifteen eventful years there before leaving forever. I never missed it. When I try to tell that to my American friends, they don't believe me. They suspect me of concealing my homesickness because I cannot bear the pain. Allegedly, my nightmarish wartime memories have made me repress how much dear old Belgrade meant to me. My wartime memories may have been terrifying, but I had a happy childhood despite droning planes, deafening explosions, and people hung from lampposts. I mean, it's not like I knew better and dreamed of a life of quiet strolls with my parents along tree-lined boulevards or playing with other children in the park. No. I was three years old when the first bombs fell and old enough to be miserable when the war ended and I had to go to school.

The first person who told me about the evil in the world was my grandmother. She died in 1948, but I recall her vividly because she took care of me and my brother while my mother went to work. The poor woman had more sense than most people. She listened to Mussolini, Hitler, Stalin, and other lunatics on the radio, and since she knew several languages, she under-

Charles Simic, c. 1940.

stood the imbecilities they were saying. What upset her even more than their vile words was their cheering followers. I didn't realize it then, but she taught me a lesson that has stuck. Beware of the so-called great leaders and the collective euphorias they excite. Many years later I wrote this poem about her:

Empires

My grandmother prophesied the end
Of your empires, O Fools!
She was ironing. The radio was on.
The earth trembled beneath our feet.
One of their heroes was giving a speech.
"Monster," she called him.
There were cheers and gun salutes for the monster.
"I could kill him with my bare hands,"
She announced to me.
There was no need to. They were all
Going to the devil any day now.
"Don't go blabbering about this to anyone,"
She warned me.
And pulled my ear to make sure I understood.

When people speak of the dark years after the war, they usually have in mind political oppression and hunger, but what I see are poorly lit streets with black windows and doorways as dark as the inside of a coffin. If the lone lightbulb one used to read by in bed late into the night died suddenly, it was not likely to be replaced soon. Every year, we had less and less light in our house and not much heat in winter. In the evening, we sat in our overcoats listening to the rumblings of each other's empty stomachs. When guests came, they didn't even bother to remove their hats and gloves. We would huddle close whispering about arrests, a neighbor being shot, another one disappearing. I wasn't supposed to hear any of this, in case I forgot myself in school and got everyone at home in trouble.

This was the first time I heard people say that we Serbs are numskulls. There was no disagreement. Who else among the nations in Europe was stupid enough to have a civil war while the Nazis were occupying them? We had the Communists, the royalists, and at least a couple of factions of domestic fascists. Some collaborated with Germans and Italians and some did not, but they all fought one another and executed their political opponents. I didn't understand much of it at the time, but I recall the exasperation and anger of the grown-ups.

Of course, the mood was most likely different in other homes where they welcomed the Communists. We were, after all, members of a mummified, impoverished, middle-class family that would have preferred that everything had remained the same. My mother and grandmother hated wars, distrusted national demagogues, and wanted the kind of government that left everybody alone.

In other words, they were the kind of people, as we were lectured in school, destined to be thrown on the garbage dump of history.

Occasionally, one of our visitors would start defending the Serbs. Our history is one of honor, heroic sacrifice, and endless suffering in defense of Europe against the Ottoman Empire, for which we never got any thanks. We are gullible innocents who always think better of our neighbors than they deserve. We sided with England and America when the rest of Europe was already occupied by the Nazis and it was suicidal to go against them.

Yes, my grandmother would say, we did that because we are conceited fools with exaggerated notions of our historical importance. A rabble of thieving and dimwitted yokels who were happiest under the Turks when they had no freedom, no education, and no ambition, except to roast a suckling pig on some holiday.

"Mrs. Matijevic, how can you talk like that?" our visitors would object. My grandmother would just shrug her shoulders. Her husband had been a military hero in World War I, a much-decorated colonel who had lost his enthusiasm for war. I recall being shocked when I first heard him say that Serbs should not have kicked out the government that signed the nonaggression pact with Hitler in 1941. Look what the war had brought us, he would say.

I wonder what my unknown great-uncle in America thought about all that. I bet he had his own ideas on the subject as he sat in some outhouse in Kansas or Texas reading in last month's papers how on March 27, 1941, the heroic Serbs walked the streets of Belgrade shouting "better death than a pact" while Hitler threw a fit. I reckon he must have tried to explain to his wife now and then about Serbs.

If she was an Apache, or a member of some other Native American tribe, she may have understood more quickly. Serbs are a large, quarrelsome tribe, he would have said, never as happy as when they are cutting each other's throats. A Serb from Bosnia has as much in common with a Serb from Belgrade as a Hopi Indian does with a Comanche. All together, they often act as if they have less sense than God gave a duck.

On second thought, he probably never brought up the subject. The Balkans, with its many nationalities and three different religions, is too complicated a place for anyone to explain, or begin to make sense of, especially since each ethnic group writes its history only remembering the wrongs done to them while conveniently passing over all the nasty things they've done to their neighbors over the centuries.

When I came to the United States in 1954, I discovered that the conversation among the immigrant Serbs my parents saw now and then was identical to the one I had heard in Belgrade. The cry was still, how did we who are so brave, so honorable, so innocent end up like this?

Because of traitors, of course. Serbs stabbing each other in the back. A nation of double-crossers, turncoats, Judases, snakes in the grass. Even worse were our big allies. England, America, and France screwed us royally. Didn't Churchill say to Eden at Yalta that he didn't give a fuck what happened to Yugoslavia after the Communists took over?

Charles and his father, George Simic, 1942.

"It's exhausting to be a Serb," my father would say after an evening like that. He was a cheerful pessimist. He loved life, but had no faith in the idea that the human condition was meliorable. He had had sympathies for the chetniks, pro-monarchy Serbian nationalists, at the beginning of the war, but no more. Nationalist claptrap left him cold. He was like his father, who used to shock family and friends by ridiculing Serbian national heroes. Both he and my father went to church and had genuine religious feelings, but they could not resist making fun of priests.

Charles Simic, 1952.

"There is nothing sacred for them," my mother would say when she got angry with the Simic family. Of course, she really wasn't any better. It's just that she preferred that appearances be kept up. Her philosophy was, let the world think we believe in all that nonsense, and we'll keep our real views to ourselves.

After my parents separated in 1956, I left home. I attended university at night and worked during the day, first in Chicago and then in New York City. If someone asked me about my accent, I would say that I was born in Yugoslavia, and that would be the end of it. I saw my father frequently, but though he liked to reminisce about his youth in the old country he had an equal and even greater interest in America, and so did I. It was only when we went to visit his brother Boris that the eternal subject of Serbian national destiny came up. Boris was a successful trucking company executive who lived in a posh Westchester suburb, where he had a house, a wife, and three German shepherds. He loved to organize large dinner parties to which he'd invite his many Serbian friends, serve them fabulous food and wine, and then argue with them about politics till the next day.

Boris was a lefty in Yugoslavia, an admirer of the partisans, but as he grew older, he became more and more conservative, suspecting even Nixon of having liberal tendencies. He had a quality of mind that I have often found in Serbian men. He could be intellectually brilliant one moment and unbelievably stupid the next. When someone pointed this out to him, he got mad. Never in my life had I heard so many original and idiotic things come out of the same mouth. He was never happier than when arguing. Even if one agreed with everything he said and admitted that black was white, he would find reasons to fight you. He needed opponents, endless drama with eruptions of anger, absurd accusations, near fistfights. Boris, everyone who knew him said, would have made Mahatma Gandhi reach for a stick. Compromise for him was a sign of weakness rather than of good sense. He was not a bad man, just a hothead when it came to politics. He died before Milosevic came to power, and I have wondered ever since what he would have made of him and his wars.

Listening to Boris and his pals endlessly rehash our national history, I assumed this was just immigrant talk, old water under the bridge. Like many others, I was under the impression that Yugoslavia was a thriving country not likely to fall apart even after Tito's death. I made two brief trips to Belgrade, one in 1972 and another in 1982, had heard about ethnic incidents, but continued to believe, even when the rhetoric got more and more heated in the late 1980s after the emergence of the first nationalist leaders, that reason would prevail in the end. I had no problem with cultural nationalism, but the kind that demands unquestioning solidarity with prejudices, self-deceptions, paranoias of the collective, I loathed. I couldn't stand it in America, and even less so in Serbia.

The few friends and relatives I had in Belgrade were telling me about the rise of a new leader, a national savior, called Slobodan Milosevic, whom they all seemed to approve of. I started reading Belgrade papers and weeklies and having a huge monthly telephone bill trying to understand what was taking place. After more than forty years in America, I became a Serb again, except, as many would say, a bad Serb.

"We don't want to live with them any more," friends would tell me. They wanted a complete separation from Croats and Bosnians and at the same time a Serbia that would include all the areas where Serbs had lived for centuries. When I pointed out that this could not be done without bloodshed, they got very upset with me since they were decent people who didn't approve of violence. They simply would not accept that the leaders and the policies they were so thrilled about were bound to lead to slaughter.

"How can you separate yourselves when you are all mixed together?" I would ask and not get a straight answer. I could recall the ethnic mixture we had in our neighborhood in Belgrade and could not imagine that someone would actually attempt to do something so wicked. Plus, I liked the mix. I spent most of my life translating poetry from every region of Yugoslavia, had some idea what their cultures were like, so I could not see any advantage for anyone living in a ghetto with just their own kind.

Of course, I was naive. I didn't realize the immense prestige that inhumanity and brutality have among nationalists. I also didn't grasp to what degree they are impervious to reason. To point out the inevitable consequences of their actions didn't make the slightest impression on them, since they refused to believe in cause and effect.

The infuriating aspect of every nationalism is that it doesn't understand that it is a mirror image of some other nationalism, and that most of its pronouncements have been heard in other places and at other times. Smug in their ethnocentricity, certain of their own superiority, indifferent to the cultural, religious, and political concerns of their neighbors, all they needed in 1990 was a leader to lead them into disaster.

How did I see what many others didn't? Or as the Serbs would say, what made me an *odrod* (renegade)?

The years of the Vietnam War focused my mind. It took me a while to appreciate the full extent of the prevarication and sheer madness in our press and television and our political opinion, and to see what our frothing patriots with their calls for indiscriminate slaughter were getting us into. The war deepened for me what was already a lifelong suspicion of all causes that turn a blind eye to the slaughter of the innocent.

"Go back to Russia," I recall someone shouting to the antiwar demonstrators in New York. So, it's like that, I recall thinking then. You opt for the sanctity of the individual and your fellow citizens immediately want to string you up. Even today our conservatives argue that we lost the war in Vietnam because the protesters undercut the military, who were forced to fight with one hand tied behind their backs. In other words, if we had gone ahead and killed four million Vietnamese instead of two million, we would have won that war.

*

Milosevic struck me from the beginning, in the late 1980s, as bad news. I said as much in an interview with a Serbian paper. This provoked a reaction. I was called a traitor in the pay of Serbia's enemies, and many other things. This only spurred me on.

After the siege of the Croatian town of Vukovar in 1991, one didn't have to be Nostradamus to prophesy how badly it would all end for the Serbs. I wrote numerous pieces in Serbian and German newspapers arguing with the nationalists. Many others did the same in Serbia, and far more forcefully and eloquently than I did. We were in the minority. As is usually the case everywhere, a craven, corrupt intellectual class was unwilling to sound the alarm that war crimes were being committed, accustomed as they were under communism to being servants to power.

The belief in the independence of intellectuals, as so much of the twentieth century proves, is nothing but a fairy tale. The most repellent crimes in the former Yugoslavia had the enthusiastic support of people whose education and past accomplishments would lead one to believe that they would know better. Even poets of large talent and reputation found something to praise in the destruction of cities. If they wept, it was only for their own kind. Not once did they bother to stop and imagine the cost of these wars, which their leaders had instigated, for everybody else.

Many of my compatriots were upset with me. Serbs always imagine elaborate conspiracies. For them every event is a sham behind which some hidden interest operates. The idea that my views were my own, the product of my sleepless nights and torments of my conscience, was unthinkable. There were innuendoes about my family, hints that for years there had been suspicions about us, that we were foreigners who had managed for centuries to pass themselves off as Serbs.

My favorite one was that the CIA had paid me huge amounts of money to write poems against Serbia, so that I now live a life of leisure in a mansion in New Hampshire attended by numerous black servants.

Incapable of either statecraft or a formulation of legitimate national interest, Milosevic and his followers could only fan the flames of hatred and set neighbor against neighbor. We now know that all the supposedly spontaneous, patriotic military outfits that went to defend Serbs in Croatia and Bosnia were organized, armed, and controlled by his secret services.

There is nothing more disheartening than to watch, year after year, cities and villages destroyed, people killed or sent into exile, knowing that their suffering did not have to happen. Once newspapers and weekly magazines became available on the Internet, I'd rise early every morning to read them and inevitably fall into the darkest despair by eight o'clock.

Serbs often say in their defense that they were not the only ones committing war crimes. Of course not. If everyone else were an angel, there would not be several hundred thousand refugees in Serbia today. Nonetheless, it is with the murderers in one's own family that one has the moral obligation to deal first.

This, as I discovered, was not how a patriot was supposed to feel. The role of the intellectual was to make excuses for the killers of women and children. As for journalists and political commentators, their function was to spread lies and then prove that these lies were true. What instantly became clear to me is that I was being asked by my own people to become an accomplice in a crime by pretending to understand and forgive acts that I knew were unforgivable.

It's not just Serbs who make such demands, of course. It is not much better in America today, but that, too, is not an excuse. The unwillingness to confront the past has made Serbia a backpedaling society, unable to look at the present, much less deal with difficult contemporary problems. It's like a family that sits around the dinner table each evening pretending that Granny had not stabbed the mailman with scissors and Dad had not tried to rape one of his little girls in the bathroom just this afternoon.

The worst thing is to be right about one's own kind. For that you are never forgiven. Better to be wrong a hundred times! They'll explain it later by saying that you loved your people so much. Among the nationalists, we are more likely to be admired if we had been photographed slashing the throat of a child than marching against some war they had fought and lost.

When I went back to Belgrade in 1972, after an absence of almost twenty years, I discovered that the window above the entrance of our apartment building, through which I had kicked a ball after the war, was still broken. In 1982, it was still not repaired. Last fall, when I returned, I discovered it had been fixed after the NATO bombing, which hit the TV studio close by and broke lots of windows in the neighborhood.

The reason it was not repaired earlier is that all the tenants in the building had quarreled and were not on speaking terms. My late aunt did not acknowledge the existence of some of her neighbors for forty years, so it was unthinkable that she would knock on their doors for the sake of a window or many other things that needed to be done. That, to my mind, is pretty much the story of Serbs and Serbia—or so I intend to tell my great-uncle, whom I still hope to run into one of these days.

He'll be more than one hundred years old, sitting in a rocking chair at a nursing home in rural Alabama, deaf and nearly blind, wearing a straw hat and a string tie over a Hawaiian shirt, but still looking like a Serb despite all the guises he devised in his long life to not look like one. From time to time, he mutters some words in that strange language which his nurses take to be just old man's private gibberish.

READING ABOUT UTOPIA IN NEW YORK CITY

It's odd enough in this day and age to read about utopia; what's even stranger is to be doing it in a city like New York with its mad bustle. Hundreds of thousands of people turn up every morning to work in Manhattan out of surrounding boroughs, suburbs and the adjoining states of New Jersey and Connecticut. The traffic is backed up for miles. They pour out of subways and train stations. They take buses and taxis. Some walk over bridges. Hundreds wait at every intersection for the lights to change. Each person has his or her own routine, and they are all in a hurry. Even crossing the street they sip coffee out of paper cups and shout into their cell phones. No one has time to look at anyone else. The energy and purposefulness are breathtaking. Crowds can be oppressive, but not here. What Whitman said in a poem, "A Broadway Pageant," a hundred and fifty years ago about the whole world being here side by side is still true.

> The countries there with their populations, the millions
>   en-masse are curiously here,
> The swarming market-places, the temples with idols ranged
>   along the sides or at the end, bonze, Brahmin, and llama,
> Mandarin, farmer, merchant, mechanic, and fisherman,
> The singing-girl and the dancing-girl, the ecstatic persons,
>   the secluded emperors,

First appeared in *The Gettysberg Review* (2006).

Confucius himself, the great poets and heroes, the
    warriors, the castes, all,
Trooping up, crowding from all directions, from the
    Altay mountains,
From Thibet, from four winding and far-flowing rivers
    of China,
From the southern peninsulas and the demi-continental
    islands, from Malaysia,
These and whatever belongs to them palpable show
    forth to me, and are seiz'd by me.
And I am seiz'd by them, and friendlily held by them,
Till as here them all I chant, Libertad! for themselves
    and for you

In the midst of it all, borne by the crowd, wonderfully anonymous, here I was, lugging day after day a hefty book called *Utopian Thought in the Western World*. It was one of those works that by its sheer size and intellectual ambition gave one the feeling that an insight, guaranteed to change one's life forever, lay in wait somewhere among its 814 pages. I'd stop to buy bread still thinking about Campanella and Saint Simon, sit in a coffee shop over a third cup of coffee reading Kropotkin, or I'd make myself comfortable on the 19th floor balcony of my son's midtown apartment surrounded by a cluster of even taller buildings and try to make sense of Robert Owen:

World history past, present, and future was divisible into
two segments, one in which irrationality, even insanity,
characterized virtually all human relationships, and one whose
moment has just come in which rationality would predominate.
The whole past and most present behavior were blind to reason
in action, because men were steeped in error and were bound
by false association of ideas. Minor errors of perception and
superstitious beliefs were malignant, but one Great Error held

mankind in thrall, and this was the religious falsehood that
an individual of his own free will could choose to perform
acts that were either good or evil. In fact, man had no such
liberty. He was born into a specific environment in which evil
influences were compelling, he was reared to accept lies, and
he lived his life subject to erroneous ideas. As a consequence,
the creature was blindly selfish, cruel, lying, hypocritical,
addicted to vices, criminal, generating his own unhappiness.
Societies and religions fixed blame upon the individual for his
acts, whereas in truth he was blameless, merely a product of
circumstances and iniquitous arrangements

Owen's wish to correct once and for all the accumulated errors of
our irrational ancestors may sound laughable today. Not to me. I did
not subscribe, of course, to his notion that even my choice in reading
him on this hot afternoon was not an act of free will, but I liked the
way it made my life into a Borges story. I was also curious to find out
what further mental and moral maladies and their remedies lay in store
on the very next page. Unfortunately, I could not pay full attention to
what I was reading. One would assume that sitting on the 19th floor
balcony with the blue sky over my head would make for a peaceful
environment—but no. The sound of traffic was even louder up here.
Fire engines, police cars, ambulances rushed by seemingly every few
minutes. Park Avenue was so jammed, the vehicles barely moved so
they kept honking their horns out of anger and frustration while I sat
pondering some passionate declaration of his. Perhaps, the ideal place
to read about utopias is on a mountain in Montana? The farther from
humanity the better. There's nothing like vast empty spaces to give one
the illusion that everything is possible. In the present circumstances,
every idealistic pronouncement in the book had the noise of the streets
to contend with. The high buildings closing around me were like stage
sets, their reality verging on unreality, but I had no idea what play I
was in. Was it a tragedy or a low farce? Come to think of it, didn't

Owen just inform me that I was a mere puppet being pulled by thousands of invisible strings?

America, of course, is one of the grand utopias. Pilgrim Fathers set out to find a New Eden in the wilderness and thought that they had found it. To this day the gist of our public oratory is that we live in the greatest country in the world where things will continue to get better and better till Kingdom come. A few backcountry preachers still shout from their pulpits that we are all going to hell soon, but their voices are not very loud. Except for the usual windbags in Congress and their cheerleaders on the editorial pages of newspapers with their nuthouse optimism, there's more anxiety than confidence in the future among the general population. The promise that despite an occasional setback, that we are moving forward, that eventually we'll all be healthier, kinder and richer has pretty much ceased to be entertained as a serious possibility by most of us. The fulfillment of the American Dream seemed just around the corner, and then all of a sudden it wasn't there anymore. I suspect the only unwavering and maniacal utopia builders still at large are to be found among religious fundamentalists, nationalists and aficionados of gadgets of mass destruction. According to one of our supermarket tabloids, the Pentagon is secretly building the world's largest nuclear weapon and making plans to destroy Hell.

Were our ancestors who came down from the trees already utopians? I wouldn't be surprised if they were. They dreamt about someday returning to live in the trees. Joking aside, I bet it didn't take long for human beings to start imagining a place and a time where there's no strife. The seemingly inexhaustible human capacity for evil was the spur to such reveries. Innocents suffer and justice is rare is the story of history in a nutshell. Newspapers and television remind us of that every morning. Utopia's function is to protect life from the darkest despair. Long before philosophers such as Plato got into the act, there must've been many private visions of how to reorder the world. If one did the unthinkable and disagreed with whoever was in charge of the official metaphysics, one could expect nothing but exquisite torture and violent death for the offense of imagining a different future.

The great proliferation of utopias, as we know, comes in the wake of French and American Revolutions, Rousseau and the Romantics, *The Declaration of the Rights of Man* and the new models of egalitarian society. Previously, utopian projects were disguised as fictional narratives rather than proclaimed openly in revolutionary pamphlets and manifestos. Explorers, missionaries, curious travelers and shipwrecked sailors—or so the convention of imaginary utopias went—discovered or believed they had discovered, in the countries where they had landed, the ideal models of society. Utopias in the 19th century took a different approach; they now preached progress, not just that things ought to be different, but that it was inevitable that they *shall* be different. "A man as he ought to be," Nietzsche sneered, "that sounds to us as insipid as a tree as it ought to be." Previously, it was God who was in charge of the future, now it was man with his newfound analytic powers. The self-proclaimed prophets assumed that human nature was malleable and any contrary evidence that men are fond of their vices was ignored. The impious, thieving, copulating and murderous humanity—if its existence was ever so much as admitted—was to be collectively reeducated. Utopia was detached from reality in the groundless belief that the tug-of-war of conflicting desires can be stamped out. The meaning of life itself was to be fixed permanently and beyond further discussion. Here then was a project that recognized no human limits. It seemed that once one understood the few basic laws of human nature or history, it was possible to engineer souls so that for the sake of common good their reason will become the permanent enemy of their passions.

A utopian version of the history of mankind began with an obligatory age of innocence, followed by a long period of decadence and concluded with a gradual attainment of a state of terrestrial bliss. Since healthy society was assumed to be a return to what is natural, countless thinkers attempted to postulate what that simpler, purer and more loving human being would be like. No aspect of an individual's life no matter how personal was to be left to chance. Everything from sex to diet would be planned down to its minutest detail. Charles Fourier, for example, in the belief that one must spell out what natural drives are being frustrated and curtailed in human beings, wanted every woman to have a husband with whom she could conceive two children; after that there's to be a "breeder" with whom she could have only one child; then a lover and last, "possessors," men at random she could have a quick roll in the hay with. I remember telling that to a couple of women in New York as we sipped wine and sucked freshly shucked oysters in a bar on Second Avenue. They thought it was the funniest thing they ever heard. Then, after a brief reflection, they concluded that the universal debaucheries Fourier promised seemed more trouble than what they were worth.

By the end of the 19th century, one could take a pick among utopias to suit one's most fastidious moral and aesthetic taste. Does one prefer a life passed sighing at the feet of a pretty shepherdess, or would one like to lie on the floor covered in blood in one of the Marquis de Sade's sexual torture chambers? Even poets had their own versions of eternal bliss. On one hand, there was the democratic vision of Emerson and Whitman where every man, woman and child was already a poet, and on the other hand, there were the followers of Mallarmé, the art-for-art's-sake types who scribbled hermetic verses for a few initiates when they were not just staring at a blank page. For the painters, it was a white canvas in whose whiteness the sophisticated gallery viewer could recall the entire history of painting. Among the composers there was Alexander Scriabin with his unfinished masterpiece *Mysterium* which was supposed to bring about nothing less than the annihilation of the universe, and our own John Cage who thought that there's nothing more beautiful musically than silence.

Of course, while every progressive thinker was concocting their own utopias there were still the so-called savages in remote corners of the earth who already lived in paradise, or complete moral degradation—depending on your view. Visitors to Tahiti spoke of beautiful naked maidens who clambered aboard their ships driving the young sailors mad with lust. The sight of a gentle landscape and the profusion of Venuses, produced a philosophical dilemma. Is man in the state of nature a brute or the model of a good life we lost when we became civilized? The thinkers who idealized primitive societies remind me of the gullible visitors to the Soviet Union in the days of Stalin who returned home extolling the unparalleled freedoms the citizens there enjoyed. Neither was the idyllic picture true of Tahitian society, which it turns out was made up of two distinct classes of people, the ones on top exercising the powers of life and death over their less fortunate compatriots.

Nevertheless, there are still some in the U.S. today who believe we can reclaim the pastoral life, reacquire the wisdom of Native Americans and live happily ever after. It's not clear what will happen to the cities like New York, but they expect them somehow to disappear. These are the present-day descendants of a long line of utopian communities in the New World. In the 19th century, many followers of Fourier, Owen, or some other secular or religious prophet withdrew into wilderness where they could put their ideas into practice in peace and quiet. Except for the Mormons, the Amish and a few remaining Shakers, most of these communities did not last for very long. Envy, greed, ambition cropped up in no time, especially among the young. Reformers of humanity remind me of idealistic wardens of penal institutions who are convinced that hardened criminals can be reeducated. Personally, I'd sooner believe a tiger could become vegetarian than masses of human beings turn selfless.

When it comes to utopia, the delicious anarchy of the cities always has the last word. It's a hot and steamy night in New York. Bars and restaurants are full. A crowd of young people has spilled into the streets all along Park Avenue South. They are half-naked, glistening with sweat and more than a little drunk. There's music, laughter, dancing on the sidewalks and enough smooching in public to make every defender of decency tear their hair out. Can there be joy without disorder? No way. It made me recall something the late Brendan Gill once wrote somewhere:

> Not a shred of evidence exists in favor of the argument that life is serious, though it is often hard and often terrible. And saying that, I'm prompted to add what follows out of it: that since everything ends badly for us, in the inescapable catastrophe of death, it seems obvious that the first rule of life is to have a good time.

These young people knew that. Even the old taking their panting dogs out for a late walk seemed to approve. On a night like this every political, philosophical and aesthetic idea the society holds dear is being subverted and revised for anyone who has his or her eyes open. There's no general theory of happiness, every face I met proclaimed, and if there is, it is here in this large crowd of strangers of every race and ethnicity partying late into the night. Democracy is the only version of utopia that takes the defects of human nature into consideration. That's what makes it so unattractive to many thinkers. The United States is a democratic country some of whose leading intellects are suspicious of democracy. They want religion back, authority, militarism and uniformity of opinion, in short, all the delights of a premodern society, which the Constitution and decades of moral laxity abolished. "Never forget that the iron law of oligarchy always obtains; a few people will always run everything, no matter what the institution or what the country," James Madison, one of our Founding Fathers observed. That was always the secret hope, I guess. Still, despite its faults and hypocrisies, the democratic ideal is at least free of the myth of the perfectibility of man. It's that rejection of one and only one truth that exasperates lovers of authority everywhere. Democracy at its best protects our private idiosyncra-

sies against various collectivist Shangri-las, which are never in short
supply.

Poetry, too, is the defense of the individual against all generalizations that seek to enclose reality in a single conceptual system. In
that sense it is anti-utopian. Its core belief is that we can reach truth
through the imagination. It has no trust in abstractions, but proceeds
empirically by concrete particulars. In a lyric poem, another consciousness lives on in us as we recognize oneself in some stranger's
words. For some solitary reader, a book from another place and time
miraculously comes to life. A young man in a West Side tenement
reads an ancient Chinese poet in a book he borrowed from the library
earlier that day and falls in love with a poem, which he reads to himself over and over again as the summer night is ending. No utopian
project can hold a candle to that, as far as I'm concerned. No prophet
is interested in what happens next, but I am. He puts the book down
and steps to the window. It's still hot. The street is empty and silent at
this hour except for the faint hum of the air conditioners somewhere.
The parked cars have the air of being abandoned, as if they were all
stolen years ago and ditched here on this block. A single seagull walks
on the opposite sidewalk past a funeral home nodding as if he can see
someone inside. He appears delighted with himself, happy to be what
he is and not something else. If New York City is not already heaven,
then I don't know what is.

SALVATION THROUGH LAUGHTER

Polish Memories
by Witold Gombrowicz, translated from the Polish by Bill Johnston

Bacacay
by Witold Gombrowicz, translated from the Polish by Bill Johnston

Ferdydurke
by Witold Gombrowicz, translated from the Polish by Danuta Borchardt, with a foreword by Susan Sontag

Cosmos
by Witold Gombrowicz, translated from the Polish by Danuta Borchardt

A Guide to Philosophy in Six Hours and Fifteen Minutes
by Witold Gombrowicz, translated from the Polish by Benjamin Ivry

The World of Witold Gombrowicz, 1904–1969
by Vincent Girond

Catalog of a centenary exhibition at the Beinecke Rare Book and Manuscript Library, Yale University Beinecke Library/University Press of New England

1.

For the celebration of the centenary of his birth in Poland, the Ministry of Culture officially proclaimed 2004 "The Year of Gombrowicz," and Yale University organized an international conference that fea-

First appeared in the *New York Review of Books* (2006).

tured an exhibition of Gombrowicz materials in the Beinecke Library archives, as well as academic panels, films, and theater performances of his works. Despite these shows of deference, the translation of his books into more than thirty languages, and wide readership abroad, in the United States Gombrowicz is mainly known among writers. Susan Sontag and John Updike see him as an influential figure in modern literature, comparable to Proust and Joyce. I'm not sure if that would have pleased Gombrowicz, who had an entirely different idea of the kind of fame he wanted for himself. He in no way wanted to be compared, he said, to the Tolstoy of Yasnaya Polyana, the Goethe of Olympus, or the Thomas Mann who linked genius to decadence, and he had no use for Alfred Jarry's metaphysical dandyism or Anatole France's affected mastery. He claimed that he didn't even wish to be known as a Polish writer, but simply as Gombrowicz.

Born in 1904 on his parents' provincial estate in the town of Maloszyce in central Poland, Gombrowicz was an introverted, sickly child who said he preferred the company of maids and stable boys. He was raised a Catholic. The experience of World War I in Maloszyce, which was close to the Austrian border, made him a lifelong pacifist and an atheist. To make his lawyer father happy, he studied law at the University of Warsaw from 1923 to 1926 and then philosophy and economics in Paris. However, since he didn't bother to attend classes, his father cut off his allowance after two years and made him return to Poland where he worked for a time as a clerk in a municipal court while on the sly he began to write short stories. Although he had no interest in becoming a lawyer, he later said that he learned about the wretchedness of life in general and Polish life in particular while working for the court. He also took a close look at the upper spheres called upon to pass judgment on the lower ones—judges, prosecutors, and lawyers. When not in court, he frequented literary cafés where he began to acquire a reputation as a character, taking potshots at his contemporaries. His humor and impudence stood out.

By his own admission, associating with him was always rather difficult, because as a rule he aimed at debate and conflict, leading the discussion in such a way as to make it risky, unpleasant, embarrassing, and indiscreet. He was not a typical intellectual of the period in that he was not a nationalist, a Catholic, or a Communist. "I was a man of the cafés; I loved to spout nonsense for hours on end over black coffee and to indulge in various kinds of psychological games," he writes in *Polish Memories*. He made fun of literature too. The mental exertion of a waiter, who has to remember orders from five tables and not make a mistake, at the same time hurrying about with plates, bottles, sauces, and salads, seemed to him infinitely greater than the exertions of an author trying to arrange the different subtle threads of his plots. Gombrowicz said that whenever he encountered some mystification, be it of virtue or family, faith or fatherland, he was tempted to commit an indecent act. He called Polish culture a flower pinned to a peasant's sheepskin coat:

> The history of culture indicates that stupidity is the twin sister of reason, it grows most luxuriously not on the soil of virgin ignorance, but on soil cultivated by the sweat of doctors and professors. Great absurdities are not thought up by those whose reason hovers over daily affairs. It is not strange, therefore, that the most intense thinkers were the producers of the greatest idiocies.[1]

Gombrowicz claimed to loathe poetry. "Of all artists, poets are people who fall to their knees most persistently," he said. When visiting museums, he spent little time looking at paintings. He found the faces of people admiring the pictures far more interesting. "In the picture is beauty; in front of the picture is snobbery, stupidity, a dull-witted effort to grasp something of the beauty about which one is told that it exists." Life is always laughing at art, he said, always undermining its pretenses. He mocked all systems of thought that attempt to separate the spiritual from the physical, the fantastic from the real. His greatest pride as an artist was not his inhabiting the Kingdom of the Spirit, but his not having broken the relationship with the flesh. Years later, writing about existentialism, he had this to say:

> It seems impossible to meet the demands of Dasein and simultaneously have coffee and croissants for an evening snack. To fear nothingness, but to fear the dentist more. To be consciousness, which walks around in pants and talks on the telephone. To be responsibility, which runs little shopping errands downtown. To bear the weight of significant being, to install the world with meaning and then return the change from ten pesos.

His first book, a collection of seven stories, *Memoirs of a Time of Immaturity*, came out in 1933. The reviews were bad. The critics found the stories farcically implausible and ridiculed their author who seemed to take pride in acting immaturely. Actually, some of the stories are a lot of fun. A young fellow becomes obsessed with the dignified manners of an attorney and does everything he can to undermine that dignity by paying in advance for the pastries the attorney buys every day and tipping the attendant of a public restroom he uses. An investigative magistrate who finds no sign of foul play in a death of a man makes the argument, which prosecutors in Stalin's trials would have understood, that one must never be taken in by appearances and thus allow common sense to show the innocence of the criminal.

In the most outrageous story of all, the guests at an aristocratic vegetarian dinner party enjoy a cauliflower dish made, it turns out, with broth from a cooked peasant boy who perished from hunger. The stories read mostly like literary parodies. Their translator, Bill Johnston, compares them to Luis Buñuel's films and to Monty Python sketches. I agree, and would add Gogol and Alfred Jarry to his list. In *Polish Memories*, Gombrowicz wrote:

> One thing I do remember—that from the beginning the nonsensical and the absurd were very much to my liking, and I was

never more satisfied than when my pen gave birth to some scene
that was truly crazy, removed from the (healthy) expectations of
mediocre logic, and yet firmly rooted in its own separate logic.

Gombrowicz's heroes are not only torn between social expectations
which demand of them that they behave according to a given set of rules
and their "immaturity" (their wish to do as they please), but they also
seem to be struggling to free themselves of the literary conventions of the
plots they find themselves in. As Gombrowicz says in his memoir of this
period, his purpose was to introduce a new kind of disquiet in the reader.
What he wanted most of all was a distinct style as a writer. His purpose
in life, he said, was to make a character like Hamlet or Don Quixote out
of a man called Gombrowicz. We exist as writers, he believed, in order
to win readers to our side, to seduce, charm, and possess them, not in the
name of some higher purpose, but to assert our very existence.

His first novel, *Ferdydurke,* was published in 1937. The enigmatic
title was appropriated from Sinclair Lewis's novel *Babbitt* in which a
character mentions running into a certain Freddy Durkee in a restaurant. Gombrowicz's book owes something to both Rabelais and Vol-
taire, the comic novel tradition and the philosophical tale. It pursues
with vengeance the same theme of immaturity and youth. A thirty-
year-old man is visited by his old schoolmaster and dragged back to
school where he is reduced to being a child again and where he finds
it nearly impossible to break free. The narrative is twice interrupted
to include short stories that have little to do with the plot, each one
with a very funny preface that attempts to clarify, substantiate, ratio-
nalize, and explain the many digressions and convince the reader that
the author has not gone crazy. Not many reviewers got the joke. Both
the extreme left and the extreme right attacked the novel. There were
a few enthusiastic responses, among them that of Bruno Schulz, who
designed the cover. Vincent Girond writes that for Schulz, *Ferdydurke*
convincingly demonstrates that beneath our "official" selves, adult,
rational, socialized, respectable, cultivated, there remain elements of

immaturity, irrationality, anarchy, roguishness, which try to come to the surface and, when they do, expose the inauthenticity of established customs, manners, beliefs, ideologies, and culture.

That is not a new idea, of course. Gombrowicz's most obvious literary ancestor is the nameless narrator of Dostoevsky's *Notes from Underground* who sets out to expose his own vileness and pettiness and assault the comforting fairy tale about rational human beings that his contemporaries never get tired of hearing.

One month before the outbreak of World War II, Gombrowicz was invited to be a guest on the maiden voyage of a new Polish ocean liner bound for Argentina. It arrived in Buenos Aires on August 22, 1939, days before the Soviet Union signed a pact of non-aggression with Germany and a little more than a week before Germany invaded Poland. With the threat of war imminent, the ship was ordered to sail back to Poland immediately. At the last minute, Gombrowicz decided to disembark, an act that would have huge consequences for his life as a writer:

> I was suddenly in Argentina, completely alone, cut off, lost, ruined, anonymous. I was a little excited, a little frightened. Yet at the same time, something in me told me to greet with passionate emotion the blow that was destroying me and upsetting the order I had known up to now. War? The destruction of Poland? The fate of those close to me, my family? My own destiny? Could I take this to heart in a way, how shall I say this, in a normal way, I, who knew all this from the beginning, who had already known this? Yes, I am not lying when I say that I had been living with catastrophe. When it happened, I said something to myself like: Ah, so it has finally happened and I understood the time had come to take advantage of the capacity that I had cultivated in myself to separate and leave.

Gombrowicz had no money and no knowledge of Spanish. A complete unknown, he was of little interest to Argentine writers who were either drawn to Marxism and demanded a political literature or followed the trends of the Parisian literati. He met Borges once at a dinner party, but nothing came of it. His relationship to the large Polish community was also complicated. He depended on handouts from them during the difficult years, even going so far as to attend funerals in order to help himself to the food afterward.

At the same time, he did not fail to scandalize their conservative tastes. As he reports in his diary, he entered for a period a milieu of extreme, wild homosexuality. "They were *putos* at the boiling point, not knowing a moment's rest, in constant pursuit, 'torn to pieces by boys as by dogs.'" He frequented a seedy part of town where the harbor and the main train station were located and where he picked up sailors and soldiers. When not engaged in his amorous pursuits, he tried to find someone to translate his books into Spanish. His economic situation improved considerably when he found a job in the Banco Polaco in Buenos Aires where he worked between 1947 and 1955. Altogether, he spent twenty-three years in Argentina and grew to love the country and its people very much. He had his own intimate circle of admiring younger writers.

2.

The books he had written in Poland were no longer in print there and they were unknown abroad. His most important works, the novels *Trans-Atlantyk* (1952), *Pornografia* (1960), the play *The Marriage* (1947), and the three-volume *Diary* (1953–1967), were written in Argentina and were first published by the Polish émigré review *Kultura* in Paris. The Communist regïme in Poland briefly lifted the ban on his books in 1956 and 1957, which restored his literary prestige, but a new blacklist in 1958 removed his work from Polish bookstores. Eventually, the first translations of his work began to appear in French, followed by those in other languages. Ludicrously, the translations of his novels into English were not at first made from Polish, but from French, making him sound frequently like a painfully awkward writer.

Not that Gombrowicz is easy to translate. His semiautobiographical and satiric novel *Trans-Atlantyk*, which recounts his early years in Argentina, is composed in the strangely imagistic language the Polish nobility used in the eighteenth century. For Stanislaw Baranczak and other eminent Polish critics, this is one of the funniest and most original works in their literature, but an English reader can barely glimpse that from the translation we now have:

> But when night with its mantilla the earth embraced, and large glowing Worms under the Trees, when from the Darkness of the park sounds of divers animals, and thus this Mewing Bark, or Grunting Snort, that quietness, that listlessness of mine with Unquietness began to fill. And methinks, how is't that you do not fear when you ought to Fear?[2]

Gombrowicz's other novel from that period, *Pornografia*, poses different kinds of problems. The action takes place in 1943 in occupied Poland, which Gombrowicz could only imagine from the information that reached him in Argentina. A theater director and a writer from Warsaw visiting a country estate become entranced by the adolescent sensuality of both their host's teenage daughter and a local lad she knows. It was really unbelievable, the writer says, that nothing was going on between them—nothing, that is, but the pornography in his own mind. Unknown to the young people, the two older men connive to make them fall in love with each other. Eventually, the adults find themselves obliged to kill an important member of the local resistance who has lost his nerve and might, if captured, betray the cause. Incapable of committing the crime themselves, they entrust the murder to the boy, Frederick. This is how Gombrowicz explains his intentions in the introduction to the book:

The hero of the novel, Frederick, is a Christopher Columbus who departs in search of unknown continents. What is
he searching for? This new beauty, this new poetry, hidden between the adult and the young man. He is the poet of
an awareness carried to the extreme or, at least, that's how I
wanted him to be. But it is difficult to understand one another
nowadays! Certain critics saw him as Satan, no more, no less,
while others, mainly Anglo-Saxons, were content with a more
trivial definition—a voyeur. My Frederick is neither Satan nor
a voyeur: he is more like a theatrical producer, or even a chem-
ist, trying to obtain a new and magical alcohol by various combinations between individuals.[3]

This doesn't sound persuasive to me. For once, Gombrowicz
doesn't seem to fully grasp the implication of his own story. *Pornografia* is not a comic opera—even though at times it tries to be one. The
murderous reality of wartime Poland gives even its lighter moments a
somber quality. There's madness and violence in the air. "I am Christ
crucified on a sixteen-year-old cross," Frederick says. Gombrowicz
strives in all his novels to implicate the reader, have him admit that he,
too, is a voyeur with homoerotic feelings.

Pornografia is finally an implausible novel with many pages of fine
writing. The description of a village church service at the very beginning has great power, and so do a few other scenes in the book. At the
church, Frederick, a nonbeliever for whom the church was the "worst
place in the world," nevertheless falls to his knees and prays, for him "a
negative act, the very act of negation":

> What exactly had happened? Strictly speaking: nothing, strictly
> speaking it was as though a hand had withdrawn the substance
> and content from the Mass—and the priest continued—and the
> priest continued to move, to kneel, to go from one end of the
> altar to the other, and the acolytes rang the bells and the smoke

from the censers rose in spirals, but the whole content was evaporating like gas out of a balloon, and the Mass collapsed in its appalling impotence—limp and sagging—unable to procreate!

Gombrowicz's three-volume *Diary* is one of the indispensable literary works of the last century. Polemical, witty, immensely entertaining, genuinely moving, and often profound, the diaries are, in the view of such readers as Czeslaw Milosz, Gombrowicz's greatest accomplishment. Unlike his novels, which in their fixation on youth tend to be repetitive, the diaries range widely in subject matter. He writes about his life in Argentina, speculates about literature and philosophy, settles accounts with writers, quarrels with Polish nationalism, and in the process describes many amusing incidents. If given a choice, Gombrowicz said, he'd rather stare than think—and, indeed, that's what he usually does in the diaries, first stares and then thinks. Coming upon marching soldiers interrupting the Sunday stroll of local citizens in a small provincial town in Argentina, he comments:

> An invasion of pinioned legs, and bodies, inserted into uniforms, slave bodies, welded together by the command to move. Ha, ha, ha, ha, gentlemen humanists, democrats, socialists! Why, the entire social order, all systems, authority, law, state and government, institutions, everything is based on these slaves, barely grown children, taken by the ear, forced to pledge blind obedience (O priceless hypocrisy of this mandatory-voluntary pledge) and trained to kill and to allow themselves to be killed. . . . All systems, socialist or capitalist, are founded on enslavement, and, to top it off, on the enslavement of the young, my dear gentlemen rationalists, humanists, ha, ha, ha, my dear gentlemen democrats!

A Ford Foundation grant in 1963 permitted Gombrowicz to leave Argentina and spend a year in Berlin. Suffering from asthma, he moved to Vence in the south of France, where he lived for the five remaining years of his life. He never visited Poland or returned to Argentina, which he greatly missed. In 1967 he received the prestigious International Prize for Literature for his fourth novel, *Cosmos*. Toward the end, he was reduced to near speechlessness by asthma, which had also affected his heart. Though he survived a heart attack, and even married shortly after, a second attack took his life on July 24, 1969. Three years earlier he had written in his diary:

> No matter what we are told, there exists, in the entire expanse of the Universe, throughout the whole space of Being, one and only one awful, impossible, unacceptable element, one and only one thing that is truly and absolutely against us and absolutely devastating: pain. It is on pain and on nothing else that the entire dynamic of existence depends. Remove pain and the world become[s] a matter of complete indifference. . . .

3.

During the last five years, five new translations of Gombrowicz have appeared in the United States. There is *Bacacay*, an expanded collection of his first book of stories. *Polish Memories*, a series of autobiographical sketches that he wrote for Radio Free Europe in the late 1950s, tells of his childhood, his beginnings as a writer, and gives a lively description of literary life in Poland between the wars. Both are translated by Bill Johnston and very much worth reading. There is also *A Guide to Philosophy*, a work he dictated in the last year of his life, and which is based on the short course in philosophy that he used to give to a group of Polish women in Buenos Aires. Despite its catchy title and a few memorable quips, the book is too fragmentary to give a coherent view. The fullest discussions of Gombrowicz's philosophical views are still to be found in the pages of the three volumes of his *Diary*.

In addition to these books, there are new translations of Gombrowicz's first novel, *Ferdydurke*, and of his last one, *Cosmos*, by Danuta Borchardt. They are by far the best of his fiction, although I find it impossible to like *Ferdydurke* entirely. The problem with novels of ideas is that a single theme—here the irrational, anarchic reality buried beneath the conventional surface of life—can become insistent. Even Gombrowicz's best comic scenes, and there are some great ones in the book, go on too long. *Cosmos*, published in 1965, is a far better novel in my view. It may remind the reader of Alain Robbe-Grillet's *The Voyeur* (1955) and *Jealousy* (1957) with their claustrophobic settings, nearly plotless narratives, obsessive attention to minute details, and their air of menace, with one important exception. Gombrowicz, even at his most cerebral, is a comic writer whose jokes and wordplay are more akin to Flann O'Brien's novels than to a *nouveau roman*.

Cosmos is a story of two young men who spend their vacation in a pension run by an eccentric family in the Carpathian Mountains. They find a hanged bird in a bush and, spooked by the finding, begin to note further oddities in their surroundings, minor inexplicable events and portents. "Oh, the wild power of feeble thought!" the narrator in the novel exclaims. Nothing would have happened if the two young men weren't so bored on their holiday. One of them, upset by their inability to solve the mystery, perversely hangs the household cat. Some human deeds, Gombrowicz was convinced, seem wholly senseless, but still we have to perform them because they define us. He gives as an example a man who is prepared, for no apparent reason, to commit the wildest follies so as not to feel a coward. *Cosmos*, which Gombrowicz called a novel about a reality that is creating itself, ends with one more mysterious hanging, this time of a minor character who commits suicide during an excursion in the mountains. The plot, such as it is, is being mocked for seeming to be a plot, but all the characters in the novel are so well drawn that the most unlikely actions become credible.

"When you're bored, God only knows what you might imagine," Gombrowicz says. The young men in the novel are preoccupied with finding a meaning where there seems to be none. Meaning for Gombrowicz is what we, children of chaos, sons of darkness and blind coincidence, are forever trying to impose on the world around us:

> The most important, most extreme, and most incurable dispute is that waged in us by two of our most basic strivings: the one that desires form, shape, definition and the other, which protests against shape, and does not want form. Humanity is constructed in such a way that it must define itself and then escape its own definitions. Reality is not something that allows itself to be completely contained in form. Form is not in harmony with the essence of life, but all thought which tries to describe this imperfection also becomes form and thereby confirms only our striving for it. That entire philosophical and ethical dialectic of ours takes place against the background of an immensity, which is called shapelessness, which is neither darkness nor light, but exactly a mixture of everything: ferment, disorder, impurity, and accident.

Gombrowicz's philosophy centers on the ever-present conflict between the individual and the world in which he finds himself. Culture for him has little to do with values, truths, examples, and models, and should be seen as a set of conventions, a collection of stereotypes and roles, both social and psychological; we need them all in order to communicate with each other while our inner being remains chaotic, unexpressed, and incomprehensible. He saw literature as moral, intellectual, and ideological provocation. He wanted to perturb the reader and charm him at the same time. "Real art," he wrote, "is to manage to get someone to read what you write."

It's interesting to compare these views with those of Czeslaw Milosz, whose essays and letters from occupied Poland have just been translated. His *Legends of Modernity* is a wise book.[4] Reading it, I kept recalling the circumstances in which he wrote these thoughtful essays on Defoe, Balzac, Stendhal, Gide, Tolstoy, William James, his Wilno professor Marian Zdziechowski, and the Polish playwright, novelist, and philosopher Stanislaw Ignacy Witkiewicz. For Milosz, the horrors in which European civilization found itself were prepared by the long labor of charlatans of thought, appeasers of conscience, who draped the cloak of beauty or progress around the most nihilistic and destructive intellectual currents that did away with traditional understanding of good and evil. "The delicate hands of intellectuals are stained with blood from the moment a death-bearing word emerges from them," he writes in his essay on Gide. Milosz is suspicious of ideas that seek to realize the happiness of mankind and that in the process release the repressed "free will," the unconscious and other demons and phantoms lurking within the human mind. For him the sickness of contemporary culture derives from the repudiation of truth for the sake of action. Nietzsche and his many descendants were the main culprits. Even William James's pragmatism, which Milosz sees as a victory of relative values over absolute values, is to be condemned. Milosz sensed the demonic element in human nature. So did Gombrowicz, but for him boredom was just as much the cause of the evil we do as a head full of wrong ideas.

For Milosz, the past was neither dead nor irrelevant, but a part of ourselves that we need to remember, understand, and respect. He admitted being hostile to the "dark" tradition in twentieth-century literature. Its mockery, sarcasm, and profanation seemed cheap to him when compared with the power of Evil that we have experienced in our lifetime; he could be scathing, telling a friend in a letter, for instance, that people can get along quite well without freedom of thought. He said of Gombrowicz,

> Whenever he plays destroyer and ironist, he joins the company of writers who for decades have been letting their ears freeze just to spite their mommies, even as mommy—read the cosmos—ignored their tantrums.[5]

Milosz admired Gombrowicz's prose and his originality, but in the end his atheism and his savage blasphemies were too much for him.

Gombrowicz, not surprisingly, saw it differently. It never bothered him that we may be living in a meaningless universe. To pretend otherwise was to run away from the truth. He had no need of religion or God to make him sleep better. Being true to one's deepest convictions was a matter of keeping up one's dignity. Art for him was the most private property man had ever achieved for himself. Without it we would have no way of knowing what a person really thinks or feels. In contrast to the philosopher, the moralist, the priest, the artist is engaged in endless play, a form of play, he adds, that has the right to exist only insofar as it opens our eyes to reality—some new, sometimes shocking reality, which art makes palpable. If that meant poking fun at some earnest behavior or deeply held belief—so be it. At the same time, he warned his readers, don't make a demon out of me. The only thing that could save him, Gombrowicz wrote toward the end of his life, was laughter.

Notes

1. Witold Gombrowicz, *Diary, Vol. I,* trans. Lillian Vallee (Evanston: Northwestern University Press, 1988), 184.

2. Witold Gombrowicz, *Trans-Atlantyk,* trans. Carolyn French and Nina Karsov (New Haven: Yale University Press, 1995), 113.

3. Witold Gombrowicz, *Pornografia,* trans. Alistair Hamilton (London: Marion Boyars, 1994), ix.

4. Czeslaw Milosz, *Legends of Modernity: Essays and Letters from Occupied Poland, 1942–1943,* trans. Madeline G. Levine (New York: Farrar, Straus and Giroux, 2005).

5. Czeslaw Milosz, *The Land of Ulro,* trans. Louis Iribarne (New York: Farrar, Straus and Giroux, 1984), 42.

In one of Berenice Abbott's photographs of the Lower East Side, I recall a store sign advertising *Silk Underwear*. Underneath, there was the additional information about "reasonable prices for peddlers." How interesting, I thought. Did someone carry a suitcase full of ladies' underwear and try to peddle them on some street corner further uptown? Or did he ring doorbells in apartment buildings and offer them to housewives? I imagine the underwear came in many different sizes so he may have had to carry two suitcases. The peddler was most likely an immigrant and had difficulty making himself understood. What he wanted is for the lady of the house to feel how soft the silk was but she either did not understand him or she had other reasons for hesitating. She wore a house robe, her hair was loose as if she just got out of bed, so she was embarrassed to touch the undies draped over his extended hand. Then she finally did touch them.

The reason photographs live in my memory is that the city I continue to roam is still rich with such visual delights. Everyone who does the same is already taking imaginary snapshots. For all I know, my face briefly glimpsed in a crowd may live on in someone's memory too. The attentive eye makes the world mysterious. Some men or a woman going about their business seventy years ago either caught

First published in the *Harvard Review* (Fall, 2003).

sight of a camera pointed at them or they passed by oblivious. It was like hide-and-seek. They thought they had concealed themselves in plain view and the camera found them out. It showed something even they did not know they were hiding. Often people had the puzzled look of someone who had volunteered to assist a hypnotist on a stage and who had awakened at the sound of the applause of the audience.

I'm looking at the long-torn-down Second Avenue "El" at the intersection of Division Street and Bowery in another Abbott photograph. The date is April 24, 1936. It seems like a nice day, for the sunlight streams through the tracks and iron scaffolds of the elevated train making patterns of shadow and light on the sidewalk below. As far as I can make out, the street on both sides is lined up with stores selling cheap furs. The entire area was for years a bargain hunter's paradise. My father knew a fellow in his office, an elderly, impeccably dressed man, who claimed that he did all his shopping on Orchard and Hester Streets where he never paid more than five dollars for a suit. What interests me the most in this photograph are the shadowy couple under the El with their backs turned to us. She's willowy and taller than he is as if she were a model or a salesgirl in one of these shops. They have drawn close together as if talking over something very important, or why would they otherwise stop like that in the middle of the street? The way this woman in a long skirt carries herself gives me the impression that she is young. Not so the man. With one hand casually resting on a post and his other stuck in his pocket, he appears confident, even brash. It's the way they stand together that suggests to me that they are not casual acquaintances. Most likely they work in the same neighborhood, but there is something else going on between them too. She seems very interested in what he is saying now. No one else in view pays them any attention. The fellow standing on the sidewalk in front of the Beauty Fur Shop looks off into the distance where a portly young man with glasses wearing an open overcoat over a three-piece suit is coming into view. He has just had lunch and is glancing idly at the shop windows as he strolls lazily back to the office.

He is too young to be the boss, so he must be the son or the son-in-law of one of the storeowners. Except for the couple who elude being identified, there is nothing unusual here. A photograph such as this one, where time has stopped on an ordinary scene full of innuendoes, partakes of the infinite.

I cannot look long at any old photograph of the city without hearing some music in the background. The moment that happens, I'm transported into the past so vividly no one can convince me that I did not live in that moment. I have heard just about every recording of popular music and jazz made between 1920 and 1950. This is probably the most esoteric knowledge I possess. It's easier to talk to people about Tibetan Buddhism, Arab poetry in medieval Spain or Russian icons, than about Helen Kane, Annette Hanshaw and Ethel Waters. Or how about some Boswell Sisters or Joe Venuti and his Blue Four, Red McKenzie and his Mound City Blue Blowers, Ted Lewis and his orchestra playing "Egyptian Ella"? It scares me how much of that music is in my head. I have friends who cannot believe that I can enjoy both Mahler's symphonies and Coleman Hawkins. Young Ella Fitzgerald singing "If That's What You're Thinking, You're Wrong" with Chick Webb's band would be just right for Abbott's shadowy couple.

Can one experience nostalgia for a time and place one did not know? I believe one can. You can put me in solitary with Abbott's photograph of "Blossom Restaurant" and I wouldn't notice the months pass away as I study the menu chalked on the blackboard at its entrance. The prices, of course, are incredibly low, but that's secondary. The dishes enumerated here are what fascinates me. No one eats that kind of food today. Rare Mongolian, Patagonian and Afghanistani specialties are procurable in New York, but not lamb-oxtail stew, boiled beef or even stuffed peppers. The ethnic makeup of the city has changed in the last thirty years. Most of the luncheonettes in the 1950s and 1960s served samplings of German, Hungarian and Jewish cuisine. Pea and bean soup, stuffed cabbage, corned beef and boiled potatoes and veal cutlets were to be found regularly on the menu together with the usual assortment of sandwiches. On every table, and all along the counter, there were containers stocked with dill pickles and slices of raw onion. The portions served were enormous. A cheap dish like franks and kraut would stuff one for the rest of the day. I subsisted for years on soups and chowders cooked by a Greek in a greasy spoon on East 8th Street. They gave you two thick slices of rye bread and butter with the soup and all the pickles you could eat. After that, I could hardly keep my eyes open for the rest of the day.

Abbott's photograph of the Blossom Restaurant front also includes the barbershop next door with its own price list. Does any tonsorial establishment still offer electric massage anywhere in this country? The gadget which resembled contraptions from a horror film and which the barber placed on the customer's head was made of a mesh of spring coils and electric wires. Once the juice was turned on, the massager squirmed and shook for a minute or two over the customer's scalp supposedly providing a stimulating, healthful, up-to-date treatment while one sat back in the chair pretending to be absorbed in some article in the *Police Gazette*. That ordeal was followed by a few sprinkles of strong-smelling cologne from a large bottle and a dusting of the freshly shaved neck with talcum powder.

Which reminds me. The worst haircut I ever had in my life was at a barber college at the Union Square subway station. "Learn Barbering and Make Money," the sign said. It was the cheapest haircut in town. However, before I realized what was happening, the apprentice barber had cut off all my hair with clippers except for a tuft right up in front. The kid was clearly a hair fashion visionary decades ahead of his time, but back then I was in total panic. I rushed immediately across the street into Klein's department store and found a beret, which I wore pulled down over my ears for the next six weeks. The problem was that it was summer, hot and humid as it usually is in New York. I also wore dark glasses to give the impression that I was simply affecting the appearance of a jazz musician. I saw both Dizzy Gillespie and Thelonious Monk similarly decked out, but they tended to make their appearance only after dark while I had to go to work in the morning in a storeroom of a publishing company where everyone who saw me burst out laughing. Lunch was a hassle too. The customers at adjoining tables snickered and the waitress who knew me well gave me a puzzled look as she brought me my sandwich. I always held unpopular opinions and was not afraid to voice them, but to have people stare at me because I had a funny haircut or wore a necktie of some outrageous hue was something I had no stomach for.

"My place is no bigger than a closet" a woman said to her companion on the street just the other day as they rushed past me and I saw it instantly with its clutter of furniture and its piles of clothes on the bed and the floor. Dickinson's "Madonna dim" came to my mind and I did not even take a good look at her before she was lost in the crowd. No sooner has one seen an interesting face in the street than one gives them a biography to go along with the face. Through a small window in her room, the evening casts its first shadow on a blank wall where the outline of a picture that once hung there is still visible. She is not home yet, but there is a small bird in the cage waiting for her and so am I.

Mr. Nobody is what I call the man in the subway I catch sight of from time to time. He has labored all his life to make himself inconspicuous in dress and manner and has nearly succeeded. He sits in the far corner so we may glance at him without seeing his gray hat, gray moustache, pale collapsing cheeks and empty watery eyes as he stares off into space while the subway train grinds along and the overhead lights go out briefly and return to find us puzzled, looking up from newspapers at each other sitting there. Even more odd than these searching looks one gives strangers are the times when one catches someone doing the same to us. They see me as I truly am, one imagines—wanting both to run away from them and to ask what it is they saw.

Today dozens of people are sunning themselves on park benches, sitting close together with eyes shut as if making a collective wish. An old mutt who has done a lot of thinking and sighing in his life lies at their feet eyeing a rusty pigeon take wing as I pass by. The enigma of the ordinary—that's what makes old photographs so poignant: An ancient streetcar in sepia color. A few men holding on to their hats on a windy day. They hurry with their faces averted except for one befuddled old fellow who has stopped and is looking over his shoulder at what we cannot see, but where, we suspect, we ourselves will be coming into view someday, as hurried and ephemeral as any one of them.

THE POWERS OF INVENTION

Beyond the Visible: The Art of Odilon Redon
by Jodi Hauptman, with essays by Marina van Zuylen and Starr Figura

The large recent exhibition of the French artist Odilon Redon (1840–1916) at the Museum of Modern Art in New York brought together 140 of his paintings, drawings, prints, pastels, and illustrated books and was accompanied by the publication of a lavishly illustrated catalog. In addition to one hundred color plates, *Beyond the Visible* contains the full inventory of the museum's collection of his art, which is now the largest outside France. It also includes valuable essays on the artist's work by Jodi Hauptman, Marina van Zuylen, and Starr Figura.

Born in the same year as Monet, Redon belonged to the generation of the Impressionist painters, but he chose to make his way alone. His bizarre little drawings of the 1870s attracted almost no attention. It was the poets and writers of the Symbolist movement in the 1880s who provided the necessary ambience for the appreciation of his art. All that changed with the next generation of painters. Gauguin and Émile Bernard thought highly of him. Bonnard, Vuillard, and Maurice Denis, and even Matisse considered him one of their own. I was

Review of *Beyond the Visible: The Art of Odilon Bedon*, by Jodi Hauptman, with essays by Marina van Zuyten and Starr Figura. From the *New York Review of Books*, March 9, 2006.

surprised to learn that America had its first look at him in the famous Armory Show in 1913, where forty-one of his prints were shown and where one was allegedly sold for two dollars and fifty cents. His work drew the curious and that interest did not wane in the years following as his prints continued to be sought by collectors in the US. Still, no matter how familiar Redon's most famous images have now become, they have preserved their air of mystery. They remain as puzzling today as they were in 1884 when these words were written:

> Those were pictures bearing the signature: Odilon Redon. They held, between their gold-edged frames of unpolished pearwood, undreamed-of images: a Merovingian-type head, resting upon a cup; a bearded man, reminiscent both of a Buddhist priest and a public orator, touching an enormous cannon-ball with his finger; a dreadful spider with a human face lodged in the centre of its body. Then there were charcoal sketches which delved even deeper into the terrors of fever-ridden dreams. Here, on an enormous die, a melancholy eyelid winked; over there stretched dry and arid landscapes, calcinated plains, heaving and quaking ground, where volcanos erupted into rebellious clouds, under foul and murky skies; sometimes the subjects seemed to have been taken from the nightmarish dreams of science, and hark back to prehistoric times; monstrous flora bloomed on the rocks; everywhere, in among the erratic blocks and glacial mud, were figures whose simian appearance—heavy jawbone, protruding brows, receding forehead, and flattened skull top—recalled the ancestral head, the head of the first Quaternary Period, the head of man when he was still fructivorous and without speech, the contemporary of the mammoth, of the rhinoceros with septate nostrils, and of the giant bear. These drawings defied classification; unheeding, for the most part, of the limitations of painting, they ushered in a very special type of the fantastic, one born of sickness and delirium.[1]

The passage comes from *À Rebours*, translated as *Against Nature*, the fin de siècle novel by Joris-Karl Huysmans (1848–1907). It is a story of a bored, rich Parisian who retreats to an isolated villa in the countryside to create for himself an artificial paradise. Living alone, sleeping most of the day, he spends his waking hours indulging in his tastes in rare books and works of art, antique furniture, precious stones, rich scents, and other beautiful things. He replaces his windows with aquariums to better filter the light, gives a funeral banquet at which black food is served on black dishes by naked black girls, has gems embedded into the shell of a tortoise, and cultivates flowers that resemble artificial ones. Traveling, or even leaving the house, he considers pointless, believing that the imagination can easily compensate for the vulgar reality of the actual experience.

Duc Jean Floressas des Esseintes, as he is called, collects the work of painters like Gustave Moreau and Redon who reject realism and books by poets like Baudelaire and Mallarmé who write about dreams, mystical experiences, and other exceptional states of mind. To appeal to des Esseintes, a work of art had to possess an aura of strangeness that Edgar Allan Poe also required. He turned his house into a museum and a library of obscure works whose aesthetic ideas were at odds with prevailing notions of his day. *Against Nature* is a prophetic book in that it anticipates the spirit of negation found in art and literature of the next century.

The notoriety of Huysmans's book gave Redon whatever modest fame he had. He became a part of a group of little-known poets, writers, and artists associated with Mallarmé while continuing to work on his small black-and-white prints and drawings and on an occasional color painting in his later years. "I have made an art that is expressive, suggestive, undetermined," he wrote in his journal.[2] In the long-running battle on the relative merits of copying nature or relying on one's inner vision, he took the side of imagination. In her fine essay in the catalog, Jodi Hauptman shows how old that debate is. Already in the fifteenth century, the painter and writer Cennino Cennini made a case for the power of invention. The artist's aim, he said, was to discover things not seen, hiding themselves under the shadow of natural objects, and to present to plain sight what does not actually exist. What gives Redon's art its originality is that it is a product both of the nineteenth century and of an older tradition that goes back to Bosch, Dürer, and Grünewald. He was unlike any other French artist of his time, and he still stands apart, his vision closer to that of painters like James Ensor and Edvard Munch who came from countries to the north.

Redon narrowly missed having America as his birthplace. His father had immigrated to the United States, made a fortune in Louisiana, and married a local Creole woman. She gave birth to his older brother in New Orleans, but when she became pregnant again, the father took the family back to Bordeaux, where Odilon was born on April 20, 1840. Because of his poor health, he was sent by his parents to be raised by an old uncle who was a manager of the family's vineyard in the commune of Listrac in the Médoc. A frail, introspective child, he was happiest hiding among the curtains in dark corners of the manor house called Peyrelebade, playing with peasants' children, and listening to the tales of the supernatural told by their elders. All his life, Redon felt that he had suffered at the hands of a family who neither loved him nor ever understood him. He was like the disinherited prince in Gérard de Nerval's famous Romantic sonnet "El Desdichado," a poem whose spirit permeates more than a few of his drawings:

> I'm the dark one,—the widower,—the unconsoled,
> The prince of Aquitaine at his stricken tower:
> My sole star is dead,—and my constellated lute
> Bears the black sun of Melancholia.[3]

Nonetheless, he returned to Peyrelebade many times over the years and was heartbroken when the estate was sold in 1897. The sad faces of his childhood, an old bare wall, an old tree, and the grim, colorless landscape stretching to the horizon continued to provide him with material.

Sent to school in Bordeaux, Redon studied drawing, learned how to play violin, and developed a strong interest in literature and philosophy under the influence of the botanist Armand Clavaud, who became his friend and intellectual mentor. His vocation was undecided. From painting, he changed to studying architecture to please his father, but did not do well. He was finally allowed in 1864 to enroll at the School of Beaux-Arts in Paris where he briefly took classes with the academic painter Léon Gérôme, who strove to impose the school's aesthetic standards and failed to appreciate his student's particular gift. Redon learned far more from two artists who kept their distance from the academy, the much-acclaimed Camille Corot and the obscure artist Rodolphe Bresdin, whom he encountered upon his return to Bordeaux. Corot, who was forty-four years Redon's senior, told him to go paint the same tree each year. He also gave him another piece of advice that Redon never forgot: "Next to an unknown, place a known." In other words, strive to have "imaginary gardens with real toads in them," as Marianne Moore told poets to do.

Bresdin, who taught Redon the skills of the engraver, did not work from nature. He relied on imagination. Self-taught, poor, in chronic ill health, increasingly destitute toward the end of his life, he died of hunger and cold in 1885. The small drawings and prints he left were remarkable for their obsessive profusion of detail. This is how Huysmans describes them in *À Rebours*:

> An improbable landscape bristling with trees and bushes and tufts of vegetation that are shaped like demons and phantoms, and covered with birds with rat heads and vegetable tails, on a ground strewn with vertebrae and ribs and skulls, on which grow gnarled and cracked willows, surmounted by skeletons waving bouquets of flowers in the air. . . . A Christ figure is fleeing across a cloud-dappled sky while a hermit meditates, head in hands, deep in a grotto, and a miserable wretch lies dying,

exhausted by privations, prostrated by hunger, stretched out on his back with his feet by a pool of stagnant water.

Hippolyte Taine is supposed to have said that the beautiful was not the pretty, and Émile Zola that art was a fragment of nature seen through a temperament. Bresdin's greatest lesson to his pupil was the value of what he called "unalterable originality." "Look at this chimney flue," he told Redon. "What does it say to you? To me it tells a legend. If you have the strength to observe it well and to understand it, imagine the most strange, the most bizarre subject; if it is based and remains within the limits of this simple section of wall, your dream will be alive. Art is there." Writing about his teacher years later, Redon explains what that meant to him:

> The artists of my generation for the most part have surely looked at the chimney flue. And they saw nothing but it. They have not offered all that could be added to the wall panel through the mirage of our very nature. All that surpasses, illuminates or amplifies the object and elevates the mind into the realm of mystery, to the confusion of the irresolute and of its delicious restlessness, has been totally closed to them. They kept away, they feared everything pertaining to the symbolic, all that our art contains of the unexpected, the imprecise, the undefinable, and that gives it an appearance bordering on enigma. True parasites of the object, they cultivated art on a uniquely visual field, and in a certain way, closed it off from that which goes beyond it, and which might bring the light of spirituality into the most modest trials, even in the blacks. I mean an illumination that seizes our spirit and escapes all analysis.

In 1868 Redon published his first articles on art in a Bordeaux newspaper. One was a review of the Paris Salon of that year and the other an appreciation of Bresdin. Both assert that the art of the future will be the work of the imagination. Redon was undoubtedly familiar with Baudelaire's critical writings and especially his review of the Salon of 1859 in which the poet praised imagination as the queen of faculties and grumbled that art was losing its self-respect by prostrating itself before external reality as painters were becoming more and more inclined to paint what they saw and not what they dreamed. For Baudelaire, "A good picture, faithful and worthy of the dreams that gave it birth, must be created like a world."[4] Redon, in his own review of a later Salon, explains how this is to be done:

> The Old Masters have proved that the artist, once he has established his own idiom, once he has taken from nature the necessary means of expression, is free, legitimately free, to borrow his subjects from history, from the poets, from his own imagination, from the thousand sources of his fantasy. That makes the superior artist: face to face with nature he is a painter, but in his studio he is a poet and thinker.[5]

In September 1870, Redon was inducted into the army and fought briefly in the Franco-Prussian War. The experience of the war, he later claimed, was decisive in making him choose the life of an artist. Outside his family, no one knew or cared about that decision. Except for a single entry to the Salon of 1870 which passed without any critical mention, he was almost invisible. The work of most of his contemporaries left him cold. He found Manet superficial and facile, and the Impressionists too tied to the representation of external things. Redon had not yet read the poetry of Arthur Rimbaud and Lautréamont and so was not aware that the discovery of inner imaginative space he was fumbling toward had already been made by these poets. Rimbaud wrote as follows to a friend in May 1871 when he was just seventeen years old and already the author of several of the most beautiful poems in the French language:

> The first study of the man who wants to be a poet is the knowledge of himself, complete. He looks for his soul, inspects it,

tests it, learns it. As soon as he knows it, he must cultivate it! It seems simple: in every mind a natural development takes place; so many egoists call themselves authors, there are many others who attribute their intellectual progress to themselves!—But the soul must be made monstrous: in the fashion of the comprachicos,[6] if you will! Imagine a man implanting and cultivating warts on his face.

I say one must be a seer, make oneself a seer.

The Poet makes himself a seer by a long, gigantic and rational derangement of all the senses.[7]

In one of Redon's drawings, *The Heart Has Its Reasons*, made around 1887, a naked man stands on a balcony with his right hand reaching inside a slit in his chest to feel his heart. The title comes from Pascal, who says in full: the heart has its reasons of which reason knows nothing. In his book *The Temptation of Saint Redon*, Stephen F. Eisenman notes that the man has the high forehead characteristic of Redon's self-portraits, but that he has the ringlets, facial features, and postures of portraits of Pascal. The gesture, he claims, is onanistic. With the left hand close to his groin, the Redon/Pascal figure fondles his heart. What is troubling to me is not the meaning behind the image, but the image itself, the way in which the unthinkable has been made plausible and the boundary between the imaginary and the real blurred. Redon's intention was not to leave the viewer with a single idea. Nearly every gesture, every facial expression, every title in his art tends to be ambiguous. This was deliberate:

The designation of my drawings by a title is often, so to speak, superfluous. A title is justified only when it is vague and even aims confusedly at the equivocal. My drawings *inspire*, and are not to be defined. They determine nothing. They place us, as does music, in the ambiguous realm of the undetermined.[8]

Beginning around 1875, and for the next twenty years, Redon's work consisted mostly of black-and-white charcoal drawings and lithographs. Influenced by the noir drawings of Goya, he created the series of extraordinary images on which his reputation rests. A man runs through the woods with a huge die on his back; a head of a child lies with eyes closed on the bottom of a well; a mask rings the funeral bell; a centaur with a bow aims an arrow at the clouds; a bald, egg-shaped human head peeks out of an egg holder; an emaciated convict lies curled up with a hand over his mouth behind the bars of his cell. Some of these images are so dark that we can barely make out the background. We could be inside one of Piranesi's imaginary prisons, a corner of a cathedral, a madhouse where inmates dress up as historical personages, or we could be inside someone's nightmare. "My whole originality," Redon said, "consists in having made improbable beings live humanly according to the laws of the probable, by as far as possible putting the logic of the visible at the service of the invisible." That's what poems do too. They contrive to make us believe imagined things are real.

As striking as Redon's images appear to be, some of their comic and fantastic figural distortions of bodily proportions may have originated in the political caricature of the day, where substitutions of plant, insect, and animal parts for human ones were commonplace. As Stephen F. Eisenman demonstrates in his invaluable book, at the very least, Redon's marsh flowers with human faces are derivative of the work of Faustin Betbeder, Daumier, and Grandville. What is missing, of course, is their satirical slant. Redon is never funny. Another possible source of inspiration may be pantomime, the lost art that fascinated both Baudelaire and Flaubert. Redon's solitary figures, dressed in black with their white-painted faces and their downcast eyes, have the somberness and melancholy of old mime shows in early-nineteenth-century Paris. Redon, more than any other artist of his time, drew his material from books. Even his early Romantic landscapes and his late paintings of flowers were frequently inspired by something he read. His portfolios of lithographs all combine text and image. *In the Dream*

(1879), *To Edgar Poe* (1882), *The Origins* (1883), *Homage to Goya* (1885), *Night* (1886), and *The Temptation of Saint Anthony* (1888–1896) all use enigmatic-sounding titles and captions to stir the viewer away from any obvious interpretation of the image.

Redon is not interested in sticking closely to the original text. The captions he composed for the portfolio devoted to Poe allude far more to Baudelaire and Gérard de Nerval. Nonetheless, these bits of language contribute to the way we experience these images. A plate entitled *The Eye like a Strange Balloon Mounts toward Infinity* is said to be based on a passage from Baudelaire's essay "The Life and Works of Eugène Delacroix" in which he describes the painter's political resignation and despair in the face of the great chimera of the modern age, the monster-balloon of perfectibility and infinite progress rising over us. For me, the image has more to do with universal nocturnal fantasies than with fear of modern technology. The eye ascending silently in the dark winter sky carrying a severed head in a basket belongs to someone lying on the verge of sleep. The flight is his reverie, the eye his last glimmer of wakefulness. Beyond the visible—that's where the eye is taking the sleepyhead. The infinity of the title is the name for the imagination at its purest. One can do nothing but speculate on what still draws the gaze of that wide-open eye as it floats off into the opaque distance.

Flaubert's *The Temptation of Saint Anthony* (1874), which inspired three different portfolios of Redon's, is the least known of the great novelist's works. Flaubert started working on it before *Madame Bovary* and was still tinkering with it twenty-five years later while working on *Bouvard and Pécuchet*, which was to be his last book. Although he called it a novel, *The Temptation of Saint Anthony* reads like a play or a Surrealist opera unimaginable by the Surrealists themselves. Michel Foucault wrote that it was to literature what Bosch, Breughel, or the Goya of the *Caprichos* are to painting. Flaubert's version of the legend is a series of tableaux based on the familiar tale of a third-century hermit who lived in the Egyptian desert and who was said to have been besieged all his life by demons jealous of his piousness.

The action takes place during one night. Bands of imaginary animals and monsters attack him; he is tempted with gold, food, women, worldly power, and heretical ideas. The tale had been one of the favorite subjects of painters over the centuries. Flaubert made it into a play as difficult to stage as Goethe's *Faust*, though Robert Wilson gave it a try recently. Not only is the cast of characters huge, there's too much going on. In *The Temptation of St. Anthony* Flaubert took the opportunity to put forward in the name of the devil all the different beliefs in God that were held by various Gnostic sects and other religions. As a final joke, the Satan who appears in person at the end of the play turns out to be a believer in modern science. What attracted Redon was the carnival of fantastic imagery. Never before had so many monsters seen only in old bestiaries, natural history books, narratives of imaginary travels, and medieval diableries been brought all together and used in a literary work to convey the turmoil of inner life.

In Redon's lithographs we see vultures bearing specters; crocodiles playing upon lyres; faces of men with bodies of serpents; cowheaded women prostrating themselves before ithyphallic gods; peacocks who quench their thirst on rivers of gold dust; ancient gods seated on benches of some vast circus; creatures that are half deer, half ox; heads of alligators with hoofs of deer; owls with serpent tails; calves with two heads, one bellowing, another weeping; and many other such wonders. These fabulous creatures from mythological zoos were an early example of collage and caricature. Instead of using scraps, junk, and other odds and ends, anatomical properties of human beings and animals were freely exchanged, not only to construct allegorical figures, but, I suspect, out of the sheer love of invention. Marina van Zuylen is entirely convincing when she argues in her catalog essay that Redon's monsters are mainly inspired not by ideas but by forms. Redon always insisted that his most fantastic creatures began as an effort to faithfully reproduce something as ordinary as a blade of grass before his imagination took over.

One-quarter of Redon's lithographs (forty-one separate plates) deal with *The Temptation of Saint Anthony*. Each image corresponds to a specific line or passage in Flaubert's book and these lines serve as captions. Even so, removed as they are from any context, these demonic apparitions, erotic visions of the female body, Christ-like faces, and glimpses of the saint himself are too ambiguous to be mere illustrations or to work as a sequence in any obvious way. With their looming shadows, recessed doorways, steep stairwells, dungeon-like interiors, and paucity of light, they recall film noir stills. As much as I admire the luxurious colors of his later paintings and agree with John Ashbery, who called these realistic paintings even more fantastic than his imaginary ones, it is his black-and-white drawings that engage me the most. "One must admire black," Redon wrote. "Nothing can debauch it. It does not please the eye and awakens no sensuality. It is an agent of the spirit far more than the fine color of the palette or the prism." [9] His drawings and lithographs are like mirrors one encounters in a house almost dark in which one is unable to distinguish real things from phantoms. The blur that confounds, the unbidden, half-seen something that won't leave us alone was the experience he was after.

Now almost universally admired, Redon's art met with hostility, indifference, and misrepresentation early on. He was charged with elitism and obscurantism. Émile Hennequin, his earliest and most sympathetic critic, claimed that Redon "has conquered that desolate region which exists on the borders of the real and the fantastic—a realm populated by formidable phantoms, monsters, monads, and other creatures born of human perversity." He saw him, in other words, as a kind of super-realist who rendered clearly what to the rest of us is invisible. This view, which one still hears repeated today, leaves out the creative aspect of art. Redon fussed over his drawings, fixing and refixing the layers of charcoal, then drawing over them again, very much the way poets fuss over their poems until some unexpected image turns up.

Beauty is always inexplicable, whether the beauty of a metaphor or the beauty of a drawing. What made Redon a precursor of so much of what happened to art in the next century is that he understood the part imagination and accident play in creating a work of art. The enduring mystery of his images fits one of Baudelaire's definitions of beauty, "something slightly vague, giving rein to conjecture." [10]

Notes

1. Joris-Karl Huysmans, *Against Nature,* trans. Margaret Mauldon (New York: Oxford University Press, 1998), 52 – 53.

2. Odilon Redon, *To Myself: Notes on Life, Art and Artists,* trans. Mira Jacob and Jeanne L. Wasserman (New York: George Braziller, 1986), 96.

3. "The Chimeras of Gérard de Nerval," from *Bending the Bow,* trans. Robert Duncan (New York: New Directions, 1968), 84.

4. Charles Baudelaire, *Selected Writings on Art and Literature,* trans. P. E. Charvet (Cambridge: Cambridge University Press, 1972), 305.

5. Stephen F. Eisenman, *The Temptations of Saint Redon* (Chicago: The University of Chicago Press, 1992), 66 – 67.

6. Kidnappers of children who mutilate them in order to exhibit them as monsters.

7. Arthur Rimbaud, *Complete Works, Selected Letters,* trans. Wallace Fowlie (Chicago: University of Chicago Press, 1966), 307.

8. Robert Goldwater and Marco Treves, *Artists on Art* (New York: Pantheon, 1945), 360.

9. *The Graphic Works of Odilon Redon,* introduction by Alfred Werner (Mineola: Dover, 1969), x.

10. Charles Baudelaire, *The Essence of Laughter* (New York: Meridian, 1956), 166.

UNCOLLECTED

THE TRUE ADVENTURES OF FRANZ KAFKA'S CAGE

A cage went in search of a bird.

—KAFKA

Keep your canary under lock and key. In Seattle, a suspicious-looking empty cage was observed lurking outside of a pet store by Elizabeth Bauman, a registered nurse, whose car had broken down one night on her way back from work.

A heavily made-up elderly woman, arrested for shoplifting in a Berlin department store claimed she saw a birdcage adorned with expensive necklaces and earrings riding the escalators just a moment ago.

Despondent owing to the death of Isolda, his beloved canary, the opera tenor, Arturo Balderachi from Pisa, in a fit of rage threw her cage out of the window in the direction of the famous leaning tower.

In New York, seven violations have been issued last month to an unkempt birdcage seen begging around town for birds.

Finding her husband, François, age sixty-nine, trying to stick his head into a birdcage, Mme Santé, wearing only a flimsy white night-

First published in *Boulevard* (2007).

gown, ran out in the middle of the night into the streets of Paris to seek a doctor or a priest.

A birdcage belonging to an unknown person was found unattended by an alert usher in the first row of a cinema in Montevideo watching Alfred Hitchcock's movie *The Birds*. "I'm telling you, Angelita, the world has gone crazy," some old lady was heard to mutter on the way out.

The birdcage is lonely. It strokes itself with a bird feather and cries itself to sleep every night.

After finding an empty cage on his doorstep, Aaron Bosselaar, a schoolteacher in Antwerp, filed a complaint with the police against a dead Czech author of several incomprehensible books that only certifiable dingbats, like his wife, Laure-Anne, pretend to understand.

Too poor to buy him a bird, the parents of little Alfred Krauss gave him an empty cage for Christmas with a paper-cut of a parrot and told him to feed it crumbs of angel cake every night before going to sleep.

While the bickering of two housewives over whose son broke the window of a funeral parlor was putting the judge to sleep, a policeman brought into the courtroom a birdcage accused of propositioning a street sparrow to have a go at one of its swings.

Roderigo, a young surrealist poet, was reading in the park a poem he had just composed and which compares his love to "a cage full of wild beasts" to Amanda, an aspiring ballet dancer in the tradition of Isadora Duncan, when a flying pigeon dropped its doo-doo on his black, curly hair and his green velvet jacket.

Thinking that the cage capsizing in the Seine contained a pair of lovebirds, Théophile, a tenderhearted orphan visiting Paris from Lunéville, jumped after it, and not knowing how to swim, drowned before he could be rescued.

A bird seen fleeing on foot across the lawn with a cage in hot pursuit astonished a party of British swells who were playing croquet and sipping champagne on the lawn of a palatial country home, leaving them, in their advanced state of inebriation, short of words.

Oh, my God! A cage hanging from the ceiling in a rented room occupied by a lodger the landlady claimed never to have seen. An extensive search of the premises by the police proved fruitless in locating any possessions or a suicide note belonging to the pitiful contraption made of wire.

No one has yet researched the psychological effect an empty birdcage would have on a goldfish were it to be lowered in its aquarium, said Professor Sadoff at the imposing gathering of the Academy of Science, to which only one graybeard in attendance was seen to nod his head vigorously in agreement.

It occurred to Chairman Mao one day to find out from his chief of secret police how many empty cages there were in China and whether they were being carried about at night by suspicious individuals he was not aware of or were they ghosts of some of his old party comrades whom he had imprisoned and tortured over the years?

After robbing a bank in Kansas City, Garfield Jones, whose nickname was "Baby Face," made himself unobtrusive in the lunch-hour crowd by carrying the money in a birdcage which he had prudently covered with a dark cloth usually used to put a bird to sleep at night.

In Andalusia, a matador by the name of Pepete astounded the spectators, judges and picadors by using a red birdcage as a muleta to further enrage the charging bull.

"Birdcages of the world, free yourself from filthy birds," shouted the young Peruvian revolutionary as he was being led blindfolded before the firing squad.

Walking backwards on the street, the retired mailman, Kurt Brown, who had grown even more eccentric after he was fired from his job for having concealed decades of undelivered mail in his basement, met a birdcage going in the opposite direction.

Little ones, the cage whispered to some chickadees, look at the lovely swing, ladder and mirror I have for you. You'll live like a prince and princess, waking every morning in your palace to a breakfast of golden seeds and the admiration of every cat in the neighborhood as you take turns splashing in your bath and warbling to each other.

Bracing itself on the parapet of a schoolhouse high above the street, the cage waited for paper planes that come flying out of open windows on long, warm June afternoons when teachers doze off at their desks, to ask them, as they circle in the air, what should it do next?

Its tiller damaged, the fearless cage sailing across the Atlantic to catch a bird in the jungles of the Amazon that was reputed to be extraordinarily stupid, abandoned its voyage and returned safely to its home in a fire station in Bremen.

In a village in Transylvania, a gypsy woman found an empty cage and filled it with tarot cards and white mice in order to mystify and entice the gullible and drive away those who see the devil's hand at work even at country fairs.

"If you were a prison that didn't have a single prisoner wouldn't you yearn for one?" said the cage to the blue sky as it lay on the railroad track expecting Eurostar to come its way instead of a local rattler full of caged chickens and boxes of fresh eggs.

And what did you, dear Madame, expect the cage to look like after fifty years of searching for a bird? Waiting for years by the side of some road to hitch a ride, sleeping under bridges, drowning one's disappointment in dives from Hong Kong to San Francisco, meeting jewel thieves, burglars, bank robbers, fortune-tellers and listening to their advice without ever enticing one damn bird.

"It's because you kept searching," a wise man in India told the distraught cage. "If you had stayed in Aunt Zelda's kitchen all these years, one day when the window was open a bird would have flown in on its own and made the acquaintance of your charming self."

MY SECRET

For a lazy man I'm extremely industrious.

—WILLIAM DEAN HOWELLS

All writers have some secret about the way they work. Mine is that I write in bed. Big deal! you are probably thinking. Mark Twain, James Joyce, Marcel Proust, Truman Capote, and plenty of other writers did too. Vladimir Nabokov even kept index cards under his pillow in case he couldn't sleep some night and felt like working. However, I haven't heard of other poets composing in bed—although what could be more natural than scribbling a love poem with a ballpoint pen on the back of one's beloved? True, there was Edith Sitwell, who supposedly used to lie in a coffin in preparation for the far greater horror of facing the blank page. Robert Lowell wrote lying down on the floor, or so I read somewhere. I've done that, too, occasionally, but I prefer a mattress and strangely have never been tempted by a couch, a chaise longue, a rocker, or any other variety of comfortable chairs.

For some reason, I've never told this to anyone. My wife knows, of course, and so did all the cats and dogs we ever had. Some of them would join me in bed to nap alongside me, or to watch in alarm as I tossed and turned from side to side, occasionally bumping into them

First appeared as a post on the *New York Review of Books* blog (2012).

without intending to, in a hurry to jot something down on a small writing pad or in a notebook I was holding. I'm not the type who sits in bed with a couple of pillows at his back and one of those trays with legs that servants use to serve rich old ladies their breakfast in bed. I lie in a chaos of tangled sheets and covers, pages of notes and abandoned drafts, books I need to consult and parts of my anatomy in various stages of undress, giving the appearance, I'm certain, of someone incredibly uncomfortable and foolish beyond belief, who, if he had any sense, would make himself get up and cross the room to the small writing table with nothing on it, except for a closed silver laptop, thin and elegant.

"Poetry is made in bed like love," André Breton wrote in one of his surrealist poems. I was a very young man when I read that, and I was enchanted. It confirmed my own experience. When the desire comes over me to write, I have no choice but to remain in a horizontal position, or if I have risen hours before, to hurry back to bed. Silence or noise makes no difference to me. In hotels, I use the "Don't Disturb" sign on the door to keep away the maids waiting to clean my room. To my embarrassment, I have often chosen to forgo sightseeing and museum visits, so I could stay in bed writing. It's the illicit quality of it that appeals to me. No writing is as satisfying as the kind that makes one feel that one is doing something the world disapproves of. For reasons that are mysterious to me, I'm more imaginatively adventurous when I'm recumbent. Sitting at a desk I can't help feeling I'm playing a role. In this little poem by James Tate, you could say, I'm both the monkey and the mad doctor performing the experiment on him.

Teaching the Ape to Write Poems

They didn't have much trouble
teaching the ape to write poems:
first they strapped him into the chair,
then tied the pencil around his hand

(the paper had already been nailed down).
Then Dr. Bluespire leaned over his shoulder
and whispered into his ear:
"You look like a god sitting there.
Why don't you try writing something?"

This habit of working in bed had its beginning in my childhood. Like any other normal and healthy child, I often pretended to be sick on mornings when I hadn't done my homework and my mother was already frantic about being late for work. I knew how to manipulate the thermometer she would insert in the pit of my arm and produce a high enough temperature to alarm her and make it mandatory that I skip school. "Stay in bed," she would yell on her way out of the door. I obeyed her conscientiously, spending some of the happiest hours in my memory reading, daydreaming, and napping till she returned home in the afternoon. Poor mother. It may have been only a coincidence, but I was shocked to learn after her death that she had almost married a Serbian composer in Paris in the 1930s who used to compose in a bathtub. The thought that he could have been my father both terrifies me and delights me. I'd be in bed dashing off verses and he would be in the tub working on a symphony, while my mother would be screaming for one of us to come down and take out the garbage.

In past centuries, in unheated rooms, it made perfect sense to stay under the covers as long as one could, but today, with so many comforts and distractions awaiting us elsewhere in the house, it's not so easy, even for someone like me, to stay in the sack for hours. In the summer, I can lie in the shade under a tree, listen to the birds sing, to the leaves make their own soft, dreamy music—but that's just the trouble. The more beautiful the setting, the more abhorrent any kind of work is to me. Put me on a terrace overlooking the Mediterranean at sundown and it will never occur to me to write a poem.

In New Hampshire, where I live, with five months of snow and foul weather, one has a choice of dying of boredom, watching television, or becoming a writer. If not in bed, my next writing-place of choice is the kitchen, with its smells of cooking. Some hearty soup or a stew simmering on the stove is all I need to get inspired. At such moments, I'm reminded how much writing poetry resembles the art of cooking. Out of the simplest and often the most seemingly incompatible ingredients and spices, using either tried-and-true recipes, or concocting something at the spur of the moment, one turns out forgettable or memorable dishes. All that's left for the poet to do is garnish his poems with a little parsley and serve them to poetry gourmets.

February 10, 2012, 2 p.m.

OH, WHAT A LOVELY WAR!

In a certain sense, the ideas are villains and the people their hapless victims.

—MARY McCARTHY

"How empty, how sickish, how senseless everything suddenly seems the moment the war is over!" Edmund Wilson—who had opposed US involvement in World War II—said after a visit to England in 1945. If London looked grim, the appearance of Berlin, Cologne, Warsaw, Stalingrad, Tokyo, Hiroshima, and hundreds of other places, both in Europe and Asia, defied description. Just in Germany, where British planes attacked by night and American planes by day, the Allies dropped nearly two million tons of bombs, leaving cities and towns reduced to smoldering ruins reeking of death. There were 31.1 cubic meters of rubble for every person in Cologne and 42.8 cubic meters for every inhabitant of Dresden. "The first thing," Ian Buruma writes in *Year Zero: A History of 1945*, "that struck many visitors in the early months after the war was the eerie silence."

The buildings that remained standing often had some of their floors caved in and their windows blown out from the explosions. There were no more sidewalks, since piles of debris lay where houses

Review of *Year Zero: A History of 1945*, by Ian Buruma. From the *New York Review of Books*, October 10, 2013.

once stood. The survivors searched through the ruins for anyone still alive and for something to eat. At night, because electricity and gas no longer worked, people groped about with flashlights and candles, sticking to the middle of the street to avoid collapsing walls, leaking water pipes, and the twisted wreckage of civilian and military vehicles.

When the German officers were signing their surrender on May 8, 1945, Field Marshal Wilhelm Keitel told the Russians that he was horrified by the extent of the destruction wrought on Berlin, whereupon a Russian officer asked Keitel whether he had been equally horrified when on his orders thousands of Soviet villages and towns were obliterated and millions of people, including many children, were buried under the ruins. Keitel shrugged his shoulders and said nothing.

The numbers of dead in German cities were staggering, but they were equally ghastly elsewhere. Some 43,000 died in London during the Blitz, 100,000 in Tokyo in 1945, and over 200,000 perished in Hiroshima and Nagasaki. "I've lost everything. *Everything!*" people were heard to say. Many of them had lost not only their possessions but also their families, their homes, and their countries. With anywhere from 50 million to 70 million dead in World War II, a great majority of them civilians, the scale of human misery was so vast and so widespread that comparisons are useless and misleading, since rounded-off figures, which are often nothing more than educated guesses, convey the horror on an abstract level, while concealing the fates of individual human beings. A number like 50,000,001 would be far more terrifying to see, since that one additional man, woman, or child would restore reality to the 50 million others.

As is well known, there was an immense outpouring of joy on the day Germany capitulated, not just in the countries that had won the war, but also among millions of occupied people who were now free. In Paris, a US bomber pilot thrilled the crowd by flying his plane through the gap under the Eiffel Tower. Cities that were either completely blacked out during the war, or like New York had known "dim-outs" and then "brownouts," were flooded with light while 500,000 people celebrated in the streets.

I'm old enough to remember May 9, 1945, in Belgrade and the jubilation as the news came over the radio. Even old women I had never seen smile and men who had lost an arm or a leg in the war were beaming and chatting amiably outside of buildings pockmarked with bullets. The liberators everywhere were greeted with flowers and kisses. I got a ride in a Russian tank, and so did some girls in my neighborhood. The common reaction was that we've survived, though in many families there was someone dead or missing and no idea whether he or she was alive. Buruma's father, who had been conscripted by the Nazis in Holland to work in a factory in Berlin, was also not heard from in the confusion of the final months of the war, and my father, whom we would not see for ten years, was, unknown to us, in Milan after being freed from a Gestapo prison by the arrival of American troops.

"Scenes Worthy of Dante," the *Times* headline said after the concentration camps were liberated and the photographs of the piles of corpses and of the survivors, who themselves didn't look much better than the corpses, were first published. In London, moviegoers unable to stomach atrocity newsreels tried to walk out of a movie theater only to be blocked by British soldiers who told them to go back and face it. No one yet had any idea how many Jews were put to death by the Nazis or that some 60 million people had perished in the war. On top of that, there were eight million uprooted people in Germany, three million more in other parts of Europe, six and a half million Japanese stranded in Asia and the Pacific, a million Korean workers still in Japan, and countless POWs wherever the war was fought.

If the scale of human misery was unimaginable in 1945, it is not easier to grasp today. Perhaps the reason we never learn from history is that we are incapable of picturing the reality of war and its aftermath, for fear that if we did, we would stop believing both in God and in our fellow human beings.

.With men in defeated and occupied countries either absent or demoralized, the Allied soldiers who arrived as liberators, wearing nice uniforms and handing out luxury items like Hershey bars and cigarettes, were greeted by young girls and some older women the way the Beatles, as Buruma says, were treated twenty years later when they first became popular. Here are a few statistics:

> Reading contemporary accounts and comments in the press, one might get the impression that the summer of '45 was one long orgy indulged in by foreign servicemen and local women, out of greed, or lust, or loneliness. The impression appears to be confirmed by statistics: five times more women were hospitalized in Paris for sexually transmitted diseases (aka VD) in 1945 than in 1939. In Holland more than seven thousand illegitimate babies were born in 1946, three times the number in 1939. . . .

> The fact is that many women and men were simply looking for warmth, companionship, love, even marriage. Much as the early months of liberation offered the chance for wild abandon, people also longed for a return to normality. It should not be forgotten that the 277,000 legitimate Dutch births in 1946 constituted the highest figure in the recorded history of the nation.

Relief workers were shocked at the feverish sexual activity in DP camps—the low moral standards and unrestrained debauchery among the survivors of death camps, and the number of babies born to them every month the following year. The relief workers did not understand their all-consuming want of affection and need to prove to themselves that they were still alive. Buruma reports a story about hundreds of starving, horribly emaciated, newly liberated women in Bergen-Belsen receiving, owing to some British army screwup, not food and medicine, which they badly needed, but a shipment of large quantities of lipstick. It most certainly lifted their spirits. At last someone had done something to make them look like women again. They hobbled around, barely able to walk, wearing nothing but a threadbare blanket over their shoulders, but with their lips painted scarlet.

In defeated countries, women also sold themselves, because there was no other way to keep themselves and their families alive. I remember being more hungry after the war than during it. I'd come home from school and ask my mother what there was to eat and she'd burst into tears. Of course, there was a black market. Even during the siege of Berlin, I was told, if you could pay with gold or diamonds, you could dine on foie gras and French champagne in your private bomb crater.

It was like that after the war too. People searched their homes for something valuable to barter—a silk dress made in Paris, Grandma's wedding plates and silverware, an old oil painting, preferably with some naked ladies—and then sought some shady character or a yokel rumored to have cash, hoping to come home with a slab of bacon or a chicken. Often, these fellows were not interested in what you had to trade—or if the woman happened to be attractive, they suggested a roll in the hay to help them make up their mind. An American reporter observed the following scene on a marshy plot of land near Hamburg: an elderly German man in a business suit was seen clubbing a duck to death with his cane. In parts of Asia it was even worse. Parents offered their babies for sale.

The prospect of famine and pandemics was quite real not just in defeated nations, but in the recently occupied ones. In Japan, where the population had already been starving well before the war ended, government authorities "were advising people how to prepare meals from acorns, grain husks, sawdust (for pancakes), snails, grasshoppers, and rats." Germany had to find a way not only to feed its citizens and returning soldiers, but to deal with ten million ethnic Germans who were expelled after the war from their native lands in Eastern Europe with the full approval of the Allied governments. Understandably, there was little sympathy among the victors. Russians had fresh memories of millions of their own prisoners being deliberately starved by the German army, and the thought of cutting British rations and spending more tax dollars in Washington to feed former enemies was not popular.

Still, something urgently had to be done. "Hungry people are fertile fields for the philosophies of the anti-Christ and for those who would make God of the omnipotent state," a Democratic congressman from Pennsylvania warned Congress. Against all expectations, the United Nations Relief and Rehabilitation Administration (UNRRA) was formed to help victims of German and Japanese aggression and undeniably saved millions from starvation, including me.

Buruma wrote *Year Zero,* he tells us, to look back in time and understand the world of his father and his generation, how millions emerged from this catastrophe and restored their societies and countries to normalcy, believing as they did that a new and better world could be created from the ashes of the old with the collapse of Nazism and fascism. Before that could take place, however, there were scores to settle with the occupiers and collaborators by people bent on revenge:

> In Czechoslovakia in the summer of 1945, near the town of Budweis (České Budějovice), best known for its fine beer, was a concentration camp with a sign nailed to its main gate which read: "An Eye for an Eye, a Tooth for a Tooth." The camp was now under Czech control. It was filled with German prisoners, most of them civilians. The Czech commandant, a young man with a savage reputation, made the Germans work twelve hours a day on minimal rations, then woke them in the middle of the night and ordered them to the *Appelplatz* where they were made to sing, crawl, beat each other, dance, or any other torment that amused the Czech guards.

If this comes as a shock, one must not forget that given the opportunity, sadists in every ethnic group will have their fun. It would not surprise me to learn that some of these Germans were completely innocent and some of their torturers were Nazi collaborators. That was often the case. For turncoats, pointing fingers at others always comes easy. Hunting for traitors and leading lynch mobs was one way to cover up one's guilty past. Germans, in addition, were so hated that no one was likely to come to their defense. "At Dachau," Buruma writes,

> American soldiers stood by as SS guards were lynched, drowned, cut up, strangled, or battered to death with spades, and at least in one case beheaded with a bayonet lent by a GI to a former inmate for this purpose.

Red Army troops were explicitly told to show no pity. "If you kill one German, kill another—there is nothing funnier for us than a pile of German corpses," Marshal Zhukov stated in an order of January 1945. Collective guilt, whatever form or justification it takes, has to be one of the most evil notions the human brain has concocted, most likely the cause of more suffering of innocents than any other vile belief in history.

Among the worst examples recounted in *Year Zero* (and there are enough of them in the book to make even those who already hold a low opinion of our species lower it some more), the pogroms of Jews in postwar Poland were so despicable that they sound improbable, except they did happen. Here were Polish Jews, three million of whom were exterminated by the Germans, tormented by another suffering people who themselves had gone through hell and had almost as many killed during the war:

> [On] August 11, 1945, a rumor started in Krakow that Jews had killed a Christian child in the synagogue. This was an updated version of an age-old anti-Semitic canard. People spoke darkly

of Jewish survivors using Christian blood to revive their ravaged health. Soon, a mob gathered, led by policemen and militiamen. The synagogue was attacked, Jewish homes were plundered, and men, women and children were beaten up in the streets. Several people (the exact number is not known) were murdered. . . .

Badly wounded Jews were taken to the hospital, where some of them were assaulted again while awaiting surgery. One female survivor recalls "the comments of the escorting soldier and the nurse, who spoke about us as Jewish scum whom they had to save, and that they shouldn't be doing this because we murdered children, that all of us should be shot." Another nurse promised to rip the Jews apart as soon as surgery was over. A railway man at the hospital remarked: "It's a scandal that a Pole does not have the civil courage to hit a defenseless person." This man, true to his word, proceeded to beat a wounded Jew.

The Allies, too, did some awful things. They expelled from Germany thousands of Russians and other citizens of the Soviet Union who were prisoners of war, or were brought there to be slave workers, or had fought in General Vlasov's anti-Soviet army, none of whom wanted to return home. Lord Selborne, minister of economic warfare, cautioned Churchill that handing these people back to Russia would mean certain death for them. Nevertheless, it was done. If they couldn't trust them to get into the cattle cars and trucks, battle-hardened British soldiers, often in tears themselves, had to prod, beat, and use their bayonets to make them comply.

In a Cossack camp in Austria, after being ordered to board a train, thousands of men, women, and children came together in a massive huddle around their priests in full Orthodox regalia, carrying an altar, a large cross, and icons while praying and singing psalms. Their hope was that the soldiers would not assault their fellow Christians at prayer. They were wrong. Everyone was beaten, the weeping children, the screaming women, and even the priests who held their crosses over their heads. Without delay they were shipped to the Soviet Union along with the other Russians, where they were either summarily executed or sent to the Gulag, which only a few of them survived.

As Buruma points out, population transfers, mass expulsions, and shifting borders were commonplace in the policies of Stalin and Hitler, but Churchill's precedent was the Treaty of Lausanne in 1923, when it was agreed to move Greek Muslims to Turkey and Greek Orthodox Turkish citizens to Greece. After the war, this was done not just to Germans and Russians who were expelled en masse, but to countless individuals who found themselves without papers in a foreign country and did not wish to go back to where they came from.

My mother, my brother, and I were sent back to Communist Yugoslavia by the British in 1948 after illegally crossing into Austria, even though our father was living in Italy and working for the American army. Notwithstanding our ripped clothes and grubby appearance after two days of hiking through the Slovenian Alps, the colonel who interviewed us asked to see our passports. My mother replied that had we had passports, we would have taken a sleeping car. Her words made no impression on him. Once you have no papers, you do not exist. Anyone in authority can do what he wishes with you, as millions found out after the war.

Were the Allied governments and the more thoughtful members of the occupation forces the ones who got Germany and Japan back on their feet? They without doubt had an important part in restoring democratic institutions and changing some minds, but as we discover in *Year Zero,* that is not the whole story. Curing collective madness and restoring the economy, it turns out, involve many factors. Once defeat sinks in, and the lies people lived on for years lose their power to delude them, civic virtues and renewed interest in the welfare of fellow citizens begin to flourish.

Even that, however, was not enough. The Allies realized almost immediately that the industrial and banking elites in Germany and Japan, who had by and large handsomely profited from the various criminal enterprises their countries were engaged in, including vast empires of slave labor camps, had to be brought back to run things. A few prominent people in Germany served short prison sentences that were typically further reduced; they grumbled afterward about the mediocre food and the inferior quality of the wines they had to endure during their confinement. Their Japanese counterparts were spared even that humiliation before being restored to their former eminence.

A Japanese doctor named Shiro Ishii—whose biological warfare unit in Manchuria conducted experiments on Chinese, Russian, and American POWs by injecting bubonic plague, cholera, and other diseases into them, and then cutting them open without anesthetic and removing their organs for study—managed to convince his interrogators, led by an American general, that the data culled from his experiments would be of great interest to the US. He received immunity from prosecution and additional support when army microbiologists back in the States found his research invaluable.

Year Zero is a relatively short book that covers a great deal of history without minimizing the complexity of the events and the issues. It is well written and researched, full of little-known facts and incisive political analysis. What makes it unique among hundreds of other works written about this period is that it gives an overview of the effects of the war and liberation, not only in Europe, but also in Asia. There the defeat of Japan and the collapse of its short-lived empire accelerated and broadened the civil war in China and set in motion revolts against the colonial masters by native populations across the hemisphere. These consequences of the fall of the Japanese empire are still inadequately known. Unlike many recent books about World War II, Buruma's doesn't have a revisionist interpretation of history to advance. What he has here, instead, is a stirring account of the year in which the world woke up to the horror of what had just occurred and—while some new horrors were being committed—began to reflect on how to make sure that it never happens again.

Was this then a "good war," as we still like to call it? As one of those who had the privilege of being bombed by both the Germans and the Allies, I cringe every time I hear it called that, while never doubting for a minute that the war had to be fought. Still, reading page after page of Buruma's descriptions of death and destruction and the millions of innocent and now long-forgotten victims who were left in its wake, I can't help but cringe some more. How is it possible, I ask myself, that out of all the winners and losers in 1945, the United States is the only country in all the years since that has not experienced lasting peace, but has grown more and more enamored of military solutions to world problems and has of late come to believe, at least in some high places, that it may have to fight a global war that will go on for decades, if not forever? If anyone needs a fresh reminder of where the illusion of omnipotence and its companion, folly, lead to, with savage and often unintended consequences, this book by Ian Buruma ought to provide plenty of corroboration.

INSOMNIA'S PHILOSOPHER

Who reads E. M. Cioran nowadays? Someone must, since most of his books have been translated and are in print. At universities where graduate students and professors are familiar with every recent French philosopher and literary theorist, he's practically unknown, though he was a much finer thinker and wrote far better prose than a whole lot of them. Much of the neglect of Cioran is unquestionably due to his uncompromisingly dark vision of the human condition; his denunciations of both Christianity and philosophy read at times like the ravings of a madman. To make it even more confusing, he had two lives and two identities: the Romanian Cioran of the 1930s who wrote in Romanian and the later, better-known French Cioran who wrote in French. Since his death in 1995, the sensational revelations about his youthful sympathies for Hitler and his involvement with the Iron Guard, the Romanian pro-fascist, nationalist, and anti-Semitic movement in the 1930s, have also contributed to his marginalization. And yet following the publication in 1949 of the first book he wrote in French, he was

Review of *Searching for Cioran*, by Ilinca Zarifopol-Johnston, edited by Kenneth R. Johnston, with a foreword by Matei Calinescu; *On the Heights of Despair*, by E. M. Cioran, translated from the Romanian and with an introduction by Ilinca Zarifopol-Johnston; *Tears and Saints* by E. M. Cioran, translated from the Romanian and with an introduction by Ilinca Zarifopol-Johnston. From the *New York Review of Books*, November 11, 2010.

hailed in France as a stylist and thinker worthy of comparison to great seventeenth- and eighteenth-century moralists like La Rochefoucauld, La Bruyère, Chamfort, and Vauvenargues.

This is what makes *Searching for Cioran* by the late Ilinca Zarifopol-Johnston, who didn't live to finish her book, so valuable. It tells the story of his Romanian years and gives a fine account of the personal and political circumstances in which both his philosophical ideas and his brand of nationalism were formed. In later years, Cioran spoke rarely of that shameful period in his life and never—except to allude vaguely to his "youthful follies"—talked openly of his one political tract, *Romania's Transfiguration* (1936), a short, demented book in which he prescribed how his native country could overcome its second-rate historical status through radical, totalitarian methods. Along with Mircea Eliade, the philosopher and historian of religion, the playwright Eugène Ionesco, and many others, equally eminent but less known abroad, he was a member of Romania's "Young Generation," the "angry young men" responsible for both a cultural renaissance and apocalyptic nationalism in the 1930s. To understand what led Cioran to leave Romania and become disillusioned with ideas he espoused in his youth, it's best to start at the beginning.

Emil Cioran was born in 1911, the second of three children, in the remote mountain village of Rășinari near the city of Sibiu in southern Transylvania, which at that time was still part of the Austro-Hungarian Empire. His father, Emilian, was a Romanian Orthodox priest who came from a long line of priests, as did his mother, Elvira. He loved his native landscape with its streams, hills, and woods where he ran free with other kids, even telling one interviewer, "I don't know of anyone with a happier childhood than mine."

At other times, when not moved by nostalgia, he called it this "cursed and splendid paradise" where his people hid and slumbered for centuries, victims of the whims and slights of history, used to all kinds of masters. As Zarifopol-Johnston shows, "Cioran inherited at birth an 'identity problem.'" In Transylvania, which was annexed by Austria in 1691, Romanians, who made up the majority of the population, were mostly peasants and serfs dominated by the Hungarians and Germans, and reduced to the status of "tolerated population" under the Empire. Their struggle for political rights made Transylvania and Rǎşinari a hub of organized national resistance. Both of Cioran's parents spent time as political prisoners in Hungarian concentration camps because of their Romanian nationalist sympathies. No wonder their son felt free to roam; his parents were in prison.

Humiliations, Cioran later said, are the hardest things to forget. If Rǎşinari was a place of lost happiness, Sibiu—the town where his parents sent him to middle school at the age of ten and where for the next eight years he lived, first alone in a boardinghouse and later with his parents when they themselves moved there—was worlds apart with its Central European architecture, its fine parks, schools, and libraries, and its genteel, bourgeois life. He was not an especially outstanding student, yet he read widely, devouring Shakespeare, Novalis, Schlegel, Pushkin, Tolstoy, Turgenev, Rozanov, Shestov, and Dostoevsky, whom he admired above all the others. What better reading could there be for a rebellious youth—who had already refused to say grace with the family before dinner and left the table while they prayed— than *Notes from Underground*, in which Dostoevsky writes:

> I was nothing but a fly before all that fine society, a revolting, obscene fly—more intelligent, more cultivated, nobler than anyone else, that went without saying, but a fly nonetheless, forever yielding the way to everyone, humiliated and insulted by everyone.

Although Cioran's parents were a highly respected middle-class couple connected by marriage to many old and illustrious families in Transylvania—his father a newly appointed archpriest and adviser to the

Metropolitan bishop of Sibiu and his mother the head of the Christian Women's League—their son felt like a lost soul, a stranger in his own surroundings. The years in Sibiu were a prelude to what was going to be a lifelong identity crisis made worse by his susceptibility to chronic insomnia, from which he started suffering when he was seventeen. The only escape was in books and, when he was older, in long walks at night through the empty and silent streets of Sibiu. The town boasted of three well-established brothels where young Emil became a regular customer, once carrying in his pocket a copy of Kant's *Critique of Pure Reason* and meeting there not only his schoolmates but also his teachers. Still, he continued to be plagued by his secret, mysterious illness—an insomnia, he later said, that would make a martyr envious—which affected all his thinking, set his nerves on edge, and made him constantly irritable. Years later he was to say that he wrote all his books during his nightly walks and while lying in bed unable to sleep.

In Bucharest, where he went next to study philosophy at the university in 1928, he slept even less. Luckily for him, he could flee his cold, drab little room by reading fifteen hours a day at the library of the King Carol Foundation, situated on the city's main thoroughfare right across from the royal palace. He had come to the capital at a time of great political ferment. The liberal party, responsible for political stability and economic prosperity after the creation of Greater Romania in 1918, was shaken by the European-wide economic crisis, local strikes, and violent student protests, as well as the rise of a pro-fascist movement, the Iron Guard, which competed with the king for power.

For Cioran, reading in a library of a country in chaos with its mixed population of Romanians, Hungarians, Jews, Slavs, Greeks, Russians, Bulgarians, and Turks, with their half-Eastern, half-Western ways, the conviction that each man is alone, forced to find his own meaning in a meaningless universe, became even stronger. Stiff and awkward in his shabby dark suit, with a slightly pudgy face, piercing green eyes, and a permanent scowl furrowing his forehead, he spoke with a Transylvanian accent and kept to himself. "I've been for three years here in Bucharest and no one knows me, because I haven't tried, certainly," he wrote to a friend.

He was exaggerating. At university, he attended the seminars of the philosophy professor Nae Ionescu, a charismatic figure responsible for introducing to his students a religiously inspired, messianic nationalism. There he met many of the men who were to have a leading part in undermining the democratic state by rejecting the ideas of liberalism and eagerly replacing them with totalitarian ones. As Marta Petreu writes in *An Infamous Past: E. M. Cioran and the Rise of Fascism in Romania*, redemption through death-sacrifice in the name of the nation became the leading idea of the far right. "We were a bunch of wretched idiots," Eugène Ionesco later said.[1]

Cioran's turn at being a political idiot was still to come. Although he was preparing an undergraduate thesis on Henri Bergson, the kind of philosophy he favored was that of attack and provocation in the manner of Nietzsche. He rejected the Cartesian belief in the primacy of the intellect and reason in man and therefore had no interest in abstract speculation about the nature of being or truth. Like Schopenhauer, he abhorred the strain of optimism in thinking about history and human society and pictured mankind as doomed to an eternal round of torment and misery. Most philosophers, he claimed, pretend that insoluble problems do not exist. They have no courage to face their inner doubts and to admit that they lead an existence full of irreconcilable contradictions. In his first book, *On the Heights of Despair*, published in Bucharest in 1934 when he was twenty-three, he wrote:

> I like thought which preserves a whiff of flesh and blood, and I prefer a thousand times an idea rising from sexual tension or nervous depression to an empty abstraction. Haven't people learned yet that the time of superficial intellectual games is over, that

agony is infinitely more important than syllogism, that a cry of
despair is more revealing than the most subtle thought . . . ?

Man, for Cioran, is an unhappy beast banished from the animal kingdom with just enough imagination to make his life miserable. His
quarrel with philosophers is that they ignore the reality of the body,
that most terrible of all realities, and its mental and physical pain. He
is closer to a poet like Baudelaire, who kept insisting that the hell he
found himself in was representative of the human condition:

> How could the actor of a complicated drama of the soul in
> which, all at once, erotic anticipation clashes with metaphysical
> anxiety, fear of death with desire for innocence, total renuncia-
> tion with paradoxical heroism, despair with pride, forebodings
> of madness with longings for anonymity, screams with silence,
> aspiration with nothingness—how could he still go on philoso-
> phizing in a systematic way?

How, indeed? Cioran tackles all the major philosophical themes in his
writings, but from that anguished, personal angle. Despite passages
of Romantic bravado and self-pity undercut by his cynicism and black
humor, *On the Heights of Despair* is a book of breathtaking ambition
and courage. Made up of sixty-six chapters, most of them no longer
than a couple of pages, it explores morality, love, evil, passion for the
absurd, obsession with the absolute, suffering, melancholy, time and
eternity, solitude and death, in formulations that are both incendiary
and have a depth and originality astonishing in someone so young. The
book was awarded the prestigious young authors prize by the King
Carol Foundation in the literature and arts category. Its recipient, in
the meantime, was in Germany on a Humboldt fellowship, given by its
government to promising students from abroad, studying first in Berlin
and then in Munich. His declared purpose was to pursue his doctoral
studies, but he failed to attend a single class in both places.

Cioran was in Germany from November 1933 to July 1935. In the less than two years that he spent there, he wrote and sent back to Romania for publication many pieces on his impressions of the country. His detractors emphasize the passages in which he is most uncritically enthusiastic about the new Nazi regime, and his defenders seek to ignore them or to minimize their importance. Some, though not all, appeared in right-wing publications. Many are political, but most are not. Still, in a piece from July 15, 1934, Cioran announced that "there is no politician today who inspires me with greater sympathy and admiration than Hitler," and continued to argue that the Führer's mystique in Germany was totally justified.

His merit, Cioran amazingly claimed, consisted in his having stolen the critical spirit of the nation with his capacity to seduce. This, he further stated, was "the dramatic destiny and responsibility of any visionary, dictator, and prophet." What he witnessed both enchanted and horrified him and made him ponder the fragility of the instinct of liberty in mankind. Human beings, he told his readers, both aspire to liberty and exult each time they lose it. He saw Germans raise their hands toward their leader, asking impatiently to be enslaved and to be led to their collective ruin.

Although he was never a mindless enthusiast for Hitler, as Zarifopol-Johnston shows, he was something even worse. While he saw clearly what was happening in Germany, he had a strange affinity for things he otherwise detested. He persuaded himself that only such monsters can lead nations to greatness. He thought Romania needed just such a leader to lift it out of its backwardness, while at the same time openly declaring on another occasion that he found it impossible to feel any theoretical enthusiasm for dictatorship. His next book, *Romania's Transfiguration*, was an attempt to demonstrate, against his better judgment, how such transformation ought to be accomplished. It is a work of which he was ashamed all his life, although just before his death, and already suffering from Alzheimer's disease, he allowed it to be republished in Romania minus its two most offending chapters.

In her fine and detailed study of this foolish book, Marta Petreu cleverly observes that Cioran always made sure that his position on any given subject was his alone; consequently, he didn't fail to revile a single ethnic group in Romania. His objection to foreigners and to Jews in particular was that they were inhibiting the emergence of the Romanian nation. However, unlike the intellectuals associated with the Iron Guard who blamed the Jews for all of Romania's failures, he regarded them as superior to Romanians, who were solely responsible for their own ills. As for the Hungarians, he confessed to his "absolutely natural national hatred" of them mixed with "tenderness toward this incomplete people" who ruled Romania for a millennium.[2] *Romania's Transfiguration* is a work of a nationalist contemptuous of his own people, a fanatic without a racial doctrine.

The book was not well received among the Iron Guard leaders and its intellectuals because, I suspect, its author hinted that he had his own purposes. If he wanted to see the world turned upside down, it was because he wanted to assuage his own religious and metaphysical despair. As he wrote in "Deception Through Action," an article published in December 1940 after the Iron Guard had entered the government:

> In order to improve the situation of a nation or of a social category, some are willing to make the supreme sacrifice. Still, they do not make it for the sake of that particular nation or social category, but rather because life would be unbearable without the vibrations unleashed by those pretexts. . . . The need to tear everything down and rebuild it comes from an emptiness that can no longer live with itself.

This is a vile confession coming from a man who expressed wariness in his first book about supporting any political movement. And yet, he did. He wrote a few more execrable articles supporting right-wing causes after he left in 1937 for Paris, where, except for one short visit home in 1940, he was to remain for the rest of his life. One of his pieces at the time accused the older generation of senility, moral decay, and betrayal of national interests and claimed that the parliamentary system instituted by them had demoralized the nation and that any means of destroying it would be legitimate. One newspaper concluded that this was instigation to murder, and asked the Justice Ministry to take action. Nothing came of it, but that scandal and the unsettled political situation in Romania, where King Carol II had abolished all political parties and arrested the leaders and some of the intellectuals associated with the Iron Guard, made him want to prolong his stay in France.

His next book, *Tears and Saints*, which was published at his own expense after the publisher became worried by its blasphemous contents and appeared while he was already out of Romania, was not well received either, though this had nothing to do with politics. Friends and critics were appalled by his treatment of Christianity. Conceived back in Sibiu, when Cioran pored over the lives of mystics and saints in one of the town libraries, the book is a brilliant meditation on religious ecstasy by a man who confessed that even while he read and admired the lives and writings of these men and women, he could not bring himself to believe in God.

Still, the self-inflicted suffering of saints and religious mystics, the ways they would bury their sufferings in silence and absence, moved him immensely. He preferred pure mystics, mostly lay and mostly female, a family of existential outcasts whom he called "God's insomniacs," whose approach to the Christian faith was antitheological and anti-institutional, and whose one wish was to defeat time and the individual ego while denying the world of appearances. Compared to philosophy, he thought, their mystical revelations give precise answers to questions that philosophers do not even dare consider. "There is no heat except near God. That's why the Siberia of our souls clamors for saints," he writes. As for his own lack of belief, in his view both skepticism and mysticism are expressions of our despair at our lack of knowledge.

This book, like most of Cioran's future works, is a collage of short paragraphs recalling both Schlegel's and Nietzsche's philosophical fragments. Like his predecessors he is capable not only of great insights, but also of irreverent and marvelous flights of fancy:

> The only explanation for the creation of the world is God's fear of solitude. In other words, our role is to *amuse* Our Maker. Poor clowns of the absolute, we forget that we act out a tragedy to enliven the boredom of one spectator whose applause has never reached a mortal ear. Solitude weighs on God so much that he invented the saints as partners in dialogue.
>
> The greatest piece of good luck Jesus had was that he died young. Had he lived to be sixty, he would have given us his memoirs instead of the cross. Even today, we would still be blowing the dust off God's unlucky son.
>
> The beating of our heart threw us out of paradise; when we understood its meaning we fell into Time.
>
> All the sages put together are not worth a single one of Lear's curses or Ivan Karamazov's ravings.

Cioran's participation in political life in Romania lasted eight years. Gradually, after moving to France, he lost interest in politics. Unlike other intellectuals of his generation who held various positions in the diplomatic services during the war, the one job he got at the Romanian legation in Vichy lasted from February 1 to May 16, 1941. It's not clear whether he quit the minor position he held or was fired after he had an argument with his superiors. He never worked again anywhere. He lived in Paris on a scholarship from the French government, the money his parents sent him, and gifts and loans from well-to-do friends, striving to remain true to his ideal of an eternal parasite.

Simone Boué, a Frenchwoman whom he met in 1942 and with whom he stayed till his death, also helped. She was a teacher of English and occasional translator and must have had some income. They lived in small hotels, ate at university student restaurants and even high school cafeterias, and didn't have an apartment until 1960, when they moved into a modest one in the attic of a building on the Left Bank, where they were to stay for the rest of their lives.

In December 1946, Cioran mentioned in a letter that he had been working on a book in French called *Exercices négatifs*, a work he described as a farewell to the past and to all faiths. The book, renamed *A Short History of Decay*, didn't come out until September 1949. It was lavishly praised by reviewers and received the Rivarol Prize the following year by the unanimous decision of a distinguished committee made up of André Gide, Jules Romains, Jules Supervielle, and Jean Paulhan. More importantly, it gave Cioran a new identity as a French writer, although one living in constant fear that the secrets of his past would come to light. The book addresses his fanaticism in those years, though indirectly, without saying anything about his own biography or making any specific reference to the recent war and the death of millions of innocent human beings:

> History is nothing but a procession of false Absolutes, a series of temples raised to pretexts, a degradation of the mind before the Improbable. Even when he turns from religion, man remains subject to it; depleting himself to create fake gods, he then feverishly adopts them: his need for fiction, for mythology triumphs over evidence and absurdity alike. . . . Scaffolds, dungeons, jails flourish only in the shadow of a faith—of that need to believe which has infested the mind forever. The devil pales beside the man who owns a truth, *his* truth. . . . In the fervent mind you always find the camouflaged beast of prey; no protection is adequate against the claws of a prophet . . .[3]

There have been some who have doubted the sincerity of Cioran's change of heart. I do not, and neither do Ilinca Zarifopol-Johnston and Marta Petreu, who know both his Romanian and French writings well. When he wrote, "Youth, always and everywhere, has idealized executioners, provided they perform their task in the name of the vague and the bombastic," he was describing himself.[4]

What still needs to be better known are the rich philosophical and literary contents of the nine books he subsequently wrote (all splendidly translated from the French by Richard Howard), along with their sharp criticism of philosophers from Plato to Heidegger, and his essays on history, tyranny, utopia, Russia, and many other subjects, as well as on figures like Joseph de Maistre, Valéry, Beckett, Borges, and Scott Fitzgerald. Cioran was interested in everything. He wrote about music he heard on the radio, his views of many books he had read, his never-ending fascination with Taoism and Buddhism, his love of poets like Shelley and Emily Dickinson, and his conversations with prostitutes he encountered on his late-night walks through Paris. What these later books show is how much he grew and changed as a thinker, what he kept and what he discarded from his youth, as he went on living his quiet life, refusing every award and honor that came his way.

Notes

1. Marta Petreu, *An Infamous Past: E. M. Cioran and the Rise of Fascism in Romania*, trans. Bogdan Aldea, with a foreword by Norman Manea (Chicago: Ivan R. Dee, 2005), 58.

2. Ibid., 141.

3. E. M. Cioran, *A Short History of Decay*, trans. Richard Howard (New York: Richard Seaver/Viking, 1975), 3–4.

4. E. M. Cioran, *Anathemas and Admirations*, trans. Richard Howard (New York: Arcade, 1991), 148.

CHARLES SIMIC, poet, essayist, and translator, was born in Yugo-slavia in 1938 and immigrated to the United States in 1954. Since 1967, he has published twenty books of his own poetry, including his most recent collection, *New and Selected Poems: 1962–2012*, in addition to a memoir and numerous books of translations for which he has received many literary awards, including the Pulitzer Prize, the Zbigniew Herbert International Literary Award, the Griffin Prize, the MacArthur Fellowship, and the Wallace Stevens Award. Simic is a frequent con-tributor to the *New York Review of Books* and in 2007 was chosen as poet laureate of the United States. He is emeritus professor of the University of New Hampshire, where he has taught since 1973, and is distinguished visiting writer at New York University.